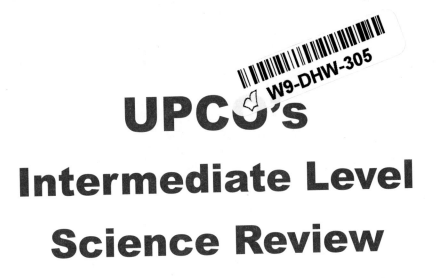

UPCO's
Intermediate Level
Science Review

PEGGY LOMAGA
Longwood Junior High School
Middle Island, New York

AMY SCHNEIDER
Longwood Junior High School
Middle Island, New York

United Publishing Company
21A Railroad Avenue
Albany, New York 12205

CONTRIBUTING EDITORS

Peter Brusoe
Earth Science Teacher
Albany High School
Albany, New York

Arnie Serotsky
Retired Department Coordinator/Teacher
Greece Athena Middle School
Rochester, New York

Nick Hejaily
Retired Department Coordinator/Teacher
Williamsville C.S.
East Amherst, New York

GRAPHIC DESIGN/ART

Kenneth G. Rainis

Ken Rando

ISBN 978-937323-23-6

PRINTED IN THE UNITED STATES OF AMERICA

1 2 3 4 5 6 7 8 9 10

CONTENTS

CHAPTER 1

SCIENTIFIC METHOD: ANALYSIS – INQUIRY – DESIGN

> - *STANDARD 1*
>   *Students will use mathematical analysis, scientific inquiry, and engineering design, as appropriate, to pose questions, seek answers, and develop solutions.*

Observation and Inference

An **observation** is a description of an object or event. For example, "this rock is shiny," "this animal has fur," and "the snowstorm lasted for six hours" are observations.

Observations are made by using the five senses. Instruments assist our senses. A telescope allows us to see objects at very long distances. Instruments are also used to make measurements. For example, "this rock has a mass of 23.4 grams" is a measurement made by using a balance.

An **inference** is a conclusion, opinion, or explanation of the observations. An inference can be a prediction about the future. The weather forecast for tomorrow is an inference.

Review Questions

1. An observation is a _____ of an object or event.

2. We observe by using our _____.

3. Our senses are helped by the use of _____.

4. An _____ is a conclusion based on observations.

5. An inference can be a _____ about a future occurrence.

6. Is the statement an *observation* (**O**) or an *inference* (**I**)?

   a. The road is 5.6 kilometers long. _____

   b. Friction slowed the car. _____

   c. This footprint was made by a dinosaur. _____

   d. It will rain tonight. _____

   e. This surface feels slippery. _____

   f. Ice melts at 0°C. _____

Scientific Method

The **scientific method** is a series of steps used to investigate and answer questions. It is an organized plan used to solve problems. Scientists are not the only ones who use this method of investigation. We all use the scientific method to find the solutions to our questions.

STEPS IN THE SCIENTIFIC METHOD OF PROBLEM SOLVING

1	Ask a Question	• State the problem which needs to be solved.
2	**Develop a Hypothesis**	• Write a possible answer to the question. • Written as an : "If . . . ., then . . . ." statement: • "if . . . .(state the factor that is to be studied)", • "then . . . (suggest a possible result)". • You can often add "because . . . (why will this happen)".
3	**Design an Experiment**	• Plan a procedure that is written as a list of steps. • Include instruments to be used and measurements to be taken. • Include appropriate safety procedures. • A **controlled experiment** will test only one factor. • The factor which you purposely change during the experiment is the **manipulated (independent) variable**. • The variable which changes as a result of the experiment is the **responding (dependent) variable**. • All other factors in the experiment remain constant.
4	**Perform the Experiment**	• Make observations and collect data. • Use a data chart.
5	**Interpret Data**	• Explain the observations. • Identify sources of error. • Include graphs, diagrams, and calculations.
6	**Form a Conclusion**	• The conclusion is based on the observations and data collected. The conclusion should answer the question and compare the results to the hypothesis.
7	**Write a Report**	• This is the way that data and results are shared with others.

During a science investigation one must be careful and cautious in the laboratory. Established rules and procedures must be followed and all safety precautions should be considered.

7. The first step in scientific method is to ask a _____.

8. A possible answer to the problem is a _____.

9. A controlled experiment tests only _____ factor.

10. The variable which you change is the _____ variable.

11. The data you collect is the _____ variable.

12. A conclusion is based on _____ and _____ collected.

13. A student wonders if the color of the light will affect how a plant grows.

    a. Write a Question: _____

    b. Develop a Hypothesis: _____

    c. State the factor that should be changed in the experiment: _____

    d. State the factor that will be observed during the experiment: _____

    e. List THREE factors that should remain the same during the experiment:

        (1) _____

        (2) _____

        (3) _____

    f. Write a procedure for an experiment to test the hypothesis : _____

_____

Metric Measurement

Measurement is an observation and description using numbers. All measurements are usually rounded to the nearest tenth and have a unit. For example, a measured mass of 35.68 should be written as 35.7 grams.

Scientific notation is a method used to write very large or very small numbers in a simpler form. In scientific notation, 2,300,000,000 kilometers would be written as 2.3×10^9 km. The number 0.000000074 meters would be written as 7.4×10^{-8} m.

The metric system is used in science and in most countries of the world. It is based on the number ten. The metric system uses prefixes with each unit of measurement.

"Milli" is the prefix used for small measurements. For example, the width of a string would be measured in millimeters. "Kilo" is the prefix used for large measurements. A horse's mass would be measured in kilograms.

Common Metric Prefixes

kilo...	1000
centi...	1/100th or 0.01
milli...	1/1000th or 0.001

COMMON MEASUREMENTS

TIME

DEFINITION	the period during which something happens
INSTRUMENT(S) USED	stopwatch, clock
UNIT OF MEASUREMENT	second (s)

FIGURE 1

TEMPERATURE

DEFINITION	average motion of molecules
INSTRUMENT(S) USED	thermometer
UNIT OF MEASUREMENT	degree Celsius (°C)

FIGURE 2

LENGTH

DEFINITION	distance between two points
INSTRUMENT(S) USED	ruler
UNIT OF MEASUREMENT	meter (m), centimeter (cm), millimeter (mm)

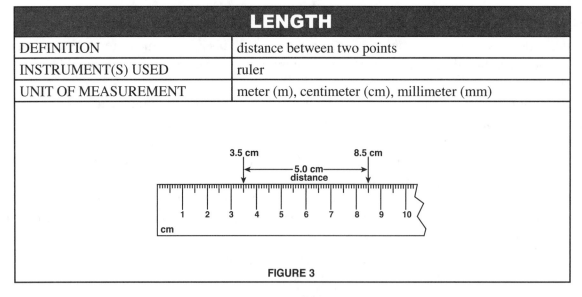

FIGURE 3

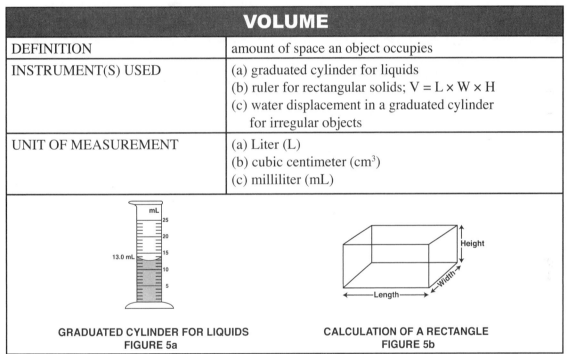

MASS	
DEFINITION	amount of matter in an object
INSTRUMENT(S) USED	balance
UNIT OF MEASUREMENT	gram (g), kilogram (kg)

FIGURE 4

VOLUME	
DEFINITION	amount of space an object occupies
INSTRUMENT(S) USED	(a) graduated cylinder for liquids (b) ruler for rectangular solids; $V = L \times W \times H$ (c) water displacement in a graduated cylinder for irregular objects
UNIT OF MEASUREMENT	(a) Liter (L) (b) cubic centimeter (cm^3) (c) milliliter (mL)

GRADUATED CYLINDER FOR LIQUIDS
FIGURE 5a

CALCULATION OF A RECTANGLE
FIGURE 5b

Review Questions

14. Round these numbers to the nearest tenth:

   a. 56.72 = _____   b. 8.37 = _____   c. 135.78 = _____

15. Write these numbers in scientific notation:

   a. 5,400,000 = _____   b. 0.00000062 = _____   c. 100,000 = _____

16. Write the number represented:

   a. 7.8×10^4 = _____   b. 4.28×10^{-3} = _____

17. One kilogram equals _____ grams.

18. Complete the following chart:

Object	Data	Measurement of ...	Instrument (method used)
Box	58.7 cm³	a.	ruler (L x W x H)
Flagpole	118.2 m	length	b.
Paper Clip	2.6 g	c.	d.
Milk	83.7 mL	e.	f.
Air in Room	20.0° C	g.	thermometer

Graphing

Graphs show the relationship between the variables. Graphs show how the responding variable has changed. They may show a pattern.

STEPS IN CONSTRUCTING A LINE GRAPH

1	**Label the X- axis**	The first factor listed in the data chart is the manipulated (independent) variable. This is labeled on the horizontal axis.
2	**Label the Y-axis**	The second factor on the data chart is the responding (dependent) variable. This is labeled on the vertical axis.
3	**Label the unit of measurement**	On each axis write the unit of measurement that was used. This is often placed in parenthesis "( )".
4	**Number each axis**	The data collected must fit along each axis of the graph. The axis must be numbered with the same interval such as by 2s (2, 4, 6,…) or 5s (5, 10, 15,…). The same interval does not have to be used on both axes.
5	**Plot the data**	Accurately place a point for each set of data.
6	**Draw a line**	Draw the best fit line for the data plotted or connect the data points.
7	**Title the Graph**	Write a title for the graph based on the type of data collected.

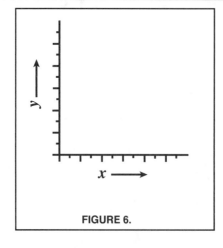

FIGURE 6.

Review Questions

19. A data chart and its corresponding graph is shown below.

   a. Name the two parts of the graph that are missing. _____ and _____.

   b. Complete the graph.

Water Temperature (°C)	Gill Movement (openings/minute)
10	15
15	25
18	30
20	38
23	60
25	57
27	25

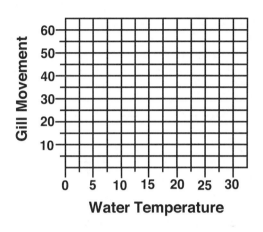

20. The horizontal axis is the _____ variable.

21. The _____ axis is the responding variable.

22. Axes are numbered using the _____ interval.

23. Each axis is labeled with the _____ and the _____.

24. Refer to the graph below:

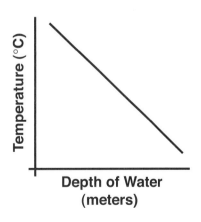

   a. The manipulated variable is _____.

   b. The responding variable is _____.

   c. A good title would be _____.

   d. As the depth of water increased, the temperature _____.

VOCABULARY

conclusion

_____

control

_____

data

_____

hypothesis

_____

inference

_____

length

_____

manipulated (independent) variable

_____

mass

_____

measurement

_____

observation

_____

responding (dependent) variable

_____

scientific method

_____

scientific notation

_____

variable

_____

volume

_____

1. A student visits a stream. The student writes down four statements in his notebook. Which statement is an inference?
    (1) The maximum water depth is 8.7 meters.
    (2) The water is so clear that I can see the bottom.
    (3) The stream was formed during the last Ice Age.
    (4) The water temperature is 16.0° C.

2. A student is rolling a ball down a ramp. Which statement is an observation?
    (1) If the ramp is steeper, then the ball will roll faster.
    (2) Friction slowed the ball.
    (3) Gravity caused the ball's motion down the ramp.
    (4) The ball rolled 86.3cm. in 3.0 seconds.

3. Which set of items could be used to make observations during an experiment?
    (1) sight, ruler, stopwatch   (3) sight, touch, textbook
    (2) sight, graph paper, calculator (4) touch, ruler, notebook

4. An orderly process used to solve problems and investigate the world is
    (1) technology   (2) scientific method   (3) prediction   (4) theory

5. A student decides to enter a science contest that requires an original research project. What is the first step she must take in doing the research?
    (1) design an experiment
    (2) write a conclusion
    (3) state the problem to which she wants to find an answer
    (4) collect data in an organized chart

6. The information that has been collected through observation and measurement is called the
    (1) data   (2) conclusion   (3) variables   (4) theory

7. In an experiment, the factor that is being tested and changed is the
    (1) data   (2) control   (3) variable   (4) inference

8. Diagrams, tables, and graphs are used by scientists mainly to
    (1) design a procedure   (3) organize data
    (2) test a hypothesis   (4) predict the independent variable

9. All of the following are safe procedures to follow when heating a beaker of water *except*:
    (1) use heat-resistant gloves
    (2) watch the beaker as it is heated
    (3) remove your goggles when you put the beaker on the hot plate
    (4) keep the counter clear of papers

10. The length of a sneaker is best measured in:
    (1) millimeters   (2) centimeters   (3) meters   (4) kilometers

11. The mass of a very large boulder is best expressed in:
    (1) milligrams   (2) centigrams   (3) grams   (4) kilograms

Base your answers to **questions 12-14** on the following paragraph:

In a science experiment, 10 bean seedlings were placed in the dark and another 10 bean seedlings were placed in sunlight. All other growth conditions were kept the same for both sets of seedlings. After one week it was observed that the seedlings in the dark were white with long slender stems. The seedlings in the sunlight were green and healthy.

12. The manipulated (independent) variable in this experiment was the:
    (1) number of bean seedlings   (3) temperature
    (2) amount of light   (4) size of the seedlings

13. The "growth conditions" that were kept the same are called:
    (1) constants   (2) predictions   (3) observations   (4) inferences

14. Which conclusion can be made from this experiment?
    (1) Plants grown in the dark can not carry on respiration.
    (2) Light is necessary for proper water absorption by roots.
    (3) Light is necessary for the germination of bean seeds.
    (4) Light is needed for the normal growth of seedlings.

15. An ecologist determined the population size of several species during May, June, and July. The results are in the data table below.

Field Species	Number of Organisms		
	May	July	August
grasshoppers	1,000	5,000	1,500
birds	250	100	100
grasses	7,000	20,000	6,000
spiders	75	200	500

Which graph best represents each specie's population for May?

(1)
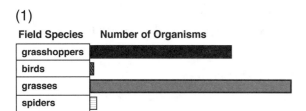

(3)
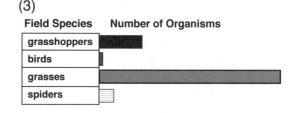

(2)

(4)
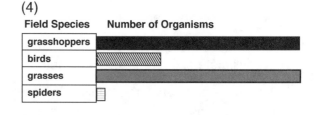

16. A student performed a laboratory experiment to determine the effect of temperature on the heart rate of a water flea. The following temperatures and heart rates were recorded:

20°C - 260 beats/min	25°C - 300 beats/min
10°C - 154 beats/min	5°C - 102 beats/min
15°C - 200 beats/min	

a. Organize the data into a data table (include title for each variable)

b. State the manipulated (independent) variable in this experiment. _____

c. Write a statement based on the data that describes the relationship between temperature and heart beat in the water flea.

_____

_____

_____

17. A student did research on the average Calorie requirements for adolescents. He organized the data table as shown below.

Calories Required Each Day

Age	Boys	Girls
11	2500	2300
12	3000	2500
13	3200	2900
14	3400	2800
15	3500	2700
16	3650	2700
17	3800	2700
18	3000	2500

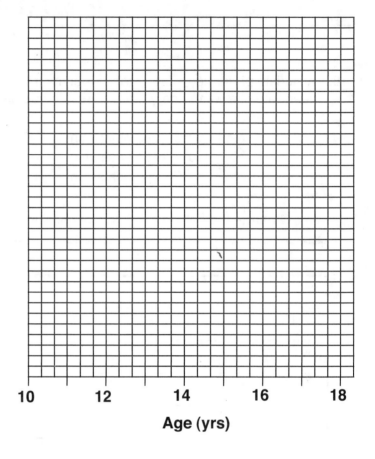

Age (yrs)

a. On the graph, label the vertical axis "*Calories per day*".

b. Mark an appropriate scale for the vertical axis.

c. Plot the data for the "boys" using a point surrounded by a circle (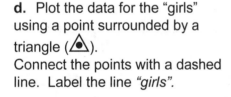). Connect the points with a solid line. Label the line "*boys*"

d. Plot the data for the "girls" using a point surrounded by a triangle (△). Connect the points with a dashed line. Label the line "*girls*".

e. State the responding (dependent) variable. _____

f. Write an appropriate title for this graph. _____

g. Contrast the Calories required for boys and for girls._____

_____

18. Determine the length of the earthworm as shown in the diagram. _____

19. Write the volume of the liquid shown.

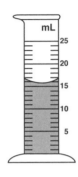

_____

20. Determine the volume of the rock.

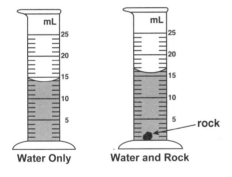

Water Only   Water and Rock

_____

21. Calculate the volume of the block of wood

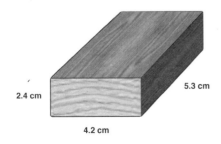

2.4 cm

5.3 cm

4.2 cm

_____

22. Record the mass indicated on the balance.

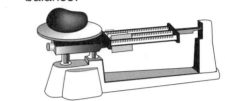

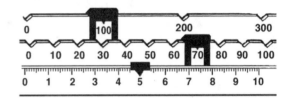

_____

23. Record the temperature indicated.

_____

24. State one safety precaution that should be used in the laboratory situation illustrated below.

_____

_____

_____

_____

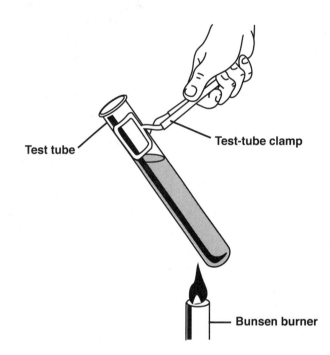

Test tube

Test-tube clamp

Bunsen burner

25. A student collects pond water in a jar. Write the steps she must follow to determine the mass of the pond water in the jar.

_____

_____

_____

_____

_____

CHAPTER 2

CHEMISTRY OF MATTER

- **THE PHYSICAL SETTING: KEY IDEA 3**
  Matter is made up of particles whose properties determine the observable characteristics of matter and its reactivity.

- **THE PHYSICAL SETTING: KEY IDEA 4**
  Energy exists in many forms and when these forms change, energy is conserved.

Elements

Matter is made of elements. For example, air contains nitrogen and oxygen. **Elements** cannot be chemically broken down into simpler substances. There are more than one hundred known elements. Most elements are solids at room temperature. Elements combine in many ways to produce compounds that make up all living and nonliving substances. Few elements are found in their pure form.

Review Questions

1. Matter can be made of combinations of different _____.

2. There are more than _____ known elements.

3. Most elements are _____ at room temperature.

4. Elements can not be physically or _____ broken down into simpler substances.

Atoms

Atoms are the smallest part of an element. Atoms are too small to be seen with a light microscope. Scientists have learned about atoms from experiments. Scientists use models as visual representations of what they are studying.

Atoms are always in motion. The higher the temperature, the more the atoms vibrate or move. The core or center of the atom is called the nucleus. The nucleus contains protons and neutrons. Protons have a positive charge. Neutrons have no charge. Surrounding the nucleus are electrons. Electrons are very small, and have a negative charge.

Atoms of one element are different from the atoms of another element. Atoms of different elements have a different number of protons. The number of protons is the atomic number. There must be an equal number of protons and electrons to keep the charge of the whole atom at zero. In an atom, the positive charges equal the negative charges. Atomic mass is expressed in atomic mass units.

5. The smallest part of an element is a(n) _____.

6. An atom with 5 protons will have 5 _____.

7. Complete the chart.

Particle	Charge	Location in atom
electron	a.	b.
c.	neutral	d.
e.	f.	in the nucleus

The Periodic Table

The Periodic Table is a model used to classify the different elements. Symbols of one, two or three letters are used to represent the names of the elements. Only the first letter of the symbol is capitalized.

Elements are arranged in order of increasing atomic number. All the elements in the same columns or groups have similar properties. Example: Li, Na, and K are all solids. The last column of elements, such as He, Ne, Ar, and Kr, are the **noble gases**. These elements are inert, they do not usually react with any other elements.

The zigzag line on the table separates two types of elements. Elements to the left are metals. **Metals** have luster (shiny) and are solid, malleable (can be hammered into a shape), ductile, and are good conductors of heat and electricity. **Non-metals** are on the right side of the line. They are dull, brittle, and are poor conductors of heat and electricity. Most of the elements that are along the line are metalloids. **Metalloids** have some properties of metals and non-metals. Most elements are metals.

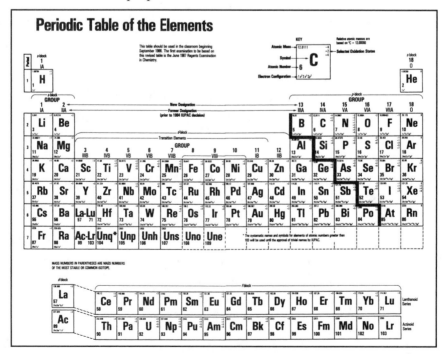

FIGURE 1

Review Questions

8. The first letter of the symbol of an element is a _____ letter.

9. Elements are arranged in order of _____ atomic number.

10. Elements in the same group have similar _____.

11. _____ are malleable, have luster, and are good conductors.

12. Non-metals are _____ conductors of heat.

13. The elements that do not react with other elements are the _____.

Matter

Matter is made of atoms. Matter has mass and takes up space (volume). Matter is not energy. Energy has no mass and does not take up space. Energy is used to change matter. For example, heat energy can change solid water (ice) to liquid water. Matter is identified by its properties or characteristics. **Physical properties** such as size, color, shape, and melting point can be observed. **Chemical properties** describe how the matter reacts with other matter. For example, iron will form rust when exposed to air.

Review Questions

14. Matter is anything that has _____ and _____.

15. Is it matter (**M**) or energy (**E**)?

    a. sunlight _____   **c.** electricity _____

    b. air _____   **d.** sand _____

16. Is it a chemical property (**C**) or a physical property (**P**)?

    a. 23.9 grams _____   **c.** combines with oxygen _____

    b. irregular shape _____   **d.** boils at 100°C _____

Phases (states) of Matter

There are three **phases of matter**: solid, liquid, and gas. In each phase the position and motion of the particles are different.

Phase	Position of particles	Motion of particles	Examples
Solid (s)	close together in fixed positions, definite volume and shape	can only vibrate	wood, rock, ice
Liquid (l)	loosely packed, can change position by sliding past each other, definite volume, no definite shape	more motion than a solid	milk, water
Gas (g)	very far apart, spread out, fills container no definite volume or shape	move freely, in constant motion	air, oxygen, helium

Matter can change phase (state) depending on the motion of its particles. The phase of matter depends on the attractive force between the particles. If heat energy is added to a solid, the particles will move apart and it will change to a liquid. This is called **melting**. If heat is removed from a liquid, it will become a solid as the particles move closer together. This is called **freezing**.

When heat is added to a liquid, it will change to a gas as the particles faster and further apart. This occurs during **boiling** or **evaporation.** If heat is removed from a gas, it will become a liquid as the particles move closer together and slower. This is called **condensation**.

Review Questions

17. A _____ has no definite shape or volume.

18. A _____ has a definite volume but no definite shape.

19. The size of the container will determine the volume of _____.

20. Particles in a _____ have the least motion or kinetic energy.

21. The change from solid to liquid is called _____.

22. If heat energy is added to a liquid it can become a _____.

23. Condensation is the change from _____ to _____.

Density

Density is a physical property of matter. Every substance has a measurable density. Aluminum has a density of 2.7g/cm^3. Gold has a density of 19.3 g/cm^3. Density can be used to identify matter. **Density** is the concentration of mass in an object. It is the amount of matter in a given amount of space. If two objects have the same volume, but one has more mass, then the one with more mass is more dense.

Density is calculated by dividing the mass of an object by its volume. Mass is measured in grams with a triple beam balance. Volume is measured in milliliters (mL) with a graduated cylinder or in cubic centimeters (cm^3) with a ruler.

$$D = \frac{M}{V}$$

The density of a substance can change. As the temperature of matter increases, its density decreases (hot air rises). As pressure increases, density increases (matter is compressed). Gases are the least dense state of matter, solids (except for ice) are the densest.

Buoyancy is the tendency of an object to float or sink. An object will float if it is less dense than the substance it is placed in. For example, cork floats in water but lead sinks. Cork is less dense than water. Lead is more dense than the water or cork.

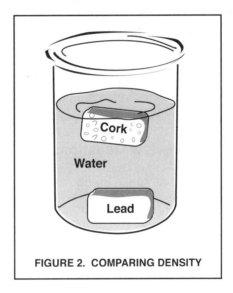

FIGURE 2. COMPARING DENSITY

Review Questions

24. Density is the amount of _____ in a unit of volume.

25. A substance with a mass of 12.0 grams and a volume of 4.0 cm^3 will have a density

    of _____.

26. Density is a _____ property of matter.

27. As temperature increases, density will _____.

28. As pressure increases, density will _____.

29. A _____ is the least dense phase of matter.

30. Buoyancy is the tendency of an object to _____ because of its density.

31. The least dense object in the container shown below is (A) (B) (C).

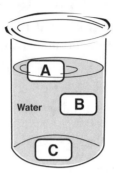

Physical and Chemical Changes

A **physical change** occurs when matter changes form but its chemical composition and properties stay the same. Sawing wood into pieces or boiling water only changes the physical appearance of the matter.

During a **chemical change**, atoms and/or molecules interact to form new substances with different physical and chemical properties. When iron is exposed to air, rust is formed which has different physical and chemical properties than the original iron. Many chemical changes are started with the addition of energy.

Chemical changes can be represented by a chemical equation. The total mass of the reactants will be equal to the mass of the products. No atoms are created or destroyed, they only change form. This is called the *Law of Conservation of Mass*.

Review Questions

32. A _____ change takes place when matter only changes its appearance.

33. During a _____ change, a new substance is formed.

34. Is it a physical (**P**) or a chemical (**C**) change?

a. burning wood _____   **c.** melting ice _____

b. sawing wood _____   **d.** making yogurt _____

Chemistry of Matter

Two or more elements can chemically combine to form a **compound**. The properties of a compound are different from the elements that make up the compound. A compound is the result of a chemical change or reaction. Most matter on Earth is made of compounds. The smallest part of a compound is a **molecule**. Compounds can be broken down into the component elements by a chemical process .

An example of a compound is calcium carbonate, $CaCO_3$, which is found in chalk. This formula, $CaCO_3$, indicates that each molecule of calcium carbonate is made of one calcium atom, one carbon atom, and three oxygen atoms. The number that follows the element symbol is the number of atoms of that element in the compound. If no number is shown, the number of atoms is one.

Mixtures are two or more substances physically combined, but not chemically changed. The substances in a mixture keep their own properties. Mixtures can be separated by simple physical means. A filter can be used to separate sand and water. A magnet can separate iron from sand.

Solutions, such as air and salt water, are mixtures in which one substance is evenly mixed with another. When a substance dissolves, it goes into solution. There are two parts of a solution. The part that dissolves is the **solute**. The part into which the solute dissolves is the **solvent**. In salt water, salt is the solute and water is the solvent. A substance that dissolves in another is soluble. **Solubility**, or the ability to dissolve, can be affected by temperature, pressure, and amount of solute. To speed up the rate of dissolving, a solution can be stirred, heated, or the solute can be broken into smaller pieces.

Review Questions

35. A _____ is a substance made up of two or more elements chemically combined.

36. The smallest part of a compound is a _____.

37. In the chemical compound : **BaCO₃**

    a. How many different elements are there? _____

    b. How many atoms of carbon (**C**) are there? _____

38. A _____ can be physically separated.

39. The part of the solution which dissolves is the _____.

40. Water is a good _____.

41. If the solvent is cold, the solute will dissolve _____.

pH

A solution can be classified as acidic, basic, or neutral. The strength of acids and bases is measured on a pH scale. This scale is a series of numbers from one to fourteen. A neutral solution has a pH of 7. Acids have a pH below 7. Bases (alkaline) have a pH above 7. An indicator, such as litmus paper, is used to test the pH. Red litmus paper will turn blue in bases, and blue litmus turns red in acids.

Review Questions

42. pH can be tested using _____ paper.

43. A pH of 4 means that the solution is _____.

44. Is the lettered position acidic, basic, or neutral ?

    A. _____   B. _____   C. _____   D. _____

1	2	3	4	5	6	7	8	9	10	11	12	13	14
	A					**B**			**C**		**D**		

VOCABULARY

atom

_____

boiling point

_____

buoyancy

_____

chemical change

_____

chemical property

_____

compound

_____

condensation

_____

density

_____

element

_____

evaporate

_____

freezing point

_____

matter

_____

metal

_____

metalloid

_____

mixture

_____

molecule

_____

noble gas

_____

non-metal

_____

phase (state) of matter

_____

physical change

_____

physical property

_____

solubility

_____

solute

_____

solution

_____

solvent

_____

1. Which term is not a form of matter?
   (1) atom   (2) compound   (3) element   (4) energy

2. Atoms are made of particles. These include:
   (1) protons only
   (2) protons and neutrons only
   (3) protons and electrons only
   (4) protons, neutrons, and electrons

3. Lithium has three protons, four neutrons, and three electrons. Which describes its nucleus?
   (1) three protons and four neutrons
   (2) three protons, four neutrons, and three electrons
   (3) three protons and three electrons
   (4) four neutrons and three electrons

4. Which pair correctly matches the atomic particle to its electric charge?
   (1) proton, neutral
   (2) electron, negative
   (3) neutron, negative
   (4) electron, positive

5. Which of the following describes an atom which is neutral?
   (1) 11 protons, 12 neutrons, and 12 electrons
   (2) 11 protons, 11 neutrons, and 12 electrons
   (3) 11 protons, 12 neutrons, and 11 electrons
   (4) 11 protons, 12 neutrons, and 6 electrons

6. Elements are arranged on the *Periodic Table* according to
   (1) density
   (2) phase of matter
   (3) number of protons
   (4) abundance on Earth

7. Which set of terms describes a non-metal?
   (1) shiny, malleable, good conductor
   (2) dull, malleable, poor conductor
   (3) dull, brittle, poor conductor
   (4) shiny, brittle, poor conductor

8. Which group of elements will not react with other elements?
   (1) metals   (2) metalloids   (3) non-metals   (4) noble gases

9. Which term describes a chemical characteristic of matter?
   (1) temperature   (2) density   (3) reactivity   (4) mass

10. Which activity best demonstrates that air takes up space?
    (1) blowing out a candle
    (2) flying a kite
    (3) seeing your breath on a cold day
    (4) inflating a balloon

11. What is the density of the object shown?

    (1) 1.3 g/cm³
    (2) 5.5 g/cm³
    (3) 3.2 g/ cm³
    (4) 0.3 g/cm³

    mass= 22.4 g
    volume= 7.0 cm³

12. Gold has a density of 19.3 g/cm³. How does the density of a bar of gold compare to a gold ring?

    (1) the bar of gold is more dense   (3) they both have the same density
    (2) the gold ring is more dense

13. As air gets hotter and expands, the density of the air will

    (1) decrease   (2) increase   (3) remain the same

14. The particles that make up a solid

    (1) can move easily   (3) can flow against each other
    (2) are closely packed together   (4) are spread far apart

15. A phase change occurs because

    (1) heat energy is absorbed or released
    (2) elements in the compound are re-arranged
    (3) two different compounds react
    (4) elements are physically combined

16. The cooling of air will cause water vapor in the air to change to liquid rain drops. This change is called

    (1) vaporization   (3) evaporation
    (2) condensation   (4) sublimation

17. Particles of a gas will do all of the following *except*

    (1) become arranged in a regular geometric pattern
    (2) spread out to fill the entire container
    (3) take on the shape of the container they are in
    (4) constantly change position

18. The following equation, **H_2O (l) + heat $\longrightarrow$ H_2O (g)**, describes a

    (1) physical change   (3) mixture
    (2) chemical change   (4) soultion

19. The following equation, $N_2 + 3 H_2 \longrightarrow 2 NH_3$, describes a

(1) physical change
(2) chemical change
(3) mixture
(4) element

20. Which describes a physical change followed by a chemical change?

(1) cutting wood then painting it green
(2) taking ice cream out of the freezer then letting it melt
(3) putting gasoline in the car then starting the engine
(4) crushing a sugar cube then dissolving it in water

21. A sample of unknown composition was tested in a laboratory. The sample could not be broken down by physical or chemical means into simpler substances. On the basis of this research, the laboratory reported that this sample was most likely a(n):

(1) compound
(2) element
(3) mixture
(4) solution

22. The compound calcium carbonate, commonly known as chalk, has the chemical formula of $CaCO_3$. How many different elements are in chalk?

(1) one
(2) two
(3) three
(4) five

23. In the formula for glucose, $C_6H_{12}O_6$, how many atoms of hydrogen are indicated?

(1) one
(2) six
(3) twelve
(4) twenty-four

24. What is the chemical formula for ethyl chloride:

$$
\begin{array}{ccc}
& H & H \\
& | & | \\
H- & C - C & -Cl \\
& | & | \\
& H & H
\end{array}
$$

(1) CHCl
(2) $C_2H_2Cl_2$
(3) C_2H_5Cl
(4) CH_5Cl

25. Which of the following will cause a lump of sugar to dissolve faster?

(1) chopping it into pieces
(2) stop stirring the water
(3) adding more sugar
(4) adding cold water

26. A student writes the following observations about aluminum in his notebook:

It is shiny and reflects light. It conducts electricity and heat. It will bend. It will not rust. It will melt at 661°C.

In the chart classify the statements as physical or chemical properties.

Physical Properties	Chemical Properties

27. A student mistakenly dumped the pencil shavings into a beaker of salt that the teacher needed for a salt water fish tank. Devise a procedure that the student could use to separate the salt from the pencil shavings.

_____

_____

_____

28. A student is eating cereal for breakfast. As the student reads the cereal box she notices that the ingredients list iron. She wonders if she can separate the iron out of a cup of cereal. Write the steps the student could follow to do this.

_____

_____

_____

29. Calculate the volume of the regular shaped object shown below. _____

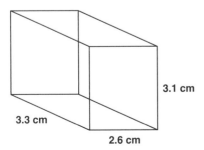

3.1 cm

3.3 cm

2.6 cm

30. Four solid objects of the same shape and size are placed into a beaker of cooking oil as shown.

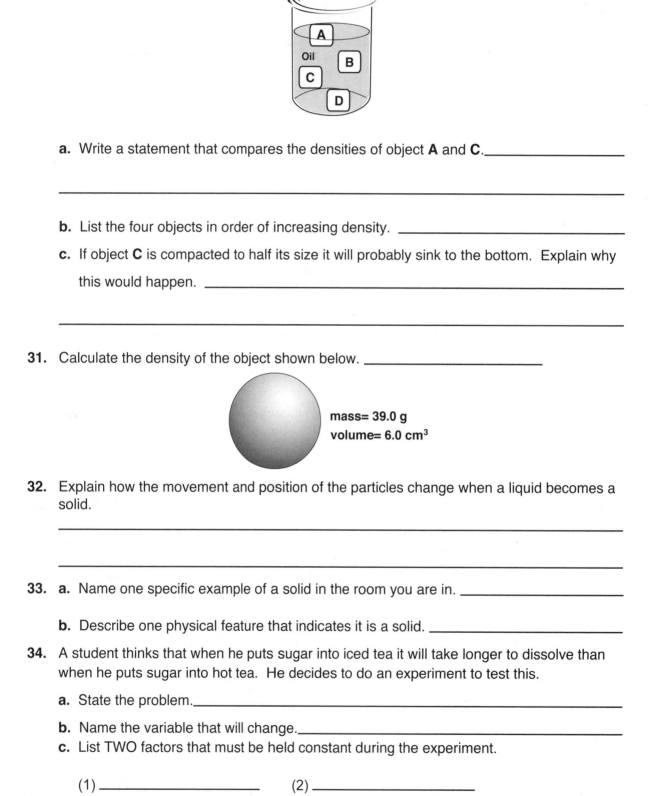

    a. Write a statement that compares the densities of object **A** and **C**._____

_____

    b. List the four objects in order of increasing density. _____

    c. If object **C** is compacted to half its size it will probably sink to the bottom. Explain why this would happen. _____

_____

31. Calculate the density of the object shown below. _____

mass= 39.0 g
volume= 6.0 cm³

32. Explain how the movement and position of the particles change when a liquid becomes a solid.

_____

_____

33. **a.** Name one specific example of a solid in the room you are in. _____

    b. Describe one physical feature that indicates it is a solid. _____

34. A student thinks that when he puts sugar into iced tea it will take longer to dissolve than when he puts sugar into hot tea. He decides to do an experiment to test this.

    a. State the problem._____

    b. Name the variable that will change._____

    c. List TWO factors that must be held constant during the experiment.

       (1) _____   (2) _____

35. Two friends are melting chocolate to make fudge. They do not have much time and want the chocolate to melt faster. Suggest TWO ways they can get the chocolate to melt faster.

(1) _____

(2) _____

36. In class a student states, "Wood always floats." The teacher says, "There are different types of wood and some types of of wood will sink in water."

Design an experiment that the student could perform to prove that the teacher's statement is correct.

a. State the question. _____

b. Identify the manipulated variable: _____

c. Identify the responding variable: _____

d. State THREE factors that should be constant during the experiment.

(1)_____ (2)_____ (3)_____

e. Write the steps of the *procedure*:

_____

_____

_____

_____

37. The data table below shows the amount of a substance that will dissolve in water at each temperature.

Temperature °C	Mass of Solute dissolved in grams
10	22
25	40
30	58
60	107
70	135

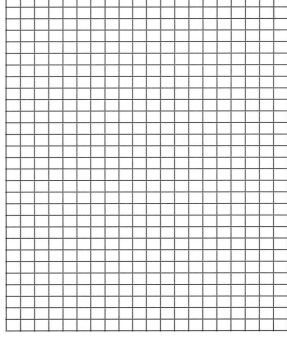

a. Construct a line graph for this data. Use "**x**" when plotting the data points.

b. Write a title for the graph:

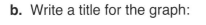
_____

c. The manipulated (independent) variable was _____.

d. Estimate the amount of the substance that will dissolve at 50°C. _____

38. Read the following:

Acid Precipitation

Acid precipitation is rain and snow that contains nitric acid and sulfuric acid. Acid precipitation forms when nitrogen oxide and sulfur dioxide gases combine with water and oxygen in the air.

Human activities which burn fossil fuels, such as driving cars and producing electricity in power plants, emit large amounts of sulfur dioxide and nitrogen oxides into the air. Natural events, such as volcanoes and forest fires, also give off these gases.

Acid precipitation affects trees, human-made structures, and surface water. Acid damages tree leaves and decreases the plant's ability to carry on photosynthesis. Acid can damage tree bark and expose the plant to insects and disease. Many statues and buildings are made of rocks which will react with acid and wear away more rapidly. Acid precipitation lowers the pH of lakes and streams which decreases the survival of plants and animals that depend on their waters.

---

a. The formation of acid precipitation is a _____ change.

b. Acid precipitation will have a pH that is (more) (less) than 7.

c. Propose one specific solution that could help decrease the formation of acid precipitation.

_____

_____

d. The map below shows the pH of precipitation in the United States.
   Shade the area that receives the most acidic rain water.

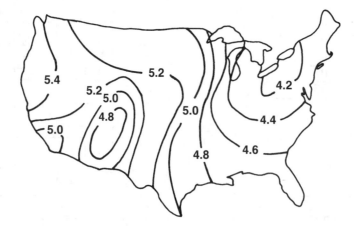

CHAPTER 3
CHARACTERISTICS OF LIFE

- **THE LIVING ENVIRONMENT : KEY IDEA 1**
  Living things are both similar to and different from each other and from non-living things.
- **THE LIVING ENVIRONMENT : KEY IDEA 5**
  Organisms maintain a dynamic equilibrium that sustains life.
- **THE LIVING ENVIRONMENT: KEY IDEA 6**
  Plants and animals depend on each other and their physical environment.

Life Processes

All living organisms need energy, which is obtained from food. Autotrophs, such as green plants, make their own food. Heterotrophs, such as animals, obtain food from other organisms.

During **respiration** energy is released from this food. All organisms need energy to survive. The amount of energy an organism needs and how it gets that energy is different from organism to organism. Most organisms use oxygen to release the energy stored in food. This is called aerobic respiration. Organisms that do not need oxygen perform anaerobic respiration.

Living organisms need water. Water enables the organism to carry on its life activities. Organisms need living space which must provide all of the organisms' needs. Every organism is adapted to the living space in which it is found.

Living things have characteristics that distinguish them from non-living things. All living organisms carry out the same basic life functions in order to maintain an internal equilibrium or balance (homeostasis). An organism's body plan and its environment determine the way that the organism carries out the life processes.

COMMON LIFE PROCESSES

Nutrition	• process of obtaining food and breaking it down into a useable form for cell absorption
Transport	• nutrients and other necessary materials are delivered to all the cells of the organism • wastes are carried away from cells
Synthesis	• chemical reactions which use the digested parts of food to make materials that the organism's cells can use
Respiration	• the release and storage of the energy from food • usually involves the use of oxygen
Excretion	• the removal of liquid and gaseous cell wastes produced by life activities
Regulation	• the control and coordination of all life functions • the response of an organism to changes in its environment
Growth	• an increase in the size or number of cells • this can cause a change in the organism's appearance
Reproduction	• to make an organism of the same kind • this is necessary for the survival of the species

Review Questions

1. The process by which an organism obtains food is called _____.

2. The release of energy stored in food is _____.

3. The removal of liquid and gaseous waste is known as _____.

4. Nutrients are carried to all parts of the body during _____.

5. Regulation is a response to changes in the _____.

6. An increase in the size of the organism is _____.

7. Reproduction is necessary for the _____ of the species.

8. All living organisms need _____, _____, and _____.

Taxonomy

Taxonomy is the science of naming, describing, and classifying organsims. Living organisms are organized into categories for easier study. They are separated into groups based on the physical characteristics they share. This includes the details of their internal and external structures. For example, vertebrates are animals with backbones and invertebrates are animals without a backbone.

The classification system of living organisms is arranged from a large general category called a **kingdom** to the smaller specific category called a **species**.

THE FIVE KINGDOMS OF ORGANISMS

KINGDOM	CHARACTERISTICS	EXAMPLES
Monera	one-celled, no organized nucleus	bacteria blue-green algae
Protist	one-celled with a nucleus, may be plant - and/or animal-like	ameba paramecium
Fungus	many-celled, heterotrophic, lacks chlorophyll	yeast, mold, mushroom
Plant	many-celled, autotrophic (contains green chlorophyll for photosynthesis so plants make their own food)	pine tree, maple cactus, grass
Animal	many-celled, heterotrophic (must obtain food from plants and/or animals)	human, cat, bird, lobster, insect

Every living organism is assigned a kingdom, phylum, class, order, family, genus, and species. For example, humans are:

Kingdom	Phylum	Class	Order	Family	Genus	species
Animala	Chordata	Mammalia	Primata	Hominidae	*Homo*	*sapiens*

Living organisms are identified by their scientific name of genus and species. The house cat is *Felis domestica*. The tiger is *Felis tigris*.

Review Questions

9. Organisms are placed into categories based on similar _____ characteristics.

10. The largest category of organisms is the _____; the smallest category is the _____.

11. Monerans are made of _____ cell.

12. Fungi do not make their own food because their cells do not contain _____.

13. Green plant cells contain _____ for photosynthesis.

14. Heterotrophs obtain food from _____ and/or _____.

The Cell

For all living things, the **cell** is the basic unit of structure and function. Life activities are accomplished at the cell level. Humans are an interactive organization of cells, tissues, organs, and organ systems. A **virus** lacks cellular organization.

Living organisms are composed of one or more cells. Cells are usually microscopic in size. The way in which cells function is similar in all living things. Cells grow and divide, making more cells. Cells take in nutrients, which provides the cell with energy and with the materials that the cell or organism needs. Cells carry on all the life processes.

Cells provide an organism with structure. Organisms composed of one cell are unicellular such as ameba and bacteria. Organisms composed of many cells are **multicellular**. Plants and animals are multicellular. Cells are organized for more effective functioning in multicellular organisms. Nerve cells carry messages and muscle cells that cause movement. **Tissues** are made of similar cells. **Organs** are made of groups of tissues that work together. A group of organs, such as the stomach, small intestine and large intestine, work together as an **organ system**.

Review Questions

15. Most cells are _____ in size.

16. Cells _____ and divide, making more cells.

17. A cell gets its energy from _____.

18. Organisms composed of more than one cell are called _____.

19. Every cell can carry on the basic _____ of life.

20. Tissues are made of _____.

21. Organs are made of _____.

22. Organ systems are made of _____ that work together.

Plant and Animal Cells

Cells are composed of many structures. The **cytoplasm** of the cell is the watery material in which specialized structures are found. Each cell structure carries out a specific function.

The **cell membrane** separates the interior of the cell from the surrounding environment. It controls the movement of materials into and out of the cell. The cell membrane keeps the internal conditions of the cell constant to maintain **homeostasis**.

The **nucleus** is the control center of the cell. It controls cell metabolism and reproduction. The nucleus contains the genetic material, DNA, which determines the inheritance of traits.

Mitochondria are the "powerhouses" of the cell. They release energy during respiration. Vacuoles store food, water, or wastes in the cell.

Animal and plant cells have many of the same cell structures. Yet there are some differences. The plant cell is surrounded by a rigid **cell wall**. It provides shape and support for the plant cell. Plant cells have **chloroplasts** which contain **chlorophyll.** Chlorophyll is the green pigment that enables the plant to absorb sunlight so it can produce food and oxygen by **photosynthesis.**

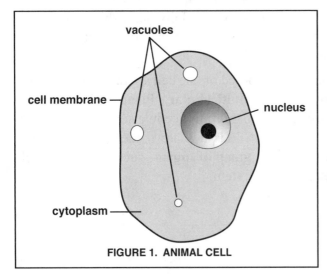

FIGURE 1. ANIMAL CELL

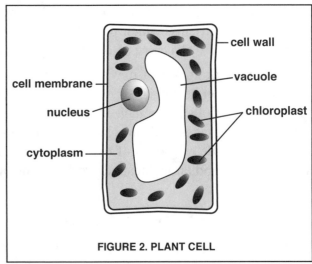

FIGURE 2. PLANT CELL

23. Complete the chart.

CELL STRUCTURE	FUNCTION	ANIMAL CELL? YES OR NO	PLANT CELL? YES OR NO
Cytoplasm	a.	b.	yes
c.	controls cell activities, contains genetic material	d.	e.
Cell membrane	f.	yes	g.
Cell wall	h.	i.	j.
k.	contains chlorophyll for photosynthesis	l.	m.

The Microscope

A microscope is an instrument used to magnify objects not visible to the naked eye such as cells. The compound microscope has more than one lens. These are called the objectives and the eyepiece. Images viewed under the microscope are upside down and reversed. If you move the slide to the right, it will appear to move left under the microscope.

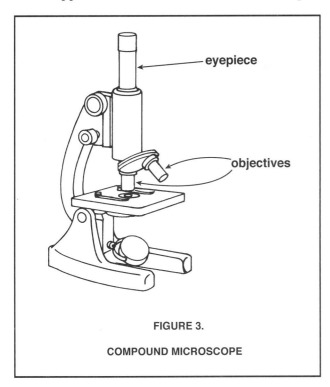

FIGURE 3.

COMPOUND MICROSCOPE

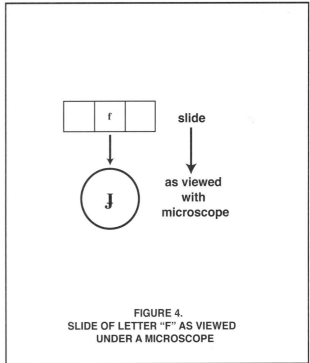

FIGURE 4.
SLIDE OF LETTER "F" AS VIEWED UNDER A MICROSCOPE

The area that you can see under the microscope is the **field of view**. The field of view is smaller under high power than low power. Under low power, more cells or parts of an organism are seen. Under high power, fewer cells, but more detail is seen.

The microscope can be used to observe the structure and the size of cells. Cell size can be measured in millimeters. If you know the diameter of the field of view you can estimate the size of a cell.

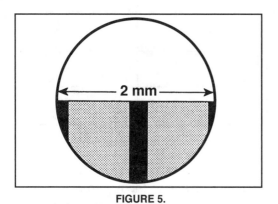

FIGURE 5.

**METRIC RULER VIEW IN
LOW POWER FIELD**

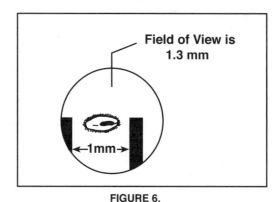

FIGURE 6.

**APPROXIMATE LENGTH OF
ORGANISM IS 0.6 mm.**

Review Questions

24. A _____ is used to enlarge the appearance of cells.

25. A compound microscope has more than one _____.

26. Images viewed under the microscope are _____ and _____.

27. The field of view is larger for _____ power.

28. Under _____ power, more cells are seen.

29. Estimate the size of the cell shown below. _____

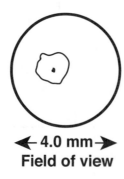

← 4.0 mm →
Field of view

cell

_____

cell membrane

_____

cell wall

_____

chlorophyll

_____

chloroplast

_____

classification

_____

cytoplasm

_____

field of view

_____

kingdom

_____

life processes

_____

multicelluar

_____

nucleus

_____

nutrient

_____

photosynthesis

_____

respiration

_____

species

_____

tissue

_____

virus

_____

1. Plants produce a variety of substances: food, flavorings, drugs, poisons. This is a result of the life process of

   (1) synthesis   (2) growth   (3) reproduction   (4) respiration

2. A migrating bird needs a large amount of energy. Which life process directly provides this energy?

   (1) synthesis   (2) respiration   (3) excretion   (4) regulation

3. All organisms have structures that remove wastes such as carbon dioxide and excess water. This life process is

   (1) nutrition   (2) regulation   (3) respiration   (4) excretion

4. A life process that must be carried on by every living organism is

   (1) photosynthesis   (2) respiration   (3) reproduction   (4) locomotion

5. A life process that is not necessary to the survival of the individual organism is

   (1) respiration   (2) reproduction   (3) nutrition   (4) excretion

6. When we exercise our bodies produce excess heat and our body temperature rises. To maintain a constant body temperature of 98.6° F our body responds by sweating. This maintenance of a constant internal environment is

   (1) homeostasis   (2) transport   (3) synthesis   (4) respiration

7. Living organisms are classified into kingdoms based on

   (1) behavior   (2) structure   (3) size   (4) habitat

8. Which is the correct order in the classification system for organisms?

   (1) kingdom, species, genus   (3) species, kingdom, genus
   (2) genus, species, kingdom   (4) kingdom, genus, species

9. Which classification group has the greatest similarity among its members?

   (1) kingdom   (2) phylum   (3) genus   (4) species

10. Which classification category has the greatest number of different types of organisms?

   (1) kingdom   (2) family   (3) genus   (4) species

Base your answers to **questions 11-13** on the following statement:

A student records the following observations of three different organisms he observed.

> **organism A:** *"one-celled, a nucleus, chloroplasts, able to move"*
> **organism B:** *"one-celled, no nucleus, able to move"*
> **organism C:** *"multicellular, nucleus in each cell, not green, able to move"*

11. To observe organisms A and B the student was probably using a

    (1) metric ruler   (3) microscope
    (2) magnifying glass   (4) graduated cylinder

12. Organism A is most likely classified as a

    (1) monera   (2) protist   (3) fungi   (4) plant

13. Organism C is most likely classified as a(n)

    (1) monera   (2) protist   (3) plant   (4) animal

14. A scientist recently discovered a new species in a rainforest. It is multicellular, has a simple root system, is non-green, and can not move on its own. This organism should be placed in which kingdom?

    (1) monera   (2) fungi   (3) plant   (4) animal

15. Which cell structure controls most cell activities and the inheritance of traits?

    (1) cytoplasm   (2) nucleus   (3) cell membrane   (4) chloroplast

16. The movement of material into and out of the cell is controlled by the

    (1) cytoplasm   (2) nucleus   (3) cell membrane   (4) chloroplast

17. Which structures are found in a cell from a dog?

    (1) cytoplasm, nucleus, chloroplast   (3) cytoplasm, nucleus, cell membrane
    (2) cytoplasm, nucleus, cell wall   (4) cytoplasm, cell membrane, cell wall

18. Which is the most common compound found in cytoplasm?

    (1) sugar   (3) carbon dioxide
    (2) water   (4) carbohydrates

19. A student examines a cell under the microscope and observes the following organelles: *cell membrane, nucleus, cell wall, chloroplasts.* This cell is most likely from

(1) an animal   (2) a plant   (3) a bacteria   (4) a fungus

20. What is the approximate size of the cell illustrated in the diagram below?

(1) 0.5 mm
(2) 1.0 mm
(3) 1.5 mm
(4) 2.0 mm

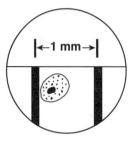

EXTENDED RESPONSE

21. The diagrams below show an animal cell and a plant cell.

Animal Cell   **Plant Cell**

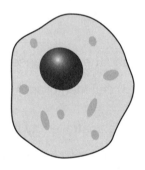 

a. Name one structure both cells have in common. _____

b. On both diagrams label this cell structure.

c. Describe the function of this cell structure. _____

_____

d. Name one structure that is found only in the plant cell. _____

e. Label this part on the plant cell using an arrow.

f. Describe the function of this structure. _____

_____

22. A student is observing green plant cells with the microscope. She notices that the chloroplasts are moving. The student wonders if temperature affects this motion.

  a. State the *question.* _____

  _____

  b. Write a *hypothesis.* _____

  c. Identify the *manipulated* (independent) *variable.* _____

  d. List the factors that should remain *constant.* _____

  e. Write the steps for a *procedure.* _____

  _____

  _____

  _____

23. A student observed a cell using the microscope. He sketched the following two diagrams in his notebook. State a reason that the same cell appeared different during his observations.

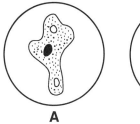
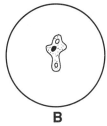

A   B

_____

_____

24. The diagram below represents the field of view of the low power objective of a microscope. Each dark line is a millimeter line on a metric ruler.

  Estimate the field of view. _____

25. The diagram below shows two cells as viewed through a microscope next to a metric measuring device.

    a. Approximate the length of one cell. _____

    b. Approximate the size of a nucleus in one of the cells. _____

1 mm

26. The diagrams below show four different animals.

A   B   C   D

    a. Separate these animals into two groups based on an observable characteristic. Place the letter of each in the box.

    b. State the reason for the separation into these two groups.

_____

_____

_____

27. A student collected some *Elodea* plants from a pond. She observed a piece of the leaf under the microscope. Write a list of steps she followed in preparing a wet mount slide of a leaf of *Elodea*.

_____

_____

_____

CHAPTER 4

ECOLOGY

Origin of the Living Environment

Living organisms depend on the **lithosphere** (rock and soil), the **hydrosphere** (water), and the **atmosphere** (air) of Earth. Throughout Earth's history these three areas have changed.

Earth's original atmosphere did not contain the gases, oxygen, and water vapor that life depends on. Volcanic eruptions released gases and water vapor from Earth's interior. As Earth cooled, water vapor condensed and precipitation filled the ocean and lake basins. This formed Earth's hydrosphere. Erosion of rock and soil added salts and minerals to the water. Photosynthesis by green plants, especially the algae in the oceans, removed the carbon dioxide from the atmosphere and released oxygen. The forces of weathering, erosion, volcanic activity, and crustal plate movement changed the shape of the land.

Review Questions

1. _____ eruptions released many gases into the atmosphere.

2. As Earth cooled, _____ condensed to water droplets.

3. The ocean basins were filled with water by the process of _____.

4. The oceans, lakes, and rivers of Earth make up the _____.

5. The solid outer layer of Earth is the _____.

6. Nitrogen and oxygen are the main gases in the _____.

7. Oxygen in the atmosphere is produced by _____ by green plants.

8. On the diagram below label the following: **atmosphere, hydrosphere, lithosphere**

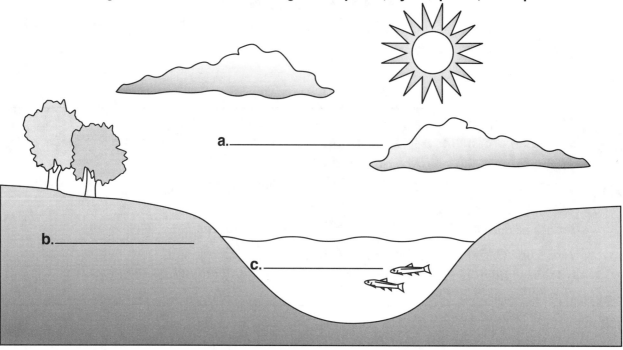

a._____

b._____

c._____

Ecosystems

Ecology is the study of the interactions between organisms and the environment. Organisms depend on their physical environment. The survival of an organism is determined by its ability to sense and respond to the environment.

The number of organisms that an ecosystem can support depends on the resources that are available and the physical features of the area. There are two parts to an **ecosystem**: the living (biotic) factors and the non-living (abiotic) physical factors. Biotic factors are the living organisms. A **population** consists of the individuals of one species living in a location. For example, all the bullfrogs that live in a pond are a population. All the different populations in one location define a **community.** A pond community could include all the frogs, fish, and plants in the water.

FIGURE 1. POND ECOSYSTEM

Some of the non-living factors in an ecosystem are temperature, light, soil, air, and water. Energy enters the ecosystem as sunlight. Energy and matter flow from one organism to another. Energy is eventually lost from the ecosystem to the environment mainly as heat.

Given enough resources and a lack of disease or predators, populations increase. Factors such as lack of resources, habitat destruction, predators, or a change in climate will limit the growth of some populations in an ecosystem. The environment may contain dangerous levels of substances called **pollutants**, which are harmful to organisms. For example, mercury in the water or carbon monoxide in the air can be harmful to organisms.

Review Questions

9. All the organisms in a forest will _____ with one another.

10. Classify the following parts of an ecosystem as (A) abiotic or (B) biotic:

    a. water _____   **d.** sunlight _____

    b. green plants _____   **e.** soil _____

    c. ants _____   **f.** bacteria _____

11. All the mountain gorillas in a rainforest are called a _____.

12. Communities are the different _____ of organisms in a location.

13. If there are adequate resources and no predators or disease, then populations will _____ in size.

14. The main source of energy for an ecosystem is _____.

15. Energy is lost from a system mainly in the form of _____.

16. Harmful substances in the environment are called _____.

Relationships Among Organisms

The organisms in an environment interact with one another. These interactions are classified as competitive, harmful, or beneficial.

INTERACTIONS BETWEEN ORGANISMS

TYPE OF INTERACTION	DESCRIPTION	EXAMPLE
Competitive	Organisms with the same needs compete for the same resources such as food and space	Foxes and hawks both eat rabbits
Harmful	One organism is harmed while the other benefits	Tapeworm in the human intestine
Beneficial	One or both organisms gain from the relationship while neither is harmed	Bacteria in the human intestine

Some species have adapted to be dependent upon each other with the result that neither could survive without the other. Some microorganisms are essential for the survival of living things. Humans could not survive if they did not have beneficial bacteria in their intestines. Bacteria live in the roots of pea plants where they convert nitrogen in the air to a useable form for the plant.

17. In an ecosystem, organisms will _____ with each other.

18. The interaction between a flea and a dog is classified as _____.

19. A snake and a hawk will _____ with each other for the same food.

20. Some species have adapted to be _____ upon each other for survival.

21. Some _____ are necessary for the survival of living organisms.

Feeding Relationships

In ecosystems two major types of nutrition occur: autotrophic and heterotrophic. Autotrophs or **producers** are organisms that make their own food. They convert light energy from the Sun into the chemical energy found in food. By the process of photosynthesis, autotrophic green plants produce sugar and oxygen from the water and carbon dioxide they absorb. They provide nutrients for all other organisms that cannot make their own food. All green plants are producers for ecosystems.

Heterotrophs or **consumers** cannot make their own food. They eat energy-rich food made by the producers. **Herbivores**, such as cows and rabbits, obtain energy by feeding on plants. **Carnivores**, such as lions and hawks, obtain energy by feeding on other animals. **Omnivores** are consumers that obtain energy by eating both plants and animals. Humans and bears are omnivores.

Decomposers obtain energy by consuming wastes and dead organisms. Bacteria and fungi are important decomposers in ecosystems. They break down the remains of dead organisms and return substances to the environment that can be reused by other organisms. This activity recycles substances for the ecosystem. For example, when leaves decay, the nutrients in the leaves are returned to the soil for plants to use for growth.

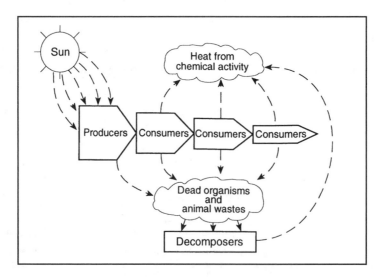

FIGURE 2. FEEDING RELATIONSHIPS

22. All organisms need _____ to survive.

23. Autotrophs _____ their own food.

24. _____ do not make their own food.

25. Substances in the ecosystem are recycled by the _____.

26. Complete the chart.

Nutrition Type	Producer or Consumer?	Description	Example
Autotroph	a.	b.	c.
Herbivore	d.	Feeds on plants	e.
Carnivore	Consumer	f.	g.
h.	i.	Feeds on plants and animals	j.
Decomposer	k.	l.	m.

Energy Flow in the Ecosystem

Matter is transferred from one organism to another and between organisms and the physical environment. Water, nitrogen, carbon dioxide, and oxygen are examples of substances cycled between the living and non-living environment. Green plants remove carbon dioxide from the air. The carbon is passed on to consumers in the form of sugar. The plants release oxygen and water vapor to the air.

Food chains illustrate the flow of energy and matter through an ecosystem. The energy flows in one direction and usually starts from the Sun. Food chains begin with producers. Energy passes from the producers to the consumers. Decomposers return the energy to the ecosystem. There are many types of organisms at each feeding level. There are many food chains in an ecosystem.

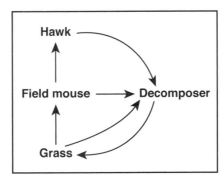

FIGURE 3. FOOD CHAIN

Food chains are interconnected at various points forming a **food web**. Food webs identify all of the feeding relationships among the producers, consumers, and decomposers in the ecosystem. The final organism in a food web is always a decomposer.

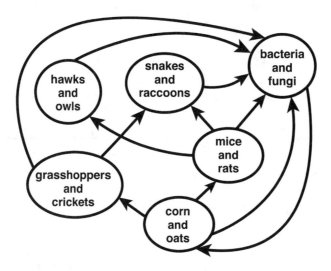

FIGURE 4. FOOD WEB

Energy pyramids show the amount of energy available in the ecosystem from one organism to the next. The greatest amount of energy is present in producers which are at the bottom of the pyramid. An ecosystem needs a large number of plants to support the other organisms. Producer plants are eaten by primary consumers known as herbivores. Herbivores are eaten by secondary consumers or carnivores.

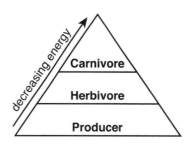

FIGURE 5. ENERGY PYRAMID

Energy is passed on and used in the food chain. Yet some energy is wasted and lost from one level to the next. The energy available decreases as one moves to the upper levels of the energy pyramid. Therefore the total mass of living organisms that can be supported at each level decreases.

Review Questions

27. Energy flows through the ecosystem in one _____.

28. The energy in the ecosystem begins with the _____.

29. The final organism in a food web or chain is always a _____.

30. Examples of substances cycled between living and non-living environment are

water, _____, _____ and _____.

31. The greatest amount of energy in the pyramid is present at the _____ level.

32. Large numbers of _____ are consumed by smaller numbers of consumers.

33. The energy available in the pyramid _____ towards the top.

34. Refer to the diagram of a desert community.

DESERT COMMUNITY

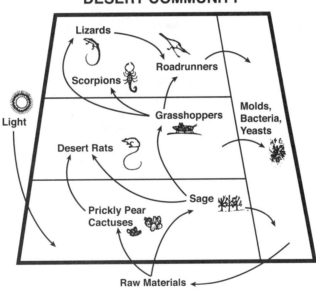

a. This diagram represents a food _____.

b. Name one producer_____.

c. Name a carnivore _____.

d. Molds are classified as _____.

e. Name a "*raw material* "_____.

f. Complete this food chain:

_____ ⟶ _____ ⟶ **scorpion**

Changes in Ecosystems

For an ecosystem to remain unchanged, there must be a constant source of energy. There must be organisms which use this energy to produce food. These are producers such as green plants. There must also be a cycling of materials between the living organisms and the environment. This is done by decomposers.

Ecosystems change over time. The environment may be altered through the activities of organisms or by forces of nature. Natural events such as volcanoes, floods, and forest fires can change environments. As the environment changes some species may replace others. This results in a gradual change called **ecological succession**. The original organisms in an ecosystem are replaced with other types. A new community replaces the old community. For example, over time a pond of fish and snails may become a swamp of frogs and large plants.

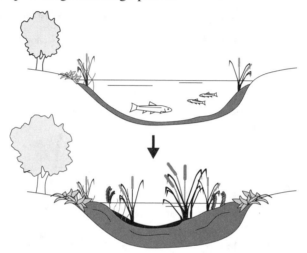

FIGURE 6. ECOLOGICAL SUCCESSION

An organism will survive only if it can adapt to its changing environment. Species that cannot adapt become **extinct**, or die out. This happens when something that is essential for the organism to survive is removed. Causes of extinction include changes in climate, natural disasters such as asteroid impacts, habitat invasion by predators, and hunting by humans. Pollution in the water can lead to a loss of habitat resulting in extinction of certain types of fish.

Evidence for extinction is found in fossils in sedimentary rock. Many organisms which lived in the past are no longer found on Earth. The dinosaur which was very abundant 70 million years ago, no longer exists.

Review Questions

35. Ecosystems will be unchanged if there is a constant source of _____.

36. Decomposers _____ material between living organisms and the environment.

37. A gradual change in the ecosystem of an area is called _____.

38. An organism will survive only if it can _____ to changes in its environment.

39. Evidence for extinction is found by studying _____ in sedimentary rock.

Human Effects on Ecosystems

The survival of living organisms on Earth depends on the conservation and protection of Earth's natural resources. **Non-renewable resources** are Earth materials which cannot be replaced by natural processes. For example, as we continue to remove and use copper ore from rocks, the amount of copper available to us becomes less. Recycling of metals can lessen this effect.

Renewable resources are replaced by natural processes within a period of time. Soil is replenished with nutrients by decomposition of plant and animal matter. Water is recycled by nature. Overuse and not allowing time for replenishment threatens renewable resources.

Overpopulation by any species affects the environment due to increased use of resources. Human activities have caused environmental degradation through resource acquisition and the use of non-renewable resources. **Urban** growth, that is the spreading of cities by humans, has caused habitat destruction as forests and wetlands have been destroyed. Land use decisions and waste disposal by humans have changed ecosystems.

Human activities have caused major pollution of the air, water, and soil. Since the start of the Industrial Revolution this impact has increased dramatically. The burning of fossil fuels for energy production and the use of Earth's natural resources in manufacturing have affected ecosystems. Pollution has had a cumulative and global impact. Acid rain, global warming, and ozone depletion impact many ecosystems worldwide.

Review Questions

40. The survival of organisms on Earth depends on the protection and _____ of natural resources.

41. _____ resources cannot be replaced in our lifetime.

42. Water is an example of a _____ resource.

43. Human activities have resulted in air, water, and soil _____.

44. The negative impact of human activities on ecosystems has increased since the

_____ began.

atmosphere

_____

carnivore

_____

community

_____

competition

_____

consumer

_____

decomposer

_____

ecological succession

_____

ecology

_____

ecosystem

_____

energy pyramid

_____

extinction

_____

food chain

_____

food web

_____

habitat

_____

herbivore

_____

hydrosphere

_____

lithosphere

_____

non-renewable resource

_____

omnivores

_____

pollutant

_____

population

_____

predator

_____

producer

_____

renewable resource

_____

urban

_____

1. An earthworm burrows in the soil. The earthworm is directly interacting with the

   (1) atmosphere   (2) hydrosphere   (3) lithosphere   (4) stratosphere

2. The oceans, lakes, and streams are part of the

   (1) atmosphere   (2) hydrosphere   (3) lithosphere   (4) stratosphere

3. Which process added oxygen to Earth's atmosphere?

   (1) volcanic eruptions   (3) erosion of rock surfaces
   (2) competition among species   (4) photosynthesis by green plants

4. The group of different organisms that live together in an area is the

   (1) community   (2) niche   (3) population   (4) species

5. Pigeons of the same species living in a city park represent

   (1) a population   (2) a biome   (3) a food chain   (4) an ecosystem

6. Which term includes the other three?

   (1) population   (2) species   (3) community   (4) ecosystem

7. The study of the interactions between organisms and their interrelationships with the environment is

   (1) ecology   (2) zoology   (3) physiology   (4) cytology

8. A non-living (abiotic) factor that might affect the types of organisms in a pond is

   (1) production of food by green algae   (3) addition of goldfish to the pond
   (2) number of offspring produced by the fish   (4) amount of oxygen in the pond

9. The relationship between fleas and a dog is most similar to the relationship between

   (1) bees and flowers   (3) foot fungus and human
   (2) fish and algae   (4) hawk and mice

10. In a natural community in New York State, the producer organisms may include

    (1) bacteria, fungi, protists   (3) fish, algae, frogs
    (2) deer, rabbits, squirrels   (4) grasses, trees, weeds

11. Bacteria of decay (decomposers) are important components of an ecosystem because they

(1) recycle organic matter
(2) carry on photosynthesis
(3) absorb sunlight
(4) produce oxygen

12. As a member of the ecological community, humans are classified as

(1) producers   (2) decomposers   (3) consumers   (4) autotrophs

13. Solar energy enters food chains through the life processes of

(1) omnivores   (2) decomposers   (3) carnivores   (4) producers

14. The decomposers that decay plant and animal matter in an ecosystem include

(1) grasses and bacteria
(2) bacteria and mushrooms
(3) grasses and insects
(4) grasses and mushrooms

15. The typical sequence for a food chain is

(1) green plants ⟶ carnivores ⟶ herbivores
(2) green plants ⟶ herbivores ⟶ carnivores
(3) herbivores ⟶ green plants ⟶ carnivores
(4) herbivores ⟶ carnivores ⟶ green plants

16. An incomplete food chain is shown below

algae ⟶ minnow ⟶ trout ⟶ X

What organism could be represented by the **X** ?
(1) human   (2) jellyfish   (3) pine tree   (4) cow

17. In a food web, the greatest amount of chemical energy is provided by

(1) producers
(2) decomposers
(3) primary consumers
(4) secondary consumers

18. The diagram shows a food web. Which organisms are most likely competitors?

(1) A and C

(2) B and C

(3) B and D

(4) D and E

Base your answers to **questions 19-24** on the food web diagram below.

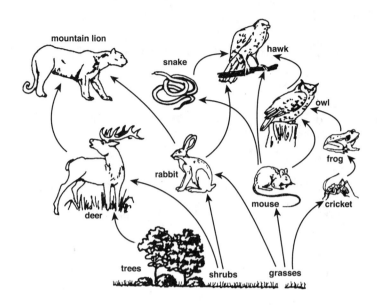

19. Which is a food chain in this web?

(1) trees, mountain lion, snake, and hawk
(2) trees, rabbit, deer, and shrubs
(3) grasses, cricket, frog, and mouse
(4) grasses, mouse, snake, and hawk

20. What is the primary source of energy for this food web?

(1) Sun   (2) grasses   (3) snake   (4) wind

21. Two herbivores (primary consumers) are the

(1) deer and mountain lion   (3) rabbit and mouse
(2) owl and snake   (4) cricket and frog

22. Which organisms not shown in this food web are important in all ecosystems?

(1) decomposers   (2) consumers   (3) producers   (4) predators

23. The snake is classified as a(n)

(1) herbivore   (2) carnivore   (3) decomposer   (4) omnivore

24. If a pesticide was sprayed that killed all the crickets, how would the food web be affected?

(1) the grasses would die
(2) the frog population would decrease
(3) the mountain lion would migrate
(4) the deer population would increase

25. Overpopulation of deer in an area will most likely cause

(1) a decrease in the number of predators of the deer
(2) a decrease in disease among the deer
(3) an increase in the amount of plants available for food
(4) an increase in competition among the deer

26. In an abandoned field, the grasses were slowly replaced by small bushes and then years later by a forest of trees. This is known as

(1) conservation of energy
(2) ecological succession
(3) competition
(4) predation

27. Which activity has a *negative* effect on the environment?

(1) recycling aluminum cans
(2) controlling air pollution
(3) establishing a wildlife preserve
(4) use of chemical pesticides

Base your answers to **questions 28-31** on the following statement:

The food pyramid below represents a pond community.

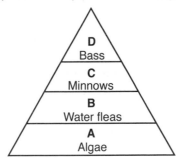

28. Which level contains the greatest amount of energy and biomass?

(1) A   (2) B   (3) C   (4) D

29. A carnivore is found at level(s):

(1) C only   (2) D only   (3) B and C   (4) C and D

30. From level **A** to **D**, the amount of energy will

(1) decrease   (2) increase   (3) remain the same

31. Acid rain causes the algae to die in the pond. As a result the water flea population

(1) decreases   (2) increases   (3) remains the same

32. Place these organisms in the correct sequence in the energy pyramid.

Hawk   Seeds   Sparrow

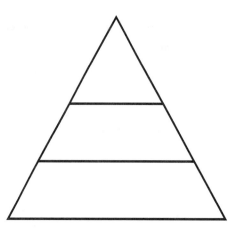

33. The characteristics of some organisms are listed below.

Trout ....carnivorous fish
Minnow .... herbivorous fish
Algae .... green plant
Osprey .... large carnivorous bird
Bacteria .... decomposer

Arrange these organisms in a food chain.

34. Aphids are insects that feed on and destroy crops. To control these pests, farmers place ladybugs in the farm fields. Ladybugs are natural predators of aphids.

   a. The aphid is a (carnivore) (herbivore) (producer)

   b. The ladybug is a (carnivore) (herbivore) (producer)

   c. State one advantage of using this method of pest control._____

_____

   d. State one possible danger of using this method of pest control.

_____

35. The diagram below shows a food web in a lake.

$$Algae \longrightarrow Zooplankton \longrightarrow Perch fish \longrightarrow Pike fish$$
$$\searrow Zebra Mussels$$

   a. State the organism that is most affected by changes in sunlight. _____

   b. Name the TWO organisms that are in competition for the same food.

   (1) _____   (2) _____

   c. Describe one effect on the food web if the *Perch fish* population increases for the next two years.

   _____

36. The diagrams below show the changes that have occurred in the ecosystem of a location. Write the letters in the correct sequence of ecological succession.

   _____ $\longrightarrow$ _____ $\longrightarrow$ _____ $\longrightarrow$ _____

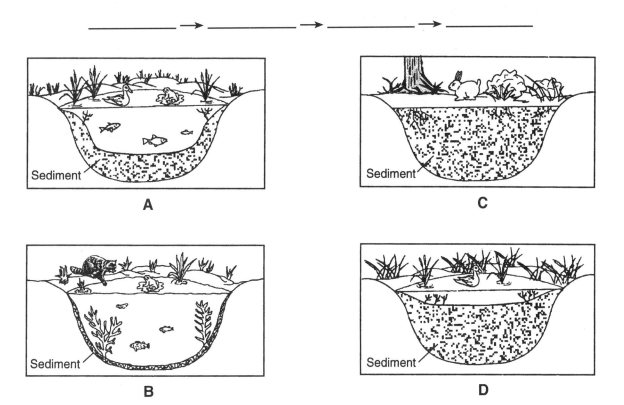

37. Refer to the diagram below of a food web.

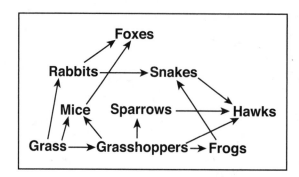

a. Select one organism and explain how its removal could affect the other species.

_____

_____

b. Name a herbivore. _____

c. Name a producer. _____

d. Name an omnivore. _____

e. Name one organism that converts light energy to chemical energy. _____

f. Name the important organism missing from the food web. _____

38. The diagram illustrates a pond ecosystem.

a. Name TWO biotic (living) factors. (1) _____ (2) _____

b. Name TWO abiotic (non-living) factors. (1) _____ (2) _____

c. Energy for this ecosystem is from the _____.

d. Carbon dioxide is removed from the water by _____.

e. The oxygen content of the water is provided by _____.

f. Bacteria in the pond are important decomposers. Explain their function in this ecosystem.

_____

_____

_____

39. Read the following passage.

> The panther is the state mammal of Florida. This large wild cat once roamed the woodlands and swamps of the southeastern states. Today this native cat of the Southeast numbers less than eighty in population and is on the endangered species list. There seems little chance that its population will increase. As more people have made Florida their home, the panther population has decreased. The forests and swamps of the South are developed for homes, hotels, malls, and golf courses. What was once home to the panther is now called home by Florida's increasing human population. The continued urban development of Florida will keep the panther on the endangered species list.

a. State the reason an organism is placed on the "Endangered Species List."

_____

_____

_____

b. Name one human activity that threatens the panther's survival in Florida.

_____

_____

_____

c. Propose one solution that will help preserve the state mammal of Florida.

_____

_____

_____

40. The deer population in a region of Montana had been studied from 1900 to 1940. During this time, hunting and ranching activities increased in this area.

DATA TABLE

Year	Deer Population (thousands)
1900	3.0
1910	9.5
1920	65.0
1924	100.0
1926	40.0
1930	25.0
1940	10.0

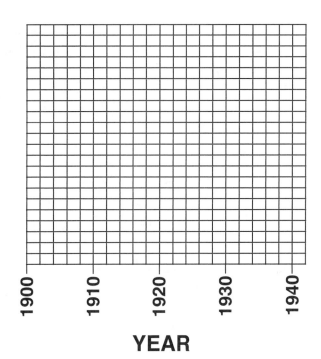

a. Set up the y - axis.

b. Construct a line graph of this data. Plot the data points using an "**X**".

c. The dependent (responding) variable for this study is the _____.

d. Write a title for this graph. _____

e. Write a sentence to describe how the deer population changed during this time.

_____

_____

f. Propose a reason for the decrease in the deer population from 1930 to 1940.

_____

_____

41. A student sets up the following experiment using tomato plants in potting soil.

a. State the manipulated variable. _____.

b. Write the question for which the student is trying to find the answer.

_____

_____

c. Name THREE factors that should be kept the same during this experiment.

(1)_____ (2) _____ (3) _____

CHAPTER 5

PHYSIOLOGY

> • **THE LIVING ENVIRONMENT: KEY IDEA 1**
> **Living things are both similar to and different from each other and from non-living things.**
>
> • **THE LIVING ENVIRONMENT: KEY IDEA 5**
> **Organisms maintain a dynamic equilibrium that sustains life.**

Cells to Organ Systems

Cells are organized in multicellular organisms into **tissues**. For example, blood tissue is made of red and white blood cells and platelets. The red blood cells carry oxygen to other body cells, white blood cells fight disease and infection, and platelets help in blood clotting.

Organs are made of tissues. The heart is made of cardiac tissue. Organs that function together make up **organ systems**. The circulatory system is made up of the heart, veins, and arteries. The excretory system includes the lungs, kidneys, and bladder.

Each organ system is composed of organs that perform specific functions. Organ systems interact with each other. The nervous system sends impulses to the skeletal-muscle system to cause movement of body parts. The respiratory system adds oxygen to the blood of the circulatory system.

Tissues, organs, and organ systems provide each cell with nutrients and oxygen, and perform the task of removing wastes. Diseases break down the structure or function of an organism. Some diseases are the result of the failure of an organ system. Kidney failure, caused by a disease of the kidneys, can make the whole organism fail to function properly.

Review Questions

1. Cells organized together to perform the same function make up _____.

2. Organs are made of _____ that act together.

3. The stomach, small intestine, and large intestine are part of an _____ system.

Nutrition

Nutrition is the activity by which the body obtains food and changes it into a form that is useable by the organism. Food provides the molecules that are the "fuel" for the body and the "building materials" for cells. Nutrients provide energy at the cell and body level. Food energy is measured in **Calories**. The total Calorie value of each type of food varies. The number of Calories an organism requires depends on the species, age, sex, size, and level of activity of the organism. Teenagers have the greatest daily Calorie requirement.

Nutrients provide chemicals needed for metabolism which regulates body processes and maintains homeostasis. **Metabolism** includes all the chemical reactions in an organism. Metabolism can be influenced by hormones, diet, exercise, and aging. Nutrients also provide the building materials for the organism. For example, proteins obtained through nutrients provide the materials necessary to make hemoglobin, an essential part of the blood.

Review Questions

4. The activity by which the body obtains food is called _____.

5. Nutrients are the useable parts of _____.

6. The energy in food is measured in _____.

7. Nutrients provide _____ needed for metabolism.

8. All the chemical reactions in an organism is _____.

Types of Nutrients

Organisms need food for energy, growth and repair, and as a source of chemicals. There are several major types of nutrients which supply needed energy and chemicals to the organism.

NUTRIENT	EXAMPLE(S)	FUNCTION(S)
Carbohydrate	sugar, starches	main source of energy for life processes
Fat	oils, butter, cream	a reserve energy supply, building material for certain cell structures
Protein	meat, eggs, beans, milk, fish	supplies amino acids which make new cells and body chemicals, repairs and maintains body tissues
Vitamins	A, B, C, D, K	necessary for good health and a healthy body, lack of a vitamin can cause disease
Minerals	calcium, iron, potassium	regulate body functions, needed for structure of body parts, maintain good health
Water	water	dissolves and transports materials in the body which is 70% water, needed for chemical reactions in the body

The indigestible part of food is roughage. It is removed from the digestive tract. An unbalanced diet leads to malnutrition, disease, and weight gain or loss. All organisms have a minimum daily requirement of each type of nutrient to maintain good health.

Review Questions

9. Carbohydrates such as sugar and starch are a source of _____.

10. The amino acids found in _____ build and repair cells.

11. Calcium and iron are examples of _____ needed for good health.

12. Water will _____ and _____ materials in the body.

13. A disease such as rickets can be caused by an improper amount of _____ in the diet .

Human Physiology

Each organ system is composed of organs which perform specific functions. The organ systems interact with each other. The respiratory and excretory systems work together to rid the body of wastes. Tissues, organs, and organ systems help to provide all cells with nutrients, oxygen, and waste removal.

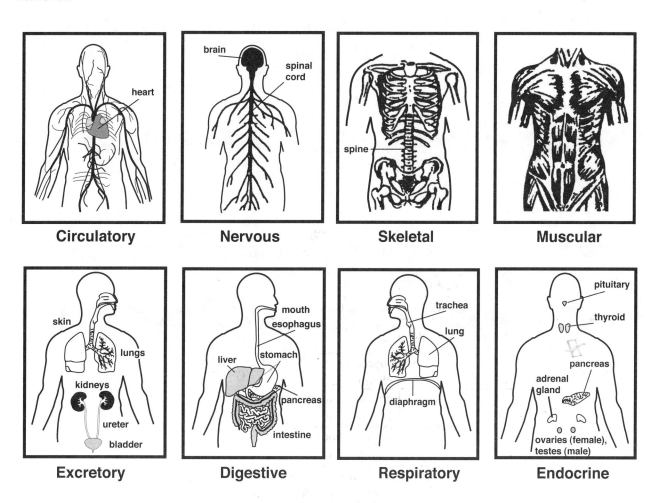

FIGURE 1. HUMAN BODY SYSTEMS

HUMAN BODY SYSTEMS

DIGESTIVE

ORGANS	FUNCTION(S)	INTERACTION(S) WITH OTHER SYSTEMS
Mouth	Physical and chemical breakdown of food	
Esophagus	Connects the mouth and stomach	
Stomach	Chemical breakdown of food	
Small Intestine	Completes chemical digestion, results in smaller molecules that can be absorbed and transported to cells	Interacts with the cirulatory system when nutrients are absorbed into the blood and transported to all body cells
Liver	Produces chemicals needed for digestion	
Pancreas		
Large Intestine	Absorbs water, collects undigested food for removal from body	Interacts with circulatory system to absorb and transport water

RESPIRATORY

ORGANS	FUNCTION(S)	INTERACTION(S) WITH OTHER SYSTEMS
Nose/mouth	Inhale oxygen and exhale carbon dioxide	
Trachea	Connects nose and lungs	
Bronchial tubes	Connect trachea to lungs	Interacts with the excretory system to rid the body of gaseous waste
Lungs	Site of gas exchange in air sacs called alveoli; oxygen goes into the blood, carbon dioxide is removed from the blood	Interacts with the circulatory system to exchange O_2 for CO_2 in the blood
Diaphragm	Muscle that helps to move air into and out of the lungs	

EXCRETORY

ORGANS	FUNCTION(S)	INTERACTION(S) WITH OTHER SYSTEMS
Kidneys	Filter out liquid waste from the blood	Interacts with the circulatory system and respiratory system to eliminate liquid and gaseous wastes from the body
Liver	Removes harmful substances from blood	
Ureters	Connect kidneys to bladder	
Bladder	Stores and eliminates liquid waste	
Lungs	Elimination of gaseous waste (carbon dioxide)	
Skin	Elimination of excess heat	

CIRCULATORY

ORGANS	FUNCTION(S)	INTERACTION(S) WITH OTHER SYSTEMS
Heart	Pumps blood through the body and the lungs	Interacts with the digestive and respiratory system to move substances to and from the cells
Arteries	Move blood away from the heart to the body	
Capillaries	Allow for the exchange of nutrients, oxygen, and wastes between the blood and body cells	
Veins	Move blood to the heart from the body	
Blood which includes: plasma	Immunity, antibodies	
platelets	Blood clotting	
white blood cells	Fight disease	
red blood cells	Transport oxygen and carbon dioxide	
Lymph Nodes	Remove bacteria, cancer cells, and disease - causing microorganisms before they enter the blood stream	

SKELETAL

ORGANS	FUNCTION(S)	INTERACTION(S)
Bones	Support body	Interacts with muscular system for movement of the body
	Protects organs	Coordinated by the nervous system
	Produce new red blood cells in the bone marrow	
Cartilage	Cushions bones	
Tendons	Attach muscles to bones	
Ligaments	Connect bone to bone	

MUSCULAR

ORGANS	FUNCTION(S)	INTERACTION(S) WITH OTHER SYSTEMS
Muscles	Motion of organs	Interacts with all organ systems causing movement of tissues and ogans
	Locomotion of body	Interacts with skeletal and nervous systems so that organism can move to escape danger, obtain food and shelter, and reproduce

NERVOUS

ORGANS	FUNCTION(S)	INTERACTION(S) WITH OTHER SYSTEMS
Brain	Interprets stimuli, sends impulses to the body	Interacts with the endocrine system to regulate the body's responses to changes in the environment
Spinal cord	Sends impulses to the brain	
Nerves	Send messages to the spinal cord, muscles and glands for response	
Sense organs	Detect changes in the environment	

ENDOCRINE

ORGANS	FUNCTION(S)	INTERACTION(S) WITH OTHER SYSTEMS
Glands which include: Pituitary	Produces hormones that control the actions of other glands	Interacts with all organ systems to chemically regulate and control each body function
Thyroid	Produces hormones that regulate metabolism	
Pancreas	Produces insulin, hormone that controls blood sugar	
Adrenal	Produces hormones that help the body deal with stress	

REPRODUCTIVE

ORGANS	FUNCTION(S)	INTERACTION(S) WITH OTHER SYSTEMS
Female: ovaries	Produce egg cells	Interacts with the endocrine system by producing hormones
Male: testes	Produces sperm cells	

14. The _____ system transports substances throughout the body.

15. Changes in the environment are noticed by _____ organs.

16. The excretory system eliminates liquid and gaseous _____.

17. The _____ system mechanically and chemically breaks down food.

18. Sex cells are produced by the _____ system.

19. Hormones are chemicals produced by the _____ system.

20. The alveoli in the lungs are part of the _____ system.

21. Liquid and gaseous wastes are removed from the body by the kidneys, _____ and _____.

22. Bone marrow produces _____.

23. Nutrients are provided to the cells by the interactions of the _____ and _____ systems.

Disease

Disease breaks down the structures or functions of an organism. Disease can affect the internal balance (**homeostasis**) of the organism. Disease in the human body can be infectious or non-infectious. **Infectious** disease is caused by microorganisms (**microbes**) and can be spread from person to person, such as influenza virus, or from animal to person, such as West Nile disease. We can have immunity from an infectious disease like measles because we have been vaccinated against it. Or perhaps we had a disease, like chicken pox, which caused us to produce antibodies against it. Specialized cells found in the blood protect the body from some infectious diseases. Chemicals produced by these cells identify and destroy microbes that enter the body.

Non-infectious diseases can not be transmitted from organism to organism. Some of these diseases are the result of failure of an organ or organ system. Kidney failure, caused by a malfunction of the kidneys, causes the entire system to fail. Personal behaviors involving the use of toxic substances such as alcohol and tobacco may cause disease. Emphysema is a disease of the lungs caused by the inhalation of tobacco smoke or chemicals. Poor dietary habits such as overeating (obesity) or under-eating (malnutrition) will interfere with one's internal dynamic equilibrium (balance) and affect the health of the person. Cancer is caused by abnormal cell division.

Other non-infectious diseases are hereditary. These diseases are a result of a genetic change in the chromosomes which may be passed to future generations. Cystic fibrosis, a disorder of the respiratory system, and sickle cell anemia, a disease of the blood, are hereditary.

During pregnancy poor personal behaviors by the mother may affect the development of her unborn child. Some of these effects can be seen immediately at birth, other effects may not appear for years.

Review Questions

24. Disease breaks down the structure or _____ of an organ system.

25. Disease can upset the internal balance or _____ in the organism.

26. Microbes that can be passed from organism to organism cause _____ disease.

27. Specialized _____ in the blood protect the body from infectious disease.

28. The chemicals produced by some specialized cells identify and destroy _____.

29. A poor diet can cause a _____ disease that can not be passed to another organism.

Plants

Green plants must carry out all the life functions through unique structures. The most important structures of the plant are the roots, stems, leaves, and flowers.

The **roots** absorb water and nutrients from the soil that the plant needs to stay alive. The roots anchor the plant to the ground.

The **stem** transports water and nutrients from the roots to the leaves. It also transports the food made in the leaves throughout the plant body. The stem supports the plant and its structures such as branches, leaves, and flowers.

The **leaf** is where the processes of gas exchange and photosynthesis take place. Through pores in the leaf, water vapor and carbon dioxide are exchanged with the air. In sunlight, chloroplasts in the leaf cells use carbon dioxide and water to produce oxygen and food by the process of **photosynthesis**.

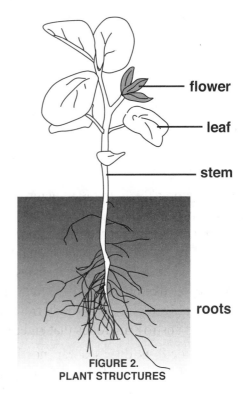

FIGURE 2.
PLANT STRUCTURES

Photosynthesis is a chemical reaction that occurs when chlorophyll in the chloroplasts absorbs light energy. Oxygen is eliminated from the plant through the leaf pores. The food, glucose, is then transported throughout the plant.

$$6CO_2 + 6H_2O \xrightarrow[\text{chlorophyll}]{\text{light}} C_6H_{12}O_6 + 6O_2$$
$$\text{(glucose)}$$

FIGURE 3. CHEMICAL REACTION OF PHOTOSYNTHESIS

Reproduction in flowering plants takes place in the flowers. Here fruits and seeds are produced.

Review Questions

30. Water and nutrients are taken out of the soil by _____.

31. The plant structures, such as branches and leaves, are supported by the _____.

32. Photosynthesis occurs in the _____ of the leaf cells.

33. Photosynthesis uses the compounds _____ and _____.

34. Green plants excrete _____ gas through their leaves.

35. The life process that occurs in flowers is _____.

VOCABULARY

Calorie

_____

carbohydrate

_____

chloroplast

_____

circulatory system

_____

diet

_____

digestive system

_____

disease

_____

endocrine system

_____

excretion

_____

fat

_____

gas exchange

_____

homeostasis

_____

hormone

_____

infectious disease

_____

leaf

_____

locomotion

_____

metabolism

_____

microbe

_____

nervous system

_____

non-infectious disease

_____

nutrition

_____

organ

_____

organ system

_____

photosynthesis

_____

protein

_____

reproductive system

_____

respiratory system

_____

root

_____

skeletal system

_____

stem

_____

stimulus

_____

tissue

_____

vitamin

_____

1. Which term includes the other three?

   (1) cell   (2) tissue   (3) organ   (4) organ system

2. Which term refers to all the chemical activities carried out by a living organism?

   (1) homeostasis   (2) regulation   (3) excretion   (4) metabolism

3. A nutrient needed for the growth and repair of cells is

   (1) carbohydrate   (2) fat   (3) vitamin   (4) protein

4. Most of the energy needed for body activities comes from

   (1) carbohydrates   (2) fats   (3) vitamins   (4) proteins

5. Fish is to protein, as vegetable oil is to

   (1) carbohydrate   (2) fat   (3) mineral   (4) vitamin

6. A person who consumes fewer calories than they need will

   (1) lose weight   (2) gain weight   (3) stay healthy   (4) have a lot of energy

7. The body system illustrated will interact with the

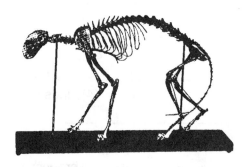

   (1) excretory system to eliminate wastes   (3) muscular system to cause locomotion
   (2) digestive system to absorb nutrients   (4) endocrine system to circulate hormones

8. Which part of the blood helps to fight disease causing microbes?

   (1) red blood cells   (2) white blood cells   (3) platelets   (4) plasma

9. Which is an appropriate heading for column **X**?

Organism	X
earthworm	moist skin
fish	gills
humans	lungs

(1) Structures Used in Gas Exchange   (3) Endocrine Systems

(2) Sensory Organs   (4) Structures Needed for Digestion

10. Which body system is functioning improperly when not enough of the hormone insulin is produced?

(1) digestive   (2) endocrine   (3) nervous   (4) reproductive

11. Kidney stones will affect the

(1) excretory system   (3) circulatory system

(2) digestive system   (4) respiratory system

12. Which is the first system affected when you hear a loud sound?

(1) excretory   (2) skeletal   (3) nervous   (4) endocrine

13. Which system is associated with transmission of impulses to the muscles?

(1) excretory   (2) skeletal   (3) nervous   (4) respiratory

14. The ribs protect the

(1) spinal cord and brain   (3) heart and kidneys

(2) lungs and heart   (4) lungs and spinal cord

15. Structures which return blood to the heart are the

(1) arteries   (3) bronchial tubes

(2) veins   (4) capillaries

Base your answers to **questions 16 – 24** on the following diagram:

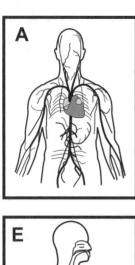
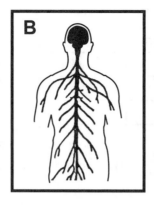
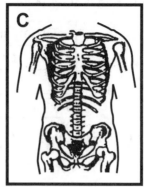
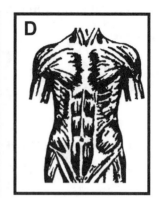
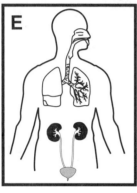
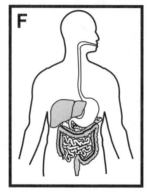
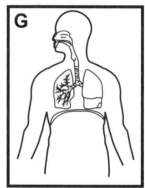
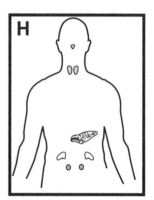

16. Which two systems work together to cause body motion?
    (1) A and B   (2) A and C   (3) C and D   (4) B and F

17. Which system exchanges oxygen for carbon dioxide?
    (1) B   (2) C   (3) D   (4) G

18. Which system coordinates and regulates all body activities?
    (1) A   (2) B   (3) C   (4) D

19. Which system includes the kidneys and bladder?
    (1) A   (2) C   (3) E   (4) G

20. Which systems release wastes from the body?
    (1) B and C   (2) C and G   (3) C and F   (4) E and G

21. Which system removes undigested food from the body?
    (1) B   (2) E   (3) F   (4) G

22. Which system circulates nutrients and oxygen throughout the body?
    (1) A   (2) D   (3) E   (4) H

23. The body system in diagram **D** is directly involved in:
    (1) blood clotting   (3) excretion of liquid wastes
    (2) causing body movements   (4) exchange of gases

24. Which systems work together to provide oxygen for all body cells and tissues?
    (1) A and G   (2) C and D   (3) C and E   (4) B and G

25. Which are organs of the human digestive system?

(1) lungs, bladder, stomach
(2) lungs, heart, small intestine
(3) stomach, small intestine, large intestine
(4) small intestine, large intestine, kidneys

26. The lungs, skin, and kidneys are all part of which system?

(1) digestive   (2) excretory   (3) respiratory   (4) circulatory

27. The chemicals that are secreted by the endocrine system to regulate organs and body activities are

(1) enzymes   (2) platelets   (3) hormones   (4) plasma

28. The main function of the human digestive system is to

(1) rid the body of wastes
(2) break down food so that nutrients can enter the body cells
(3) provide energy for the cells
(4) control and coordinate all body activities

29. A decrease in chlorophyll will affect a plant's ability to

(1) excrete wastes   (3) carry on reproduction
(2) carry on photosynthesis   (4) absorb oxygen

30. In a tree, light energy is converted to chemical energy in the

(1) root   (2) leaf   (3) stem   (4) seed

31. Which is *not* needed for photosynthesis?

(1) chlorophyll   (2) light   (3) oxygen   (4) carbon dioxide

32. Eating a sweet potato provides energy for human metabolism. The original source of this energy came from

(1) minerals in the soil   (3) water absorbed by the plant
(2) sunlight absorbed during photosynthesis   (4) absorption of carbon dioxide by the leaf

33. A stalk of celery is placed in water dyed blue. After a few days the blue dye is found in the upper part of the celery. Which life process occurred?

(1) respiration   (2) excretion   (3) reproduction   (4) transport

34. Read the passage below.

> ### Lyme Disease
>
> Since 1980, the number of reported cases of Lyme disease in New York State has been increasing. The carrier of this disease is a small deer tick, *Ixodes dammini*. The disease is spread from infected animals to ticks that bite them. Humans bitten by these ticks may become infected.
>
> The symptoms of Lyme disease do not always occur immediately. After an infected tick bite, a person may develop a skin rash several days or weeks later. Flu-like symptoms such as headache, muscle ache, joint pains, and fever may also develop. Sometimes these symptoms clear up and the person may not seek medical help. Sometimes there are no symptoms other than the sudden onset of arthritis. In a small number of cases if the person is not treated, they may develop chronic arthritis or disorders of the heart and nervous systems.
>
> A simple blood test can diagnose Lyme disease. Antibiotics are effective in treating the disease. People can take precautions to lower their risk of getting this disease. They should check themselves and pets for ticks. When walking outside wear light colored clothing, tuck pants into socks, wear long sleeves and use insect repellant. People should seek immediate medical treatment if they suspect they have the disease.

a. This disease is considered (infectious) (non-infectious).

b. Name ONE activity that would put you at risk for Lyme disease.

_____

c. There is concern about increases in the deer population in some communities. Explain, based on this reading, why this would be so.

_____

_____

d. State ONE way that you can protect yourself from getting Lyme disease.

_____

e. State TWO symptoms of Lyme disease.

(1)_____ (2)_____

f. Name TWO body systems that could be affected by Lyme disease.

(1)_____ (2)_____

35. A scientific study showed that the depth at which green algae is found in a lake varies from day to day. On a sunny day, the algae is found as much as 6 meters below the surface. On a cloudy day, the algae is nearer the surface.

Explain a possible reason for this.

_____

_____

_____

36. In an investigation, three young plants of the same species were placed in three different locations. Each plant had the same type and amount of soil and received the same amount of water each day. At the end of one week the following data was collected.

Location	Height (cm)	Leaf Color
Sunny windowsill	11.0	Green
Indirect sunlight	9.0	Green
Closed closet	7.0	Whitish Yellow

a. Write the hypothesis that was being tested by this experiment.

_____

_____

b. Explain the reason that the plant in the closet did not have green leaves.

_____

_____

c. Write a conclusion based on this data.

_____

_____

_____

37. The graph below indicates the amount of protein digested in 10 hours.

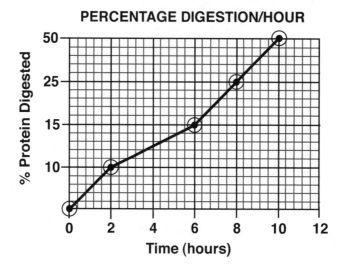

PERCENTAGE DIGESTION/HOUR

y-axis: % Protein Digested (50, 25, 15, 10)

x-axis: Time (hours) (0, 2, 4, 6, 8, 10, 12)

a. Explain ONE error that was made in preparing the graph.

_____

b. Name the responding variable. _____

c. Name ONE organ that is involved in protein digestion. _____

38. You are the head of the research division of the Leafy Lettuce Company. You are experimenting with growing lettuce using hydroponics. Hydroponics involves growing plants in a nutrient solution rather than soil. The nutrient solution that the company uses contains water, nitrogen, and phosphorous. The company wants to know if adding iron to the solution will improve the lettuce growth.

a. State the problem that is being tested.

_____

_____

b. State TWO factors that must be held constant during the experiment.

(1) _____ (2) _____

c. State the data that should be collected.

_____

39. Many human organ systems interact to carry out the life processes.

Digestive	Respiratory	Excretory	Circulatory	Nervous	Endocrine	Muscular	Skeletal

    a.   Select TWO organ systems and explain how and why they interact with each other.

_____

_____

_____

    b.   Describe ONE malfunction or disease associated with ONE of the systems.

_____

_____

40.   For each statement select the human body system involved.

    a.   The hormone adrenaline is produced when you are excited. _____

    b.   Prepares nutrients for absorption in to the body. _____

    c.   Protects the major body organs. _____

    d.   Blood returns to the heart through the veins. _____

    e.   You listen to a music concert. _____

    f.   During a bicycle ride you sweat. _____

    g.   You read and interpret a poem. _____

    h.   The kidneys filter wastes from your blood. _____

41. Select ONE structure labeled on the tree and describe its function.

    a. Structure:_____

       Function:_____

       _____

    b. Name ONE human body part that has a similar function: _____

       Explain: _____

       _____

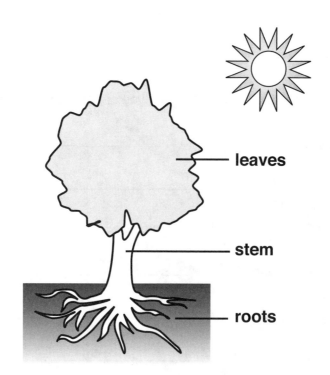

                  leaves

                  stem

                  roots

CHAPTER 6

REPRODUCTION AND DEVELOPMENT

> • *THE LIVING ENVIRONMENT: KEY IDEA 4*
> *The continuity of life is sustained through reproduction and development.*

Reproduction

Reproduction is the life process by which new cells arise from existing cells. Reproduction can occur asexually or sexually. Some organisms are able to reproduce both sexually and asexually.

Reproduction replaces cells. When you cut your finger, new skin cells are produced to repair your finger. Reproduction adds more cells for growth. As you grow, you need more cells. Reproduction also produces new organisms. This is essential for the survival of the species, but not the individual.

Review Questions

1. The life process by which new cells arise from existing cells is _____.

2. Reproduction is essential for the survival of the _____.

3. Some _____ can reproduce both sexually and asexually.

4. Describe THREE functions of reproduction.

    (1) _____

    (2) _____

    (3) _____

Asexual Reproduction

Asexual reproduction produces a new identical cell. Asexual reproduction results in more cells for an organism to grow and replace damaged cells.

Asexual reproduction involves only one parent cell. All the genetic material comes from a single parent cell. The offspring is genetically identical to the parent. Cancer cells are a result of abnormal cell division. This uncontrolled cell division is harmful to the organism.

Asexual reproduction can occur in two ways. The first is **cell division** or mitosis. This is the division of one cell into many identical cells. It is one of the methods of reproduction for unicellular organisms such as the paramecium. The genetic material, DNA, in the chromosomes of the cell's nucleus is **duplicated** or copied, and then separated. Each identical set of genetic material is passed to the two resulting cells. The heredity information is identical in all the resulting cells, they are exactly alike.

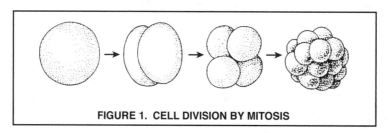

FIGURE 1. CELL DIVISION BY MITOSIS

Asexual reproduction can also take place by the separation of a part of a plant or animal. The ability of an organism to regrow lost body parts is called **regeneration**. Some animals, such as starfish, can replace lost arms. Some plants and animals produce small buds that will grow into new individuals. A piece of a branch or stem cut from a plant can grow into a new identical plant.

FIGURE 2. REGENERATION

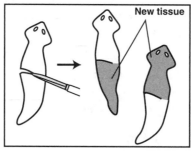

Review Questions

5. Asexual reproduction begins with _____ parent cell.

6. Asexual reproduction produces a cell that is _____ to the parent cell.

7. Due to asexual reproduction, the heredity information in each new cell is _____ to the parent cell.

8. A branch of a forsynthia bush is planted in the ground and grows into a new plant. This is an example of _____ reproduction.

9. Regeneration is the ability to _____ lost body parts.

Sexual Reproduction

The function of sexual reproduction is to produce new individuals. **Sexual reproduction** requires two parent cells coming together. It is most common in multicellular organisms. It begins with the production of sex cells. The female sex cell is the **egg**. The male sex cell is the **sperm**. Each sex cell contains half the heredity information, DNA, for the offspring. The sex cells join together to produce a new organism. This process is called **fertilization**. The resulting cell is a zygote that has genetic material from each parent. Sexual reproduction causes variation in the traits of a species, which could help in the survival of the species.

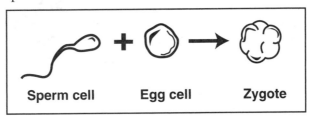

FIGURE 3. FERTILIZATION

Fertilization can take place either externally, outside the body, or internally. Frog eggs are fertilized in the water, outside the body. In mammals, fertilization takes place inside the female's body.

Review Questions

10. Sexual reproduction requires _____ parent cells.

11. The male sex cell is the _____.

12. The female sex cell is the _____.

13. During fertilization, the two parent cells will _____ together.

14. In cats, fertilization is _____.

15. Fertilization in most fish takes place _____.

Development

Multicellular organisms exhibit complex changes in development which begins after fertilization. The fertilized egg, or zygote, undergoes many cell divisions that will result in a multicellular organism. Each cell has identical genetic information.

In humans, the fertilized egg grows specialized tissue which develops into organs and organ systems before birth. Each type of cell grows using a set of specific instructions. For example, nerve cells grow differently than muscle cells.

Patterns of development vary among plants and animals. Some fertilized eggs develop outside of the female's body, such as those of birds. Others develop inside the female's body, such as those of humans. In seed-bearing plants, the young plant begins to develop inside the seed.

In some species the young resemble the adults. In other species the young do not resemble the adults. Some insects and amphibians undergo **metamorphosis** as they mature. This is a series of changes the organism undergoes during its development from egg to adult. The moth undergoes four stages of development: the egg, larva (caterpillar), pupa, and adult.

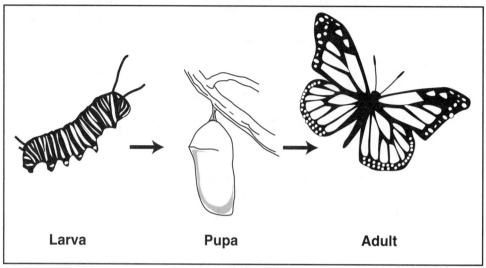

Larva   **Pupa**   **Adult**

FIGURE 4. METAMORPHOSIS

Development into adulthood is characterized by varying growth patterns. Various body structures and functions change as an organism goes through its **life cycle**. After the adult stage is reached, the structures and functions of the body systems weaken. This is called aging, which is a natural part of development.

Review Questions

16. The fertilized egg undergoes many _____ divisions as it becomes a multicellular organism.

17. Each body cell has _____ genetic information.

18. In humans, tissues and organ systems develop before _____.

19. Some insects and amphibians undergo body changes called _____.

20. As an organism ages, many structures and organ systems will _____.

Reproduction in Plants

Some plants reproduce asexually so that each offspring is exactly like the parent. Vegetative reproduction is the process by which the roots, stems, and leaves of a plant give rise to a new plant. The new plant has the same exact hereditary information as its parent. A bulb is a short underground stem containing stored food. As the plant grows, new bulbs sprout from the old one. Daffodils and garlic reproduce by bulbs. A runner is a horizontal stem with buds, a new plant grows where the runner roots into the ground. Strawberry plants reproduce from runners.

Plants can also reproduce sexually. The **flower** of a plant is the reproductive organ. Female eggs are in the ovary at the base of the flower bud. **Pollen** produced in the flower contains male sperm cells. **Pollination** is the transfer of pollen to the ovary. Fertilization occurs when the sperm in the pollen merges with the egg cell in the flower's ovary. Some plants self-pollinate when pollen grains join with the eggs of the same flower. Cross-pollination is the transfer of pollen from one plant to another. Wind, insects, rain, and birds carry pollen from one plant to another.

FIGURE 5.

FLOWER

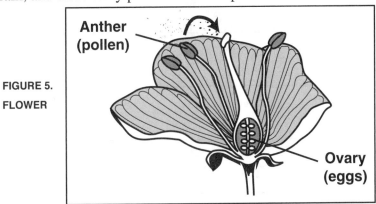

The fertilized egg develops into a young plant found in the **seed**. The seed contains food for the new plant. In order for the seed to sprout or germinate and develop into a plant, it needs the proper temperature, oxygen, and water.

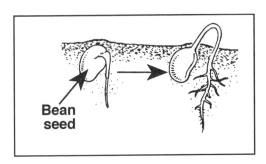

FIGURE 6. GERMINATION OF A SEED

Review Questions

21. A _____ is a short, underground stem containing stored food.

22. The _____ is the reproductive organ of a plant.

23. Pollen contain _____ cells

24. The transfer of pollen from one plant to another is _____.

25. Wind, water, and animals carry _____ from one plant to another.

26. The THREE conditions necessary for seeds to germinate are (1)_____

    (2) _____ (3) _____.

asexual reproduction

_____

cell division

_____

duplicated

_____

egg cell

_____

external fertilization

_____

fertilization

_____

flower

_____

internal fertilization

_____

life cycle

_____

metamorphosis

_____

offspring

_____

pollen

_____

pollination

_____

regeneration

_____

reproduction

_____

seed

_____

sexual reproduction

_____

sperm cell

_____

CHAPTER REVIEW

1. Reproduction would not occur if which part of a cell was removed?
   (1) cell membrane   (2) chloroplast   (3) nucleus   (4) cytoplasm

2. Uncontrolled cell division of abnormal cells is characteristic of
   (1) cancer cells   (2) regeneration   (3) sperm cells   (4) fruits and seeds

3. In a hen house, the length of daylight is prolonged by using indoor lighting.
   The stimulus for egg laying is
   (1) food   (2) warmth   (3) light   (4) amount of water

4. Female is to egg, as male is to
   (1) embryo   (2) sperm   (3) offspring   (4) spore

Base your answer to **questions 5-7** on the diagram below which illustrates sexual reproduction and early development of a new organism.

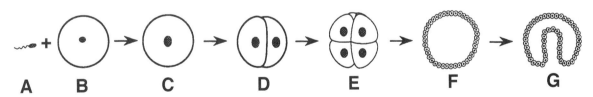

A   B   C   D   E   F   G

5. The structure **A** is most likely the
   (1) egg cell   (2) embryo   (3) sperm cell   (4) nerve cell

6. Fertlization of the egg will occur between diagrams
   (1) A, B and C   (2) C and D   (3) E and F   (4) F and G

7. Identical twins would result if
   (1) cells at **E** join with **F**   (3) two cells at **A** unite
   (2) cells at **D** separate from one another   (4) two **A** cells unite with one **B** cell

Base your answers to **questions 8-10** on the diagrams below which illustrate reproduction in several organisms.

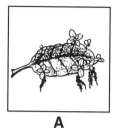 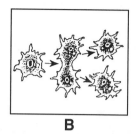 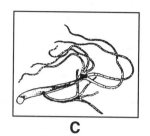 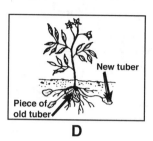

| A | B | C | D |

8. All of these diagrams represent
   (1) asexual reproduction
   (2) sexual reproduction
   (3) metamorphosis
   (4) regeneration

9. Budding is illustrated in diagram
   (1) A   (2) B   (3) C   (4) D

10. A protist, such as a paramecium, will most likely reproduce as shown in diagram:
    (1) A   (2) B   (3) C   (4) D

11. Organisms, such as fish, which reproduce by external fertilization and development usually
    (1) have eggs that are very large
    (2) produce a very large number of eggs
    (3) produce a very small number of eggs
    (4) have all eggs survive

12. The diagram to the right illustrates
    (1) asexual reproduction
    (2) sexual reproduction
    (3) metamorphosis
    (4) regeneration

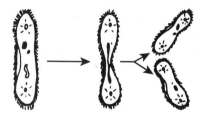

13. Which diagram illustrates regeneration?

A   B   C   D

(1) A   (2) B   (3) C   (4) D

14. Which set of phrases best lists the characteristics of sexual reproduction?
    (1) one parent, merging of cells, offspring are identical to the parent
    (2) one parent, no merging of cells, offspring are identical to the parent
    (3) two parents, no merging of cells, offspring are identical to the parents
    (4) two parents, merging of cells, offspring are not identical to the parents

15. Large numbers of genetically identical offspring can be produced by
    (1) asexual reproduction   (3) metamorphosis
    (2) sexual reproduction   (4) mutation

16. In plants sexual reproduction occurs in the
    (1) flower only   (2) flower and leaf   (3) flower and stem (4) stem only

17. The fertilized eggs in a flower will become
    (1) fruits   (3) seeds
    (2) flowers   (4) bulbs

18. When a lizard is caught by a predator, it can escape by losing its tail. The lizard's tail will regrow by the process of
    (1) regeneration   (3) pollination
    (2) metamorphosis   (4) fertilization

19. In humans the healing of a cut occurs by the process of
    (1) asexual reproduction by budding   (3) sexual reproduction by regeneration
    (2) asexual reproduction by cell division   (4) asexual and sexual reproduction

20. Which of the following is an example of sexual reproduction?
    (1) a starfish regrows a missing arm
    (2) roots develop on a stem cutting from a plant
    (3) an ameba splits in half
    (4) a seed is produced in a flower

21. Which is true about the offspring from asexual reproduction?
    (1) genetically different and larger than the parent cell
    (2) genetically different and smaller than the parent cell
    (3) genetically the same and smaller than the parent cell
    (4) genetically the same and larger than the parent cell

22. A female fish produces
    (1) egg cells   (2) sperm cells   (3) clones   (4) pollen

23. Which conditions are necessary in order for a planted seed to begin to grow into a plant?

(1) sunlight, warmth, soil

(2) sunlight , moisture, warmth

(3) moisture, warmth, oxygen

(4) moisture, carbon dioxide, oxygen

24. Which statement describes asexual reproduction?

(1) it involves two parent cells

(2) it involves one parent cell

(3) it causes variation in the offspring

(4) it involves egg and sperm cells

EXTENDED RESPONSE

25. The graph below shows data on the average life span of humans.

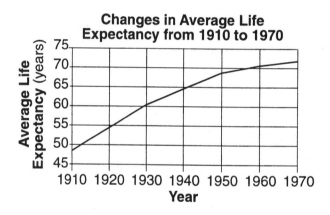

Changes in Average Life Expectancy from 1910 to 1970

a. Describe the change in human life span from 1910 to 1970.

_____

_____

b. Propose a possible reason for this change.

_____

_____

26. A student draws the following diagram in her notebook after observing a one-celled organism for an hour. The student concludes that she had observed asexual reproduction. Explain how you know this is true.

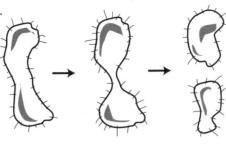

_____

_____

_____

27. Drinking alcohol during pregnancy can cause birth defects known as Fetal Alcohol Syndrome (FAS). Scientists do not know the process by which alcohol causes this damage to the unborn child. There is evidence that even low levels of alcohol consumption can cause physical and mental problems to the child. The chart below compares infant characteristics of two categories of mothers: drinker and nondrinker.

Infant Characteristics

Characteristics (Average)	Alcohol Use During Pregnancy	
	Drinker	Nondrinker
Weeks of development before birth	36.9	38.7
Birth weight (g)	2,555	3,094
Birth length (cm)	46.8	50.1
Head circumference (cm)	32.1	34.5

Physical Abnormalities Detected in Infants at Birth

Physical Abnormalities	Alcohol Use During Pregnancy	
	Drinker (Percentage of 40 Infants)	Nondrinker (Percentage of 80 Infants)
Low birth weight	73	12
Small brain	33	0
Flattened nasal bridge	8	0
Abnormal facial features	15	0
Spinal defects	8	0
Heart defects	8	0

Explain how the data supports the scientists' conclusion that alcohol is harmful to the unborn child.

_____

_____

_____

28. The diagram shows the life cycle of a frog.

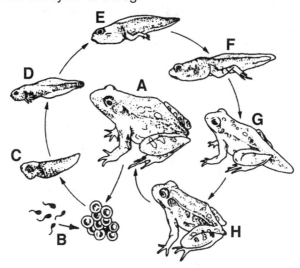

a. Write the letter at which sexual reproduction occurs. _____

b. Name the process that is occurring from letters **D** through **G.** _____

29. There are two methods of reproduction: asexual and sexual.

a. Explain ONE way the two are similar. _____

_____

b. Explain ONE way the two are different. _____

_____

30. Select the type of reproduction (*asexual or sexual*) described by each statement.

a. Two different parent cells combine. _____

b. The offspring are identical to the parent cell. _____

c. Budding. _____

d. A lobster regrows a lost claw. _____

e. The same traits appear in every generation. _____

f. A cut branch from a bush grows roots when placed in water. _____

g. There are many varieties of tomatoes. _____

CHAPTER 7

GENETICS

The Science of Heredity

Heredity is the passage of **genetic traits** from one generation to the next. It is controlled by the **chromosomes** in the nucleus of cells. Chromosomes are made of **DNA.** Chromosomes are composed of smaller units called **genes.**

During reproduction genes move from one generation to the next on the chromosomes. Genes control the development of a trait. A pair of genes control each trait. Sometimes genes mutate or change. Genetic mutations are hereditary and result in new characteristics in an organism.

In asexually reproducing organisms, all the genes come from one parent. This results in offspring that are genetically identical to the parent. In sexual reproduction, each parent contributes half of the genes. Therefore the offspring are not identical to the parents. They are a mixture of the genetic material from both parents.

Review Questions

1. Hereditary information is contained in the _____ of the cell's nucleus.

2. Chromosomes are made of the compound _____.

3. In all organisms, genetic traits are passed from one _____ to the next.

4. Every trait is controlled by at least _____ genes.

5. In sexual reproduction, _____ of the genes come from each parent.

6. In _____ reproducing organisms, all the genes come from one parent.

7. Variation in traits are found in offspring from _____ reproduction.

Probability of Inheritance

Most genes are either dominant or recessive. **Dominant genes** are the traits that will usually appear in the individual. An offspring with a gene for brown eyes and a gene for blue eyes will have brown eyes because brown eyes are a dominant trait.

Recessive genes are hidden by the dominant gene. If an offspring has one gene for blue eyes and one gene for brown eyes, they will have brown eyes because blue eyes are a recessive trait. A blue-eyed person must have both recessive genes for blue eyes.

Some recessive traits are common in populations. For example having five fingers is controlled by a recessive gene. Since most of us have five fingers, this recessive gene is the most common in the human population. Type O blood type is another example of a recessive gene being most common in the human population.

In completing genetic problems, the trait studied is represented by a letter such as "A". The dominant gene is represented by a capital letter ("A") and the recessive gene is represented by the lower case letter ("a"). In a pair of genes the following possibilities exist:

Description of a pair of genes	Gene pair	Appearance of individual
Both are dominant	AA	Shows the dominant trait
Both are recessive	aa	Shows the recessive trait
One is dominant, the other recessive	Aa	Shows the dominant trait

The **Punnett square** shows the probable results of a genetic cross of two parents. It shows the probability of a trait being expressed in the offspring. The chart below shows the possible results when two purple flowered plants are crossed (purple flowers "**F**" is dominant over yellow flowers "**f**").

	F	f
F	FF	Ff
f	Ff	ff

According to this Punnett Square, 75% ($3/4$) of the offspring could have purple flowers and 25% could have yellow flowers.

Pedigree charts trace a genetic trait in a family tree. It shows the presence or absence of a particular trait in each member of a generation. The following pedigree chart shows the inheritance of handedness in humans over three generations. The gene for right-handedness (**R**) is dominant over the gene for left-handedness (**r**).

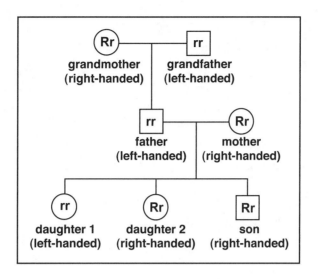

FIGURE 1. PEDIGREE CHART FOR HANDEDNESS

Review Questions

8. The traits that usually appear in the offspring are controlled by a _____ gene.

9. Recessive genes are _____ when the dominant gene is present.

10. For the offspring to show a recessive trait, both inherited genes must be the _____.

11. Complete the Punnett Square for wing type in flies. Long wings (**L**) is dominant over short wings (**l**).

x	L	L
L		
l		

a. According to this Punnett Square, what is the probability of an offspring with short wings?

_____

b. Describe the wing type of both parents? _____

12. The Punnett Square shows a cross between tomato plants. Red (**R**) fruit is dominant over yellow (**r**). The probability of producing red tomatoes is _____%.

x	R	r
r	Rr	rr
r	Rr	rr

13. Refer to the pedigree chart for hair color. Brown hair (**B**) is dominant over blond hair (**b**).

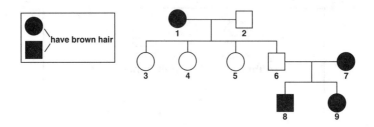

have brown hair

    a. How many children did parent **1** and parent **2** have? _____

    b. Write the gene pair for individual #**2**. _____

    c. Write the gene pair for individual #**8**. _____

Human Inheritance

Each human cell contains a copy of all the genes needed to produce a human being. A human cell has thousands of different genes found on 46 chromosomes in each cell. Each parent contributes 23 chromosomes. One of these pairs of chromosomes determines the gender of the offspring. In females the chromosome pair is XX, in males the pair is XY.

Some human diseases are the result of recessive genetic defects. These disorders are usually sex-linked because they are inherited on the X-chromosome. Hemophilia, the inability of blood to clot, and red-green color blindness are both recessive genetic disorders. Other genetic diseases are linked to certain cultures. Sickle cell anemia is a genetic disease linked to African Americans.

Review Quesions

14. A human cell has thousands of different _____.

15. In humans, each parent contributes _____ chromosomes to the offspring.

16. Some diseases are the result of _____ genes that are defective.

17. Some genetic diseases are linked to the _____ chromosome.

Gene Mutation

A **mutation** is a change in a gene which can cause the sudden appearance of a new trait in the offspring. Some genes never mutate, others do. The mutation can occur naturally or spontaneously. Most mutations are harmful and therefore the offspring do not survive.

Mutations can be caused by factors in the environment such as chemicals, x-rays, or radiation. Mutations have been important in evolution since they provide variation in a species. A new trait may cause the individual to be better adapted to the environment or to any changes that may occur in the environment .

The processes of mutation and sexual reproduction cause a variety of traits in a species. Small differences between parents and offspring can accumulate in successive generations, so that the descendants are very different from their ancestors. These genetic differences can result in a new species. This change in a species over time is known as **evolution.**

Review Questions

18. A gene mutation is a _____ in a gene.

19. Most mutations are _____ to the offspring.

20. Mutations cause the appearance of _____ in a species.

21. A mutation may enable the new individual to _____ to changes in the environment.

22. Small differences between parent and offspring can accumulate over time and result in a new _____.

23. A change in a species over long periods of time is known as _____.

Evolution

Change in most species is usually gradual. Most life forms evolved over millions of years. Some species of insects and bacteria can undergo significant changes in a few years. For example, antibiotic-resistant bacteria mutate very quickly.

There are more than 4 million species of organisms on Earth today. Evolution explains the diversity of life forms which we see today. Changes in the environment have affected the survival of organisms. New inherited traits may make the species better **adapted** to its surroundings. Biological adaptations include new structures, behaviors, or physiology that enhance the survival or reproductive success of the individual. Sexual reproduction results in variation in traits through the combining of two different parent cells. Therefore species which sexually reproduce are better able to adapt to changes in the environment .

The evolution of a species is caused by genetic **variations** which persist. Organisms with favorable variations are better able to adapt and survive. This is called **natural selection**. Today human activities such as genetic engineering and selective breeding affect the variation in some species. **Selective breeding** is choosing plants and animals with desirable traits to reproduce. For example, a farmer may choose to only grow disease-resistant plants. **Genetic engineering** involves changing the genes in a cell.

Living organisms have changed from their ancestors. These changes are mostly physical changes. Organisms have gone from simple unicellular organisms to complex multicellular organisms. Fossils found in sedimentary rock show that many organisms that existed millions of years ago no longer exist. These ancient **fossils** are very different from today's organisms. Recently deposited rock layers have fossils that are more similar to existing species.

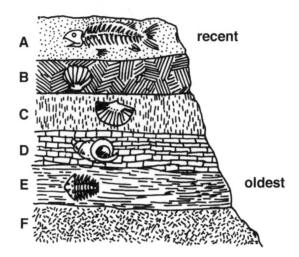

FIGURE 2. SEDIMENTARY ROCK LAYERS WITH FOSSILS

Comparative anatomy, which is the study of the structural similarities and differences among living things, provides evidence for evolution. Vestigial parts are remnants of structures that were functional in some ancestors and prove that organisms have changed. In humans, wisdom teeth and the appendix were once functional structures, but we have no use for them today.

Review Questions

24. The time needed for change in a species is usually _____.

25. Evolution causes _____ species to appear.

26. Evolution of a species enables the new organism to _____ to changes in the environment.

27. Natural selection is when organisms with _____ characteristics survive.

28. Human activities, such as _____ engineering, may affect the variation of a species.

29. Evidence of evolutionary change is found in _____ in sedimentary rocks.

30. Organisms evolved from unicellular to _____.

VOCABULARY

adapt

chromosome

DNA

dominant gene

evolution

fossil

gene

genetic engineering

genetic trait

heredity

inherited

mutation

natural selection

offspring

pedigree chart

Punnett square

recessive gene

_____

selective breeding

_____

survival of the fittest

_____

variation

_____

CHAPTER REVIEW

1. DNA is most closely associated with the
    (1) cytoplasm   (2) cell membrane   (3) chromosomes   (4) cell wall

2. The chromosomes are found in the
    (1) cytoplasm   (2) cell membrane   (3) nucleus   (4) cell wall

3. A gene is a small part of a
    (1) chromosome   (2) cell wall   (3) cell membrane   (4) chloroplast

4. The diagram below represents the organization of genetic information within a cell nucleus.

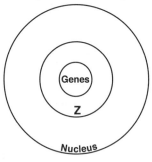

    The circle labeled "**Z**" most likely represents
    (1) vacuoles   (2) chromosomes   (3) chloroplasts   (4) amino acids

5. A change in the structure of DNA in the egg cell could result in a
    (1) clone   (2) new trait   (3) bud   (4) spore

6. The greatest genetic variation in species is found in offspring that result from:
    (1) budding   (3) sexual reproduction
    (2) regeneration   (4) asexual reproduction

7. In the joining together of two different genes for the same trait, the one that appears is
   (1) dominant   (2) recessive   (3) pure   (4) mutant

8. Only red tulips result from the cross between pure red and pure white tulips. Which statement is true?
   (1) Red is a dominant trait.
   (2) Red is a recessive trait.
   (3) Red is more common in the warmer spring weather.
   (4) Red is a gene mutation.

9. In squirrels gray (**G**) is dominant over black (**g**) fur color. If a **Gg** squirrel is crossed with a **gg** squirrel, what is the probability that the offspring will have black fur?
   (1) 0 %   (2) 25 %   (3) 50 %   (4) 100 %

10. The pedigree chart traces the appearance of earlobes through three generations of a family. Based on this chart, attached earlobes is a

    (1) dominant trait
    (2) recessive trait
    (3) mutated trait
    (4) trait common in females

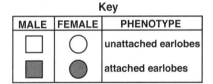

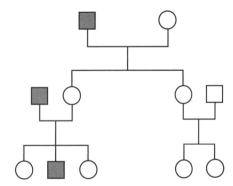

11. Most cells in the human body contain 46 chromosomes. How many of these chromosomes were contributed by each parent?
    (1) 15   (2) 23   (3) 46   (4) 92

12. A change in genetic material that produces a variation in a species may be caused by
    (1) a mutation   (3) overproduction of egg cells
    (2) competition   (4) a struggle for survival

13. Mutations of genes can be caused by

(1) x-rays, chemicals, water

(2) x-rays, chemicals, temperature changes

(3) x-rays, chemicals, ultraviolet radiation

(4) x-rays, ultraviolet radiation, temperature changes

14. Which process is a common practice that has been used by farmers for hundreds of years to develop new plant and animal varieties?

(1) cloning

(2) genetic engineering by moving DNA

(3) selective breeding for desirable traits

(4) asexual reproduction

15. Which statement is best supported by the fossil record?

(1) Many organisms from the past are extinct.

(2) Early life forms were very complex.

(3) Many early life forms are similar to today's organisms.

(4) Early organisms did not have to adapt to changes in the environment.

16. The variety of organisms present on Earth today proves that over time

(1) the environment has not changed causing rapid evolution

(2) new genetic traits have allowed species to adapt to new environments

(3) competition among species has forced organisms to evolve

(4) organisms carefully plan for the changes they need to make

17. If the rock layers have not been disturbed, which layers would contain the oldest fossil ?

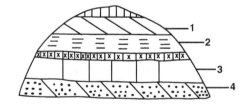

(1) 1   (2) 2   (3) 3   (4) 4

18. Which concept is illustrated by the physical changes in the size and structure of the horse over time?

TIME

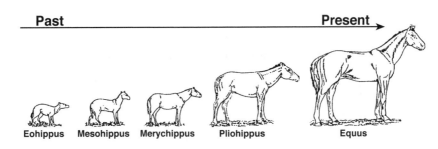

Past   Present

Eohippus   Mesohippus   Merychippus   Pliohippus   Equus

(1) genetic engineering   (3) evolution
(2) succession   (4) cloning

19. The changes in the foot structure in a bird population over many generations are shown below.

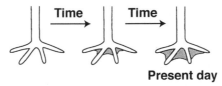

Time   Time

Present day

These changes can best be described by the concept of:

(1) evolution   (3) stable genes
(2) extinction   (4) use and disuse

20. Many plant and animal species have become extinct because they could not

(1) migrate to warmer climates   (3) reproduce
(2) adapt to environmental changes   (4) hibernate

21. Traits that enable an organism to survive and reproduce in its environment are known as

(1) adaptations   (3) recessive
(2) hybrid characteristics   (4) clones

22. The fact that offspring may have characteristics somewhat different from those of their parents is mainly due to

(1) metamorphosis   (3) sexual reproduction
(2) regeneration   (4) asexual reproduction

23. Which statement best explains the significance of sexual reproduction in the process of evolution in a species?

(1) the egg and sperm are identical   (3) variation in traits occurs
(2) many offspring are produced   (4) few offspring are produced

24. Survival of the fittest refers to organisms that can

(1) grow faster

(3) develop large muscles

(2) adapt to the environment

(4) live in cold climates

25. Sexually reproducing organisms show a greater variation in traits than asexually reproducing organisms. This is because when organisms reproduce sexually

(1) more mutations occur

(2) the offspring inherit half of the genes from each parent

(3) only the genes from the mother appear in the offspring

(4) only the genes from the father appear in the offspring

EXTENDED RESPONSE

26. Read the passage below.

> Before the Industrial Revolution, a light-colored variety of peppered moth was well camouflaged on the light-colored bark of trees near London. A dark-colored variety of peppered moth probably existed but was rare because it was so easily seen by birds and eaten. When industry was introduced in London, soot blackened the barks of the trees. As a result, the dark-colored variety of the moth was the better camouflaged of the two moth varieties and became more abundant.

a. Name the human activity that changed the population of the peppered moth.

_____

b. Explain how this is an example of natural selection.

_____

_____

c. If strict air pollution controls were put into effect, explain how the peppered moth population would be affected.

_____

_____

27. State what could happen to a species in a changing environment if the offspring do *not* have any genetic variations.

_____

_____

28. In pea plants, the trait for tall (**T**) is dominant over the trait for short (**t**) stems.

    a. Complete the Punnet square below:

	T	t
t		
t		

    b. If 100 pea plants were produced, state the amount that could probably be short stems.

    _____

29. In summer squash, white-colored fruit is dominant over yellow-colored fruit. Complete the Punnett square between pure yellow and hybrid white.

    (**W** = white; **w** = yellow)

W		
w		

30. The chart indicates a method of representing traits in pea plants.

Symbol for Gene	Trait Represented
T	tall
t	short
Y	yellow
y	green

    a. Write the gene composition for a short pea plant. _____

    b. The dominant trait for height in pea plants is _____.

    c. A plant that is **TTYy** would appear as _____.

    d. A plant that is **Ttyy** would appear as _____.

31. Short hair (**H**) in dogs is dominant over long hair (**h**). Buster has short hair and Cody has long hair.

    a. Name the dog that has both the same genes for hair length. _____

    b. Explain your choice. _____

_____

32. Pedigree chart for length of eyelashes where "**E**" is the gene for long eyelashes and "**e**" is the gene for short eyelashes.

Key

□ ○	short eyelashes
■ ●	long eyelashes

    a. State the eyelash length for individual **#2**. _____

    b. State the number of children that parents **1** and **2** had. _____

    c. State the individuals which have gene type "**ee**". _____

    d. Individual **#5** can have the gene type **EE** or **Ee**. Explain. _____

_____

    e. Individuals **#6** and **#7** both have long eyelashes but have children with short eyelashes. Explain how this is possible.

_____

_____

    f. How many children are in the third generation. _____

33. For many years, the dogs of several breeds had their tails clipped off when they were puppies. Therefore the adult dog had no tail. The offspring of these dogs were born with tails. Explain why the offspring had a tail when their parents did not have a tail.

_____

_____

CHAPTER 8

ASTRONOMY

> • *THE PHYSICAL SETTING: KEY IDEA 1*
> *Earth and celestial phenomena can be described using principles of relative motion and perspective.*

The Universe

The universe is composed of empty space, energy, and matter. Most of the universe is empty space. Matter in the universe includes gas molecules, mainly hydrogen, and dust particles. Some of this matter has come together to form stars, planets, moons, meteors, asteroids, and comets. The unaided eye can see a few of these objects. Others can only be seen with scientific instruments such as telescopes.

Stars are spherical masses of hot gases that produce energy. These luminous bodies look small because they are so far away. The distances between stars is vast and can not be measured in ordinary distance units such as kilometers. Astronomers use the unit "light year" to measure distances in space. A light year is the distance light travels in a year.

The objects in the universe are in motion relative to Earth and to each other. Astronomers have evidence that our universe is expanding. Most stars and galaxies of stars are moving away from each other.

Review Questions

1. The universe is mostly _____.

2. Light, heat, and ultraviolet radiation are types of _____ produced by stars.

3. The most common gaseous element found in stars is _____.

4. Large distances in space make stars appear very _____.

5. In the universe all objects are in motion and moving _____ each other.

6. The graph below shows the temperature and brightness of some types of stars.

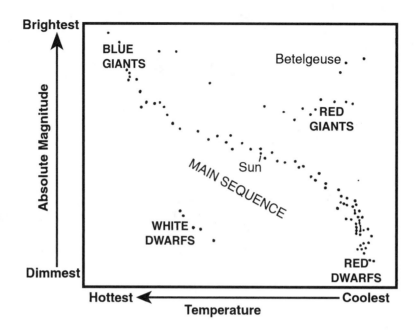

a. The brightest stars are called _____.

b. The color of the coolest stars is _____.

c. Compared to a red dwarf, a white dwarf is _____.

d. The Sun is classified as a _____ star.

e. Compared to a red dwarf, a red giant _____.

The Solar System

Our Sun is about 4.6 billion years old. It is the central and largest body of our solar system. The Sun is the nearest star to Earth. It is an average sized, yellow star which produces energy by the fusion of hydrogen gas. Some of the features on the Sun's surface are eruptions called solar flares and dark, cool areas known as sunspots.

Planets are solid bodies which move in definite paths around a central star. Gravity keeps the planets in orbit around the star. There are two types of planets in our solar system. Terrestrial planets are the inner planets closest to the Sun. They are small, dense, and rocky. The Jovian or outer planets are large, gaseous, and have low densities. All planets have nearly spherical shapes. Each planet revolves around the Sun in an almost circular path called an ellipse. Each planet also rotates or spins on an axis.

Our solar system includes other solid objects. **Moons** orbit the planets. The Jovian planets have more moons than the terrestrial planets. **Asteroids** are large, irregular shaped rocks that orbit the Sun. Most asteroids are found between Mars and Jupiter. **Comets** are masses of ice and embedded rock debris. This ice is made of water, ammonia, methane, and carbon dioxide. As a comet orbits the Sun, it will begin to warm and vaporize as it gets closer to the Sun. The comet's vapor and debris trail becomes visible when it reflects sunlight. As the comet melts it leaves behind a trail of rock debris. This rock debris becomes meteoroids. **Meteoroids** are rock fragments in space that can be as big as a boulder or as small as dust. When a meteoroid enters our atmosphere, the heat from friction causes it to disintegrate in a visible streak across our sky. Many meteoroids and asteroids have hit planets and moons forming craters.

   Most objects in the solar system have regular and predictable motions. Most of these objects rotate and revolve in a known pattern. These motions helps us to explain the occurrences of a day, a year, phases of the moon, eclipses, tides, and meteor showers.

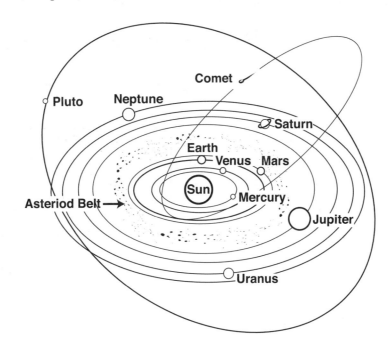

FIGURE 1. SOLAR SYSTEM (not to scale)

Review Questions

7. Compared to other stars, our Sun is an _____ sized star.

8. The planets stay in orbit around the Sun because of _____.

9. Jupiter is a large planet of low density; it is classified as a _____ planet.

10. Solid objects which orbit planets are called _____.

11. The phrase "dirty snowball" could best describe a _____.

12. Smaller rock particles in the solar system are _____.

13. Impacts of asteroids and meteors on a planet's surface will form a _____.

14. All objects in the solar system _____; they rotate and revolve.

15. Refer to the chart below which compares the members of the solar system. Name the planets described by the following statements.

Solar System Data

Object	Mean Distance from Sun (millions of km)	Period of Revolution	Period of Rotation	Eccentricity of Orbit	Equatorial Diameter (km)	Mass (Earth = 1)	Density (g/cm³)	Number of Moons
SUN	—	—	27 days	—	1,392,000	333,000.00	1.4	–
MERCURY	57.9	88 days	59 days	0.206	4,880	0.553	5.4	0
VENUS	108.2	224.7 days	243 days	0.007	12,104	0.815	5.2	0
EARTH	149.6	365.26 days	23 hr 56 min 4 sec	0.017	12,756	1.00	5.5	1
MARS	227.9	687 days	24 hr 37 min 23 sec	0.093	6,787	0.1074	3.9	2
JUPITER	778.3	11.86 years	9 hr 50 min 30 sec	0.048	142,800	317.896	1.3	16
SATURN	1,427	29.46 years	10 hr 14 min	0.056	120,000	95.185	0.7	18
URANUS	2,869	84.0 years	17 hr 14 min	0.047	51,800	14.537	1.2	21
NEPTUNE	4,496	164.8 years	16 hr	0.009	49,500	17.151	1.7	8
PLUTO	5,900	247.7 years	6 days 9 hr	0.250	2,300	0.0025	2.0	1
EARTH'S MOON	149.6 (0.386 from Earth)	27.3 days	27 days 8 hr	0.055	3,476	0.0123	3.3	—

a. smallest planet _____

b. fastest rotation _____

c. longest revolution _____

d. about 10 times further from the Sun than Earth _____

e. shortest day _____

f. closest to the Sun _____

g. largest planet _____

h. has two moons _____

i. almost the same density as Earth _____

j. almost the same size as Earth _____

k. smaller than Earth's Moon _____

The Moon

The Moon is a natural satellite of Earth. It revolves around Earth in a nearly circular, or elliptical path. Its period of revolution is 27$\frac{1}{3}$ days, and its period of rotation is also 27$\frac{1}{3}$ days. The same side of the Moon always faces Earth because the rate of rotation is equal to the rate of revolution.

We see the Moon because it reflects light from the Sun. The amount of reflected sunlight that we see from the Moon varies during the month as the Moon revolves around Earth. This monthly cycle is observed as the **Moon phases**. The phases include: *new moon*, when the Moon is between the Sun and Earth and is not visible from Earth, *first quarter* when half the Moon appears to be lit, *full moon* when the Moon appears fully illuminated , and *last quarter* when the Moon appears again as half lit.

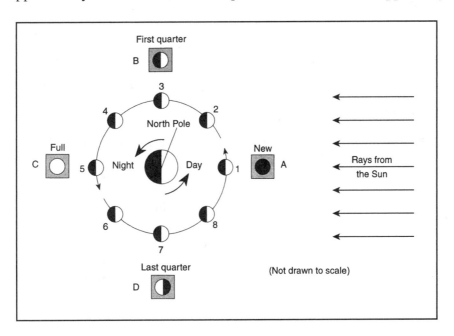

FIGURE 2. MOON PHASES

The interactive movements of the Moon and Earth relative to the Sun cause **eclipses**. Eclipses only occur when the Moon, Earth, and Sun are exactly lined up in space. During a solar eclipse the Moon is between Earth and the Sun. In this position the Moon's shadow falls on Earth so that the Sun is not visible. During a lunar eclipse, Earth is between the Moon and the Sun so that Earth's shadow darkens the full moon.

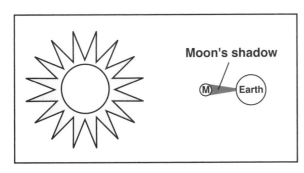

FIGURE 3. SOLAR ECLIPSE

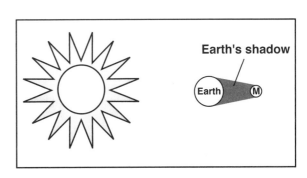

FIGURE 4. LUNAR ECLIPSE

Tides are the cyclic pattern of water rising and falling along the ocean shoreline. They are caused by the gravitational pull of the Moon and Sun on Earth's oceans. Since the Moon is closer to Earth, the Moon has more effect on the tides.

Review Questions

16. The Moon revolves around Earth once every _____ days.

17. We see the Moon because it reflects light from the _____.

18. Moon phases describe the part of the Moon that is _____ to us on Earth.

19. Phases of the Moon occur because the Moon _____ around Earth.

20. The cycle of Moon phases repeats about once every _____.

21. During a lunar eclipse, the _____ is not visible to observers on Earth.

22. Tides are caused by the gravitational pull of the _____ on the oceans.

23. Refer to the diagram which shows eight positions of the Moon relative to Earth and the Sun.

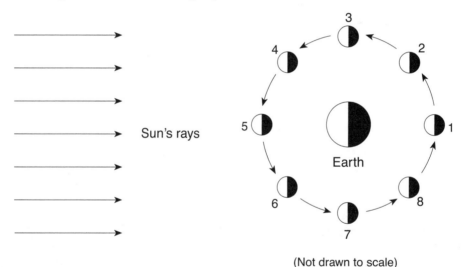

Sun's rays

Earth

(Not drawn to scale)

a. Full moon phase is at position. _____

b. A lunar eclipse could occur at _____

c. More of the Moon becomes visible as it goes from position _____ to _____.

d. The arrows indicate the motion called _____.

e. The Moon at position **8** is visible during the (daytime) (nighttime) on Earth.

Earth's Motions

Earth is in motion. Earth's motions include rotation (spinning on its axis) and revolution (orbiting around the Sun).

Earth **rotates** or spins on an imaginary axis about once every 24 hours (one day). The axis is tilted at an angle of 23½°. Earth rotates from west to east, or counterclockwise. Earth's rotation causes the Sun, Moon, and most stars to appear to rise toward the east and set toward the west. Celestial objects, such as the Sun, Moon, planets and stars, appear to move across our sky due to the rotation of Earth.

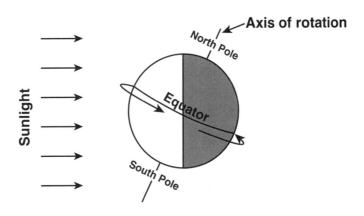

FIGURE 5. EARTH'S ROTATION

Earth **revolves** or orbits around the Sun every 365¼ days (one year). The path of revolution is nearly circular (elliptical) in a counterclockwise direction. Earth's revolution around the Sun causes apparent yearly changes in the celestial objects that are seen from Earth.

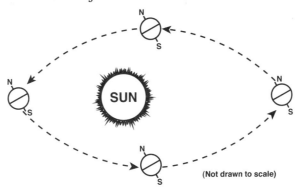

FIGURE 6. EARTH'S REVOLUTION

Review Questions

24. A planet is _____ when it spins on its axis.

25. Planets are _____ when they orbit the Sun.

26. Most stars appear to rise towards the _____ and set towards the _____.

27. Earth rotates once every _____.

28. One Earth revolution around the Sun takes _____ days.

Locating Positions on Earth

To locate a position on Earth's surface a coordinate system is used. Every location has a unique address which includes two numbers: latitude and longitude. The latitude and longitude system and our system of time are based on celestial observations.

Latitude is the angular distance north and south of the **Equator**. Latitude ranges from 0° at the Equator to 90° North or South at the Poles. The lines of latitude are drawn east and west and parallel to each other beginning at the Equator. Latitude divides Earth into Northern and Southern Hemispheres. Latitude is based on the observation of the Pole star, *Polaris*. The altitude of the Pole Star above your horizon is your latitude in the Northern Hemisphere.

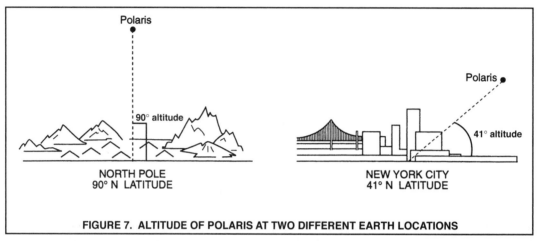

FIGURE 7. ALTITUDE OF POLARIS AT TWO DIFFERENT EARTH LOCATIONS

Longitude is the angular distance east and west of the Prime Meridian. Longitude ranges from 0° to 180° East or West. Meridians of longitude are drawn north to south meeting at the poles. The Prime Meridian (0°) divides Earth into Eastern and Western Hemispheres.

Longitude is based on observations of the Sun. Every 15 degrees of longitude is equal to one-hour time difference. This is the basis for the twenty-four time zones of the world. Locations with the same longitude are usually in the same time zone.

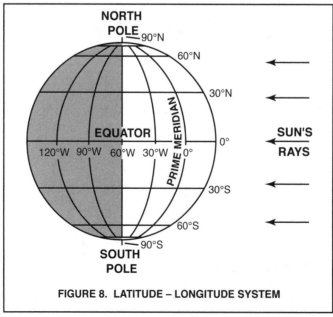

FIGURE 8. LATITUDE – LONGITUDE SYSTEM

Review Questions

29. Parallel lines that are drawn east and west on the globe measure _____.

30. Lines of _____ meet at the poles.

31. Latitude is based on a measurement of the _____.

32. The range of longitude is 0° to _____ East or West.

33. Use the map below. Determine the latitude and longitude of the following points.

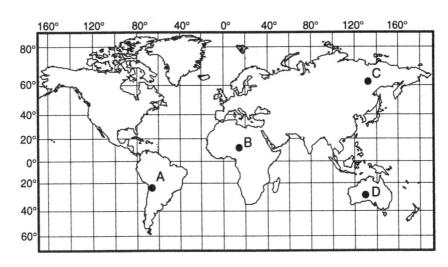

   a. A = _____, _____

   b. B = _____, _____

   c. C = _____, _____

   d. D = _____, _____

   e. The two points that are most likely in the same time zone are _____

   and _____.

Seasons

Seasons are caused by the tilt of Earth's axis relative to the Sun as Earth revolves. **Summer solstice** usually occurs on June 21st when the Northern Hemisphere is tilted toward the Sun. The Northern Hemisphere then receives the most direct Sun rays and the longest hours of daylight. The summer Sun is highest in the sky and casts the shortest shadows. The North Pole has 24 hours of daylight, while the South Pole is in darkness .

Winter solstice usually occurs on December 21st. The Southern Hemisphere is tilted toward the Sun while the Northern Hemisphere leans away from the Sun. As a result, the Northern Hemisphere receives the least direct sunlight and daylight hours are the shortest. The winter sun is lowest in the sky casting very long shadows. Those that live south of the Equator have direct Sun rays, long daylight hours, and high Sun. In winter the North Pole is in darkness, while the South Pole has 24 hours of daylight.

March 21st is usually the spring equinox, and September 21st is usually the fall equinox. On an **equinox** the Sun is most direct at the Equator. There are 12 hours of daylight and 12 hours of night worldwide.

If Earth were not tilted the seasonal change in the Sun's position and resulting weather changes would not occur. All planets in the solar system are tilted.

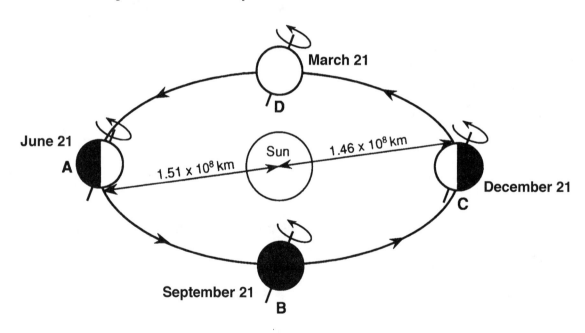

FIGURE 9. EARTH REVOLUTION AND TILT FOR SEASONAL DATES

Review Questions

34. Seasonal changes on Earth are caused by the _____.

35. The Sun is most direct in New York when the axis leans _____ the Sun.

36. When the Sun is highest in the sky, shadows are _____.

37. When it is summer in the United States, South America has _____.

38. A planet that has no axis tilt would not experience _____ change.

39. In the chart, place an "**X**" in the column(s) for which the statement is correct.

	Statement	Winter	Summer	Fall/Spring
a.	Equinox season			
b.	Sun is lowest in the sky in NY			
c.	In New York, the Sun is most direct			
d.	Longest shadows cast by the Sun in New York			
e.	12 hours of daylight worldwide			
f.	Longest daylight hours in New York			
g.	Occurs on December 21			
h.	Earth's axis tilts towards the Sun			
i.	North Pole has 24 hours of daylight			

40. The diagram shows the tilt of Earth relative to the Sun for one season.

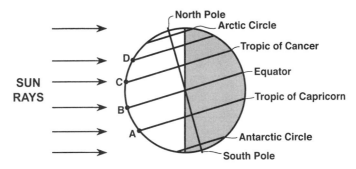

a. The season in the Northern Hemisphere would be _____.

b. The North Pole would have _____ hours of daylight.

c. The Sun is highest in the sky for the _____ Hemisphere.

d. Longest daylight hours will occur in the _____ Hemisphere.

e. Position **A** will have _____ season.

f. The South Pole will have _____ hours of daylight.

g. The latitude of position **B** is _____.

asteroid

_____

axis of rotation

_____

comet

_____

eclipse

_____

Equator

_____

equinox

_____

latitude

_____

longitude

_____

meteoroid

_____

Moon

_____

Moon phase

_____

orbit

_____

revolve

_____

rotate

_____

Solar System

_____

spherical

_____

star

_____

summer solstice

_____

tides

_____

winter solstice

_____

1. The area between stars is mainly
   (1) hydrogen gas
   (2) empty space
   (3) dust particles
   (4) planets and their moons

2. Compared to distances between planets in our solar system, the distance between stars is
   (1) much less   (2) much greater   (3) about the same

3. The Sun's position in space is best described as the approximate center of
   (1) a constellation
   (2) the universe
   (3) the Milky Way galaxy
   (4) our solar system

4. Which diagram most accurately shows the shape of Earth?

   (1)   (2)   (3)   (4)

5. Which diagram best represents the motions of objects in the solar system?

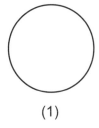
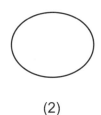
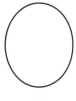

Key:
P● = Planet
M● = Moon
Ⓢ = Sun

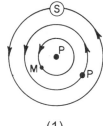
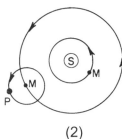
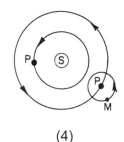

   (1)   (2)   (3)   (4)

6. A planet is viewed from Earth for several hours. The diagrams show the planet at four different times.

   DIAGRAM A   DIAGRAM B   DIAGRAM C   DIAGRAM D

   The best explanation for these observations is that the planet is
   (1) tilted on its axis
   (2) changing seasons
   (3) revolving
   (4) rotating

7. The diagram below shows Earth's orbit and the orbit of a comet around the Sun.

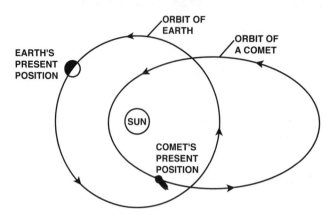

A comet is similar to Earth in that they both
(1) have liquid water
(2) are the same size
(3) orbit the Sun
(4) are frozen

8. How would the stars appear through the night if Earth did **not** rotate?

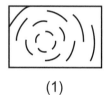 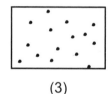 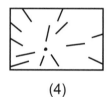

(1)   (2)   (3)   (4)

9. Which group is outside the solar system?
(1) planets   (2) asteroids   (3) moons   (4) Andromeda galaxy

10. Which force keeps the planets in orbit around the Sun?
(1) friction   (2) electrical   (3) magnetism   (4) gravity

11. The diagram below shows three planets in orbit. What object is represented by the letter **X**?

(1) comet
(2) moon
(3) star
(4) asteroid

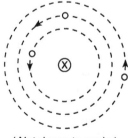

(Not drawn to scale)

12. Which motion causes the apparent rising and setting of Sun each day?
(1) Earth revolving around the Sun
(2) Earth rotating on an axis
(3) Moon rotating on an axis
(4) Moon revolving around Earth

13. The phases of the Moon are caused by the

    (1) Earth's revolution around the Sun   (3) Moon's rotation on its axis

    (2) Moon's revolution around Earth   (4) Earth's rotation on its axis

14. Which object would orbit a planet?

    (1) an asteroid   (2) a comet   (3) a star   (4) a moon

15. The Moon's gravitational force has a greater effect on the ocean tides of Earth than the Sun's gravitational force. What is the reason for this?

    (1) The Moon has a greater mass than the Sun.

    (2) The Moon is closer to Earth than the Sun.

    (3) The Moon's mass is less than the Sun.

    (4) The Moon is a solid.

Base your answers to **questions 16-18** on the diagram below which shows eight positions of the Moon as it revolves around Earth.

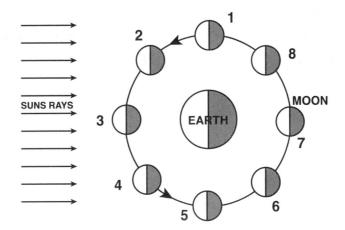

16. The time it takes for the Moon to completely orbit Earth is approximately a

    (1) day   (2) week   (3) month   (4) year

17. At which position would the Sun be eclipsed if Earth, Moon, and Sun were exactly lined up?

    (1) 1   (2) 3   (3) 5   (4) 7

18. As viewed from Earth when the Moon is at position **7** it would appear as

    (1)   (2)   (3)   (4)

19. Which diagram would represent the first day of winter in the Northern Hemisphere?

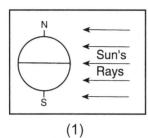
(1)

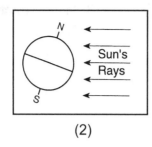
(2)

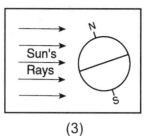
(3)

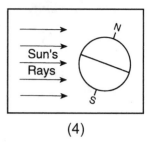
(4)

20. The apparent daily motion of the Sun across the sky is caused by
(1) Earth's rotation on its axis
(2) Earth's revolution around the Sun
(3) Sun's revolution around earth
(4) Sun's rotation on its axis

21. The length of an Earth day is equal to one:
(1) Earth rotation
(2) Earth revolution
(3) Moon rotation
(4) Moon revolution

22. Which change would occur if Earth rotated faster?
(1) The year would be shorter
(2) The day would be shorter
(3) The day would be longer
(4) The year would be longer

23. The diagram represents part of Earth's latitude-longitude system. What is the latitude and longitude of point **L** ?

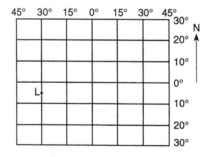

(1) 5°E, 30°N   (2) 5°W, 30°S   (3) 5°N, 30°E   (4) 5°S, 30°W

24. Which diagram is most similar to Earth's latitude-longitude system?

(1)

(2)

(3)

(4)

25. A student accurately measures the altitude of the noon Sun from the same location on four days during the school year. Which is the correct sequence?

(1)
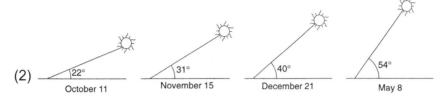

(2)

(3)
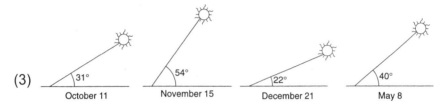

(4)
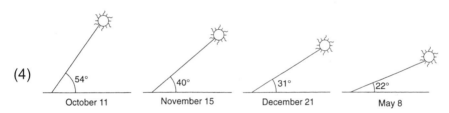

26. Summer days are hotter than winter days because in the summer
(1) Earth is closer to the Sun
(2) the number of sunspots increases
(3) the Sun's rays are more direct
(4) the Sun gives off more energy

27. Which is true of winter in New York?
(1) The Sun is higher in the sky, daylight is shorter
(2) The Sun is higher in the sky, daylight is longer
(3) The Sun is lower in the sky, daylight is longer
(4) The Sun is lower in the sky, daylight is shorter

28. In what general direction does an observer look to see the sunset each day?
(1) north   (2) south   (3) east   (4) west

29. The diagram shows a vertical post which casts shadows A, B, C, and D at four different times during the day. Which shadow was cast when the Sun was highest in the sky?

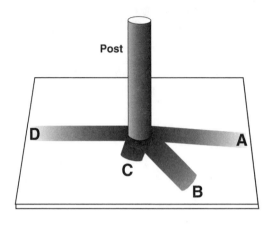

(1) A   (2) B   (3) C   (4) D

30. Seasonal changes on Earth are caused by the revolution of Earth and
(1) its rotation on its axis   (3) the Moon's revolution
(2) the tilt of its axis   (4) the distance to the Sun

31. A student in New York State collected the following data for the length of his shadow.

Date	Jan 15	Feb 15	Mar 15	Apr 15	May 15	June 15	July 15
Shadow Length	189.5 cm	165.6 cm	146.8 cm	123.3 cm	101.6 cm	78.9 cm	101.2cm

a. State the problem the student was investigating.

_____

b. State TWO factors that must have remained constant during this experiment.

(1) _____ (2) _____

c. State the manipulated (independent) variable. _____

d. State the responding (dependent) variable. _____

e. Write one sentence which describes the pattern shown by the data.

_____

_____

f. If the student continues this experiment from July to December, the length of the shadow

will _____.

g. Propose the reason that the shadow length changes. _____

_____

_____

_____

32. The diagram below shows the Moon in different positions as it revolves around Earth.

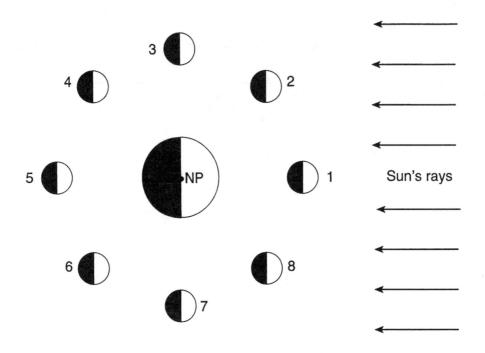

a. **Draw** an arrow between positions 6 and 7 to show the direction of the Moon's orbit.

b. Place an **"X"** over the Moon position where a solar eclipse could occur.

c. **Circle** the Moon position that would appear as a full Moon to observers on Earth.

d. Place a **"D"** at an Earth location that is in daylight.

e. The approximate time for the Moon to move from position 1 back to position 1 is a (day) (week) (month) (year)

33. The diagram below shows four positions of Earth as it revolves around the Sun.

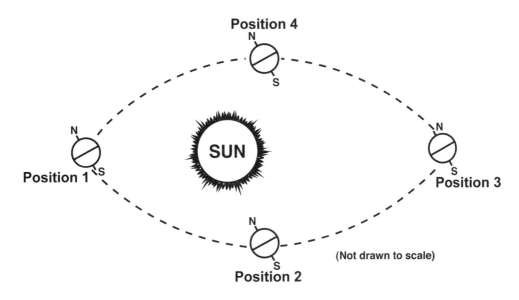

a. On position 1 **shade in** the half of Earth that would be in darkness.

b. **Write** Dec 21 at the position that represents that date.

c. **Draw** an arrow to show the direction of Earth's revolution.

d. State the numbered position that would be summer for the Southern Hemisphere._____

e. State the approximate length of time it takes Earth to move from position **1** to position **3**. _____

f. Write ONE sentence to explain the effect on Earth's seasons if Earth were not tilted.

_____

_____

_____

34. The diagram represents the latitude and longitude lines on Earth.

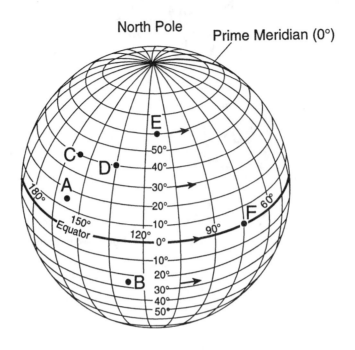

a. State the Earth motion shown by the arrows. _____

b. Name TWO points that have the same latitude. _____ and _____

c. Name TWO points that have the same longitude. _____ and _____

d. Write the letter of the position furthest north. _____

e. Write the letter of the position in the Southern Hemisphere. _____

f. Write the letter of the position with the lowest longitude. _____

g. Write the latitude-longitude of D. _____ , _____

h. Write the letter of the position with the earliest time. _____

35. The data table below gives the distance of each planet from the Sun. The orbital speed of each planet is given.

Planet	Average Distance from Sun (AU)	Average Orbital Speed (km/sec)
Mercury	0.4	48.0
Venus	0.7	35.0
Earth	1.0	30.0
Mars	1.5	24.0
Jupiter	5.2	13.0
Saturn	9.6	10.0
Uranus	19.0	7.0
Neptune	30.0	5.5
Pluto	39.0	4.7

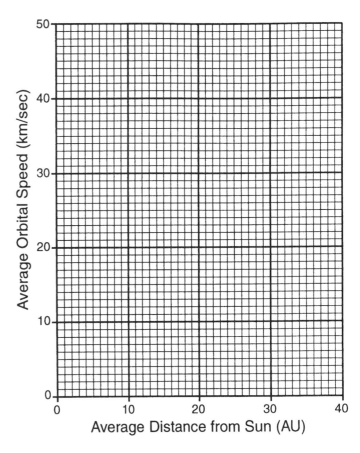

a. **Plot** the data for each planet using a point.
   Draw a line connecting each point.

b. Write a title for this graph. _____

c. Write one sentence which explains the relationship between distance to the Sun and orbital speed of the planet.

   _____

   _____

d. An asteroid is located 2.8 AU from the Sun. This asteroid is between two planets. State

   the names of the two planets. _____ and _____

e. State ONE similarity between an asteroid and a planet.

   _____

f. State ONE difference between an asteroid and a planet.

   _____

NOTES

CHAPTER 9

METEOROLOGY

- **THE PHYSICAL SETTING: KEY IDEA 2**
  Most of the phenomena that we observe on Earth involve interactions among components of air, water, and land.

The Atmosphere

The **atmosphere** is an "ocean of air." It is a mixture of gases which includes 78% nitrogen, 21% oxygen, and 1% other gases such as ozone, water vapor, and carbon dioxide.

The atmosphere contains small particles of suspended liquids and solids. These particles are from natural and human activities. For example, dust in the air can come from volcanic eruptions and building construction. Pollen, ice crystals, and water drops are from natural events. Ash and soot in the air are mainly from the burning of **fossil fuels** such as coal and oil. These air-borne solids and liquids can affect weather and climate. Dust blocks out sunlight making Earth cooler.

Nearly all the atmosphere is confined to a thin shell surrounding Earth. The atmosphere is divided or **stratified** into four layers. Each layer has its own distinct properties. The **troposphere** is the lowest, densest part. It contains most of the atmospheric gases and moisture, so clouds and storms occur here. Most weather takes place in the troposphere. As you rise through the troposphere, temperature decreases.

The **stratosphere** is the next layer. The air is very dry so clouds rarely occur here. Temperatures increase because **ozone** gas absorbs ultraviolet radiation from the Sun. The mesosphere is very clean. It has no water vapor. Temperature decreases as you rise through the mesosphere. The uppermost layer is the thermosphere. This is where meteors disintegrate. As altitude increases throughout the atmosphere, air pressure and water vapor decrease.

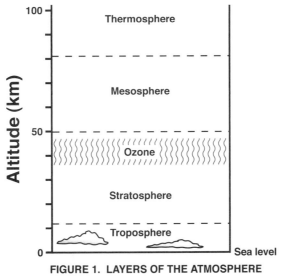

FIGURE 1. LAYERS OF THE ATMOSPHERE

Review Questions

1. The most abundant gas in the atmosphere is _____.

2. Particles can enter the air by _____ and _____ activities.

3. Earth's temperature could become cooler if large amounts of _____ block sunlight.

4. As altitude increases, air pressure _____.

5. Using the diagram in **FIGURE 1**, name the atmosphere layer described:

    a. contains ozone layer _____

    b. found at 70 km altitude _____

    c. most weather occurs here _____

    d. contains the most water vapor _____

    e. closest to sea level _____

Functions of the Atmosphere

The atmosphere supports life by providing breathing gases and moisture. It protects life on Earth from meteor impacts and dangerous **ultraviolet radiation** which is absorbed by ozone. It provides heat energy for life by absorbing heat from the Sun and Earth.

The early atmosphere of Earth had no oxygen, no water vapor, and no ozone. Volcanoes released water vapor, carbon dioxide, and nitrogen from inside Earth. As Earth cooled water vapor condensed to form clouds. Rain fell and formed the oceans, lakes, and rivers. **Photosynthesis** by green plants in the oceans absorbed carbon dioxide and released oxygen. The protective ozone layer was formed once oxygen was available.

Human activities have negatively impacted the atmosphere. Pollutants such as gases, soot, and ash from the burning of fossil fuels have been added to the air. The destruction of forests and continued burning of fossil fuels have increased the amount of carbon dioxide in the air. As a result some scientists believe that Earth's temperature has been rising. Carbon dioxide as well as methane and water vapor are known as **greenhouse gases** because they "trap" heat close to the surface.

Chlorofluorocarbons (CFCs), bromides, and nitrogen oxides also added by human activities have decreased the amount of ozone over certain portions of Earth's surface. These areas are now exposed to more harmful ultraviolet radiation which causes skin cancer in humans and hinders the growth of the plants and animals we depend on.

6. The atmospheric oxygen is produced by _____.

7. Dangerous ultraviolet rays are absorbed by _____.

8. The burning of fossil fuels adds the greenhouse gas, _____, to the air.

9. As the amount of carbon dioxide in the atmosphere increases, temperatures will _____.

10. The _____ layer is being destroyed by CFCs.

Atmospheric Conditions

Weather describes the conditions of the atmosphere at a location for a short period of time. The uneven heating of Earth's surface by the Sun cause changes in the weather. **Climate** is the average weather that prevails from season to season and year to year. Climate is more predictable than weather.

The conditions of the atmosphere are measured and recorded at weather stations. As these conditions change, the weather changes. Atmospheric conditions include air temperature, air pressure, humidity, wind, cloud cover, and precipitation.

Atmospheric temperature is caused by the absorption of heat from Earth and from the Sun. Temperatures change with time of day, time of year, latitude, and elevation. Temperature is measured with a thermometer.

Moisture exists in all three states of matter in the atmosphere. Solid moisture includes ice, snow, hail, sleet, and frost. Liquid moisture is in the form of rain, dew, fog, and water droplets. Gaseous moisture is the invisible water vapor which causes **humidity**.

Clouds are made of ice crystals and water droplets. **Precipitation** falls when the ice crystals and water droplets are large enough for gravity to pull them down. Atmospheric moisture comes from evaporation of surface waters mainly the oceans. Plants also release moisture to the air by **transpiration**. The movement of moisture between the atmosphere, lithosphere and the hydrosphere is called the **water cycle**.

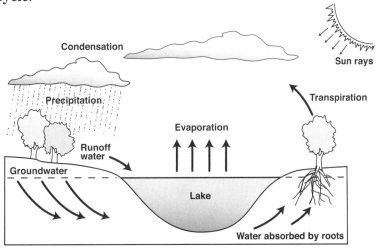

FIGURE 2. WATER CYCLE

Air pressure is caused by the weight of air pushing down. As altitude increases, air pressure decreases. **High pressure** air is cool and dry with clear, calm weather. **Low pressure** air is generally warm and moist with cloudy, unstable weather. Pressure describes the air systems which cause our weather. Air pressure is measured with a **barometer.**

Winds are horizontal air movements. They are caused by differences in air pressure. Winds move from high pressure to low pressure areas. Winds are named for the direction from which they are blowing. A wind vane indicates the direction from which the wind is blowing. An **anemometer** measures wind speed.

Review Questions

11. The conditions of the atmosphere for the day is called _____.

12. The average weather that is the same every year is called _____.

13. Clouds are made of visible _____ and _____.

14. The constant movement of water between the air, the land, and the oceans is the

    _____ cycle.

15. Atmospheric moisture returns to Earth's surface during _____.

16. Water vapor enters the air by evaporation and _____ from plants.

17. A high pressure air mass brings _____ weather.

18. Stormy, unstable weather is found in _____ pressure systems.

19. The USA map indicates the locations of the high and low pressure systems.

    The lettered position probably experiencing clear skies is _____

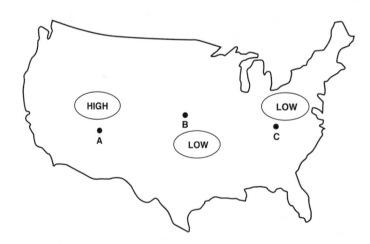

Air Masses and Fronts

Weather conditions change due to the movement of air masses. Weather conditions at a location are determined by the temperature, humidity, and pressure of the air mass over that area.

An **air mass** forms when a body of air remains nearly stationary over a large section of Earth's surface. The air acquires its temperature and humidity from that region. If an air mass forms over water, it will be moist with low pressure. If the air mass forms over land, it will be dry with high pressure. Air masses forming in polar regions are cold. Those that form in tropical latitudes are warm.

Air Mass Type	Map Symbol	Formed over...	Characteristics
Continental Tropical	cT	hot land	hot, dry air
Continental Polar	cP	cold land	cold, dry air
Maritime Polar	mP	cool ocean	cool, moist air
Maritime Tropical	mT	warm ocean	warm, moist air

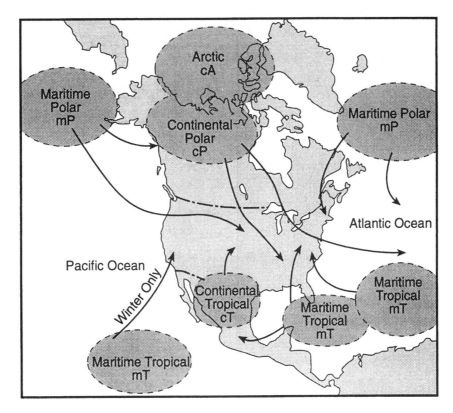

FIGURE 3. TYPES AND SOURCES OF AIR MASSES IN THE USA

Prevailing winds and upper air currents determine the movement of air masses. In the United States air masses move from west to east. This fact allows weather forecasts to be made.

Fronts are the boundaries between different air masses. Cold fronts are the leading edge of cooler air which is moving towards a region. Warm fronts are the leading edge of warmer air that is moving towards a region. Precipitation is likely to occur at these boundaries when warm, moist air rises above the cooler air. When a front passes there is a change in weather. It causes cloud formation, winds, precipitation, and air pressure and temperature changes.

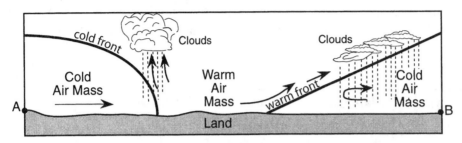
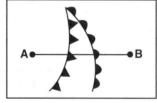

FIGURE 4. MOVEMENT OF AIR MASSES

Review Questions

20. Local weather conditions change due to the movement of _____.

21. An air mass that forms over northern Canada will be _____ and _____.

22. An air mass that is warm and dry will be classified as _____.

23. In the United States air masses move from _____ to _____.

24. A front is the _____ between different air masses.

25. Precipitation is likely to occur along _____.

26. The map shows air pressure weather systems in the USA for one day in June. Letters A, B, C, D, and E are locations in the United States.

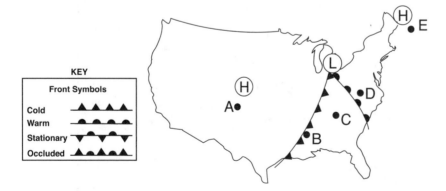

a. Locations with clear skies: _____ and _____

b. Locations probably experiencing rain: _____ and _____

c. A warm front is approaching location _____

d. The low pressure system will move towards _____

138

Technology Used to Monitor and Forecast Weather

Many instruments are used at ground-based weather stations to measure the conditions of the atmosphere.

Weather Instruments

INSTRUMENT	MEASURES ...
thermometer	air temperature
barometer	air pressure
psychrometer	humidity, dew point
anemometer	wind speed
wind vane	wind direction
rain gauge	amount of precipitation

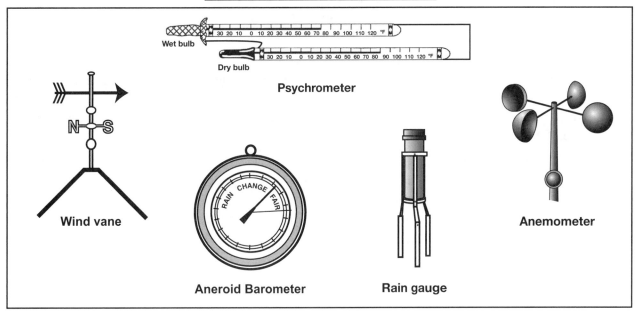

FIGURE 5. COMMON WEATHER INSTRUMENTS

Weather is monitored with weather balloons that send data to weather stations. Satellite photographs show cloud cover. Radar gives information about the intensity and speed of approaching storms. Doppler radar is especially useful in detecting tornadoes. Computers collect and store large amounts of data and compare present weather data to the past.

Review Questions

27. A _____ measures air pressure.

28. An anemometer measures _____.

29. Satellite photographs show _____.

30. Doppler radar is useful in locating _____.

31. Meteorologists store and compare weather data by using _____.

Hazardous Weather

Humans can prepare for and protect themselves against **hazardous weather** if warnings are given. Tornadoes are rapidly rotating, extremely low-pressure storms. A funnel extends down from a thunderstorm cloud. Tornadoes form when very cold air meets very warm air. They are most common in the Midwest where cold, dry air from Canada meets warm, moist air from the Gulf of Mexico. The tornado may be on the ground for a few minutes or a few hours. The path of the tornado is unpredictable. Radar monitors their formation and warnings are sent out. Tornadoes have hazardous winds and flying debris. People in the path of a tornado should seek low shelter immediately or go into or under a sturdy structure.

Thunderstorms usually form along a cold front. Rapidly rising air causes lightning and heavy rain. Thunderstorms may have strong wind, hail, deadly lightning, and the danger of flash floods. People in the path of a thunderstorm should seek shelter indoors, stay off the phone, turn off appliances, and stay away from flood prone areas.

In the winter, ice storms and blizzards pose hazards to people. Blizzards are associated with heavy snow and winds. Drifting snow can stop transportation. An ice storm can disrupt electric and phone services. Ice storms can occur suddenly as rainfall begins to freeze. There is a danger of frostbite and hypothermia. People should stay indoors, not drive, stay warm and have food, water and medical supplies available.

Hurricanes are low-pressure systems, which form over warm, tropical oceans. Winds are greater than 74 miles per hour. Hurricanes have high winds, high waves, flooding from rain, and storm surges of ocean water along coastlines. If you are in the path of a hurricane you should have food, water and all necessary supplies and stay indoors. If you live in a flood prone area you should go to an emergency shelter.

Review Questions

32. During a tornado you need to protect yourself from wind and _____.

33. Thunderstorms form along a _____ front.

34. Severe winter storms are called _____.

35. Hypothermia can be prevented by _____.

36. Hurricanes form over _____.

37. Hurricane winds are more than _____ miles per hour.

38. When a hurricane warning is issued the supplies you need should include

_____

39. Name the type of hazardous weather associated with each precaution:

   a. Leave low lying ocean shorelines in the storm's path _____

   b. Stay indoors and keep yourself warm during the storm _____

   c. Immediately go to a sturdy underground shelter _____

   d. Turn off the computer and do not use the telephone _____

40. Tornadoes are most common in the _____ section of the USA.

air mass

air pressure

anemometer

atmosphere

barometer

chlorofluorocarbon (CFC)

climate

fossil fuel

front

greenhouse gas

hazardous weather

high pressure system

humidity

low pressure system

ozone

photosynthesis

precipitation

_____

prevailing wind

_____

stratified

_____

stratosphere

_____

transpiration

_____

troposphere

_____

ultraviolet radiation

_____

water cycle

_____

weather

_____

wind

_____

1. The two most common gases in the atmosphere are

   (1) nitrogen and water vapor   (3) carbon dioxide and water vapor

   (2) nitrogen and oxygen   (4) oxygen and carbon dioxide

2. Oxygen is continually added to the atmosphere by

   (1) burning of fossil fuels   (3) photosynthesis by green plants

   (2) outgassing by volcanoes   (4) decomposition of organic wastes

3. The temperature of Earth's surface can be affected by the amount of atmospheric

   (1) oxygen   (2) nitrogen   (3) hydrogen   (4) carbon dioxide

4. Ultraviolet radiation from the Sun is absorbed in the atmosphere by

   (1) oxygen   (2) nitrogen   (3) ozone   (4) carbon dioxide

5. The weather report states "expect high humidity today." The atmospheric gas responsible for this is

   (1) oxygen   (2) ozone   (3) water vapor   (4) carbon dioxide

6. Which human activity has had the most effect on increasing air pollution?

   (1) oil spills in oceans   (3) building on the ocean beaches

   (2) burning fossil fuels   (4) disposal of wastes in a landfill

7. Water vapor is added to the atmosphere by:

   (1) evaporation only   (3) evaporation and transpiration

   (2) transpiration only

8. The main source of water for the atmosphere is Earth's

   (1) soil   (2) plants   (3) rivers   (4) oceans

Base your answers to **questions 9-12** on the diagram of the water cycle shown below.

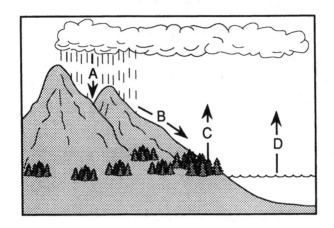

9. Which arrow represents transpiration?
   (1) A   (2) B   (3) C   (4) D

10. Which arrows represent the processes that increase humidity in the air?
   (1) A and B   (2) A and C   (3) C and D   (4) C and B

11. What provides the energy to move water along arrows **C** and **D**?
   (1) gravity   (2) the Sun   (3) ocean tides   (4) the Moon

12. At which location is condensation occurring?
   (1) at the water surface   (3) on the land
   (2) in the cloud   (4) in the forest

13. The map below shows the isotherms connecting positions of equal temperature in degrees Celsius. Which location is the coldest?

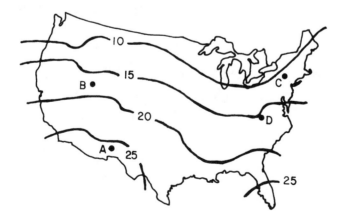

   (1) A   (2) B   (3) C   (4) D

14. Compared to a clear day, on a cloudy day the amount of sunlight reaching Earth's surface is:

(1) less   (2) more   (3) the same

Base your answers to **questions 15-18** on the diagram below which shows the path of a weather balloon released from a ship.

15. At which letter would the highest air pressure be recorded?

(1) A   (2) B   (3) C   (4) D

16. At which letter would the highest humidity be recorded?

(1) A   (2) B   (3) C   (4) D

17. If a thunderstorm was to move into the area, which position would be most affected?

(1) A   (2) B   (3) C   (4) D

18. This diagram shows that the atmosphere is

(1) clean   (3) easily polluted

(2) layered   (4) warm

19. Polar climates are colder than tropical climates, because at the Poles the

(1) Sun is lower and less direct   (3) Sun is higher and more direct

(2) Sun is lower and more direct   (4) Sun is higher and less direct

20. The map shows the path of warm and cold ocean currents in the Atlantic Ocean. Which location would have the warmest climate?

(1) A

(2) B

(3) C

(4) D

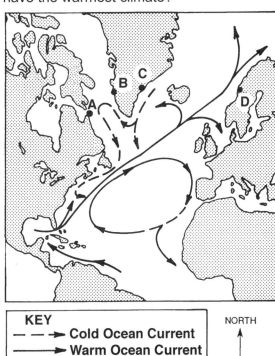

KEY

- - → Cold Ocean Current

——→ Warm Ocean Current

NORTH

Base your answers to **questions 21-23** on the diagram below, which shows the prevailing winds for each latitude zone.

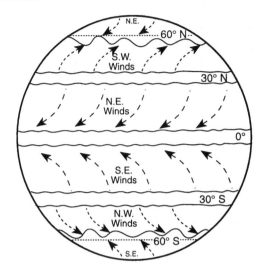

21. At a latitude of 20° N the prevailing wind is from the

    (1) northwest   (2) northeast   (3) southwest   (4) southeast

22. Which diagram shows the usual paths of low pressure systems across the United States?

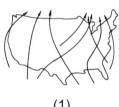         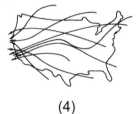

      (1)   (2)   (3)   (4)

23. Winds are caused by differences in

    (1) humidity   (2) cloud cover   (3) air temperature   (4) air pressure

24. On a weather map, an air mass that is cold and dry would be labeled

    (1) mP   (2) mT   (3) cT   (4) cP

25. The weather conditions in an air mass are determined by

    (1) the size of the air mass

    (2) the area over which the air mass formed

    (3) the wind speeds in the air mass

    (4) the amount of moisture in the air mass

Base your answers to **questions 26-28** on the diagrams below which show the location and movement of two different air masses.

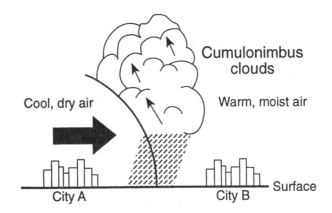

26. The air mass over city **B** would be classified as
    (1) maritime polar   (3) continental tropical
    (2) maritime tropical   (4) continental polar

27. The boundary line between the two air masses is known as
    (1) the eye   (3) a high pressure system
    (2) a front   (4) the stratosphere

28. A weather forecast for city **B** would be
    (1) clearing skies with cooler temperatures
    (2) increasing clouds with cooler temperatures
    (3) increasing clouds with warmer temperatures
    (4) clearing skies with increasing temperatures

29. Tornadoes form when a very cold, dry air mass meets a very warm, moist air mass. Which two air masses could form a tornado when they meet?
    (1) cP and cT   (3) cP and mT
    (2) cT and mP   (4) mP and mT

30. Cool, clear weather is usually found
    (1) in high pressure systems   (3) at fronts
    (2) in low pressure systems   (4) in the tropics

31. Which correctly matches the instrument with the measurement?
    (1) anemometer, temperature   (3) psychrometer, wind speed
    (2) thermometer, humidity   (4) barometer, air pressure

32. Which technology has improved our weather forecasting ability?
    (1) satellites   (3) airplanes
    (2) cruise ships   (4) internet

33. On a summer afternoon, the reading on the barometer begins to decrease. This indicates that

(1) a storm is approaching

(2) skies will stay clear

(3) weather conditions will improve

(4) it will not rain for the next three days

34. Which is a form of precipitation?

(1) frost   (2) snow   (3) dew   (4) fog

35. The climate of a region describes the

(1) daily weather conditions   (3) latitude and altitude of the location

(2) yearly weather conditions   (4) wind patterns for the area

36. Toward which point will the Low pressure system move?

(1) A

(2) B

(3) C

(4) D

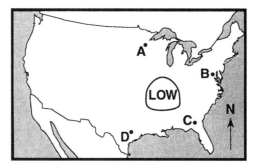

Base your answers to **questions 37-38** on the following diagram.

Locations **A** and **B** are two source regions for air masses that affect the United States.

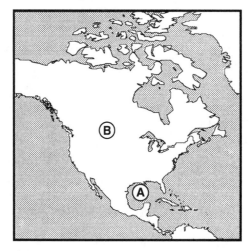

37. Compared to the air mass at B, the air mass at A is

(1) cooler and drier   (3) warmer and wetter

(2) cooler and wetter   (4) warmer and drier

38. On a weather map the air mass at location B would be labeled

(1) cP   (2) cT   (3) mT   (4) mP

39. The arrows on the map show the movement of

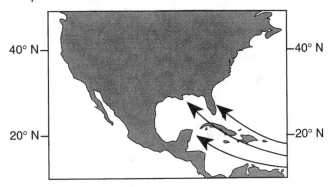

(1) Earth's rotation
(2) northeasterly winds

(3) tsunamis
(4) Atlantic Ocean hurricanes

40. The map shows the average number of thunderstorms each year in the United States. What section of the country gets the most thunderstorms?

Average Number of Thunderstorms Each Year

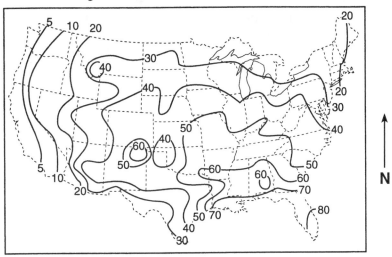

(1) northeast   (2) southeast   (3) southwest   (4) northwest

Base your answers to **questions 41-44** on the following diagram.

The diagram is part of a weather map for locations in the eastern United States. The map shows the location of the low pressure system, fronts, and weather stations **A, B, C, and D**.

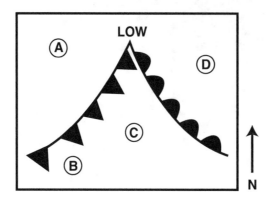

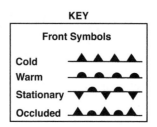

KEY

Front Symbols

Cold

Warm

Stationary

Occluded

41. At which station is it most likely raining?

(1) A   (2) B   (3) C   (4) D

42. As the front passes **D**, the air temperature will probably

(1) decrease   (2) increase   (3) remain the same

43. In the next few hours station **C** can expect cloud cover to

(1) decrease   (2) increase   (3) remain the same

44. The cold front is moving towards the

(1) northeast   (2) southeast   (3) southwest   (4) northwest

45. The data below gives the positions of a hurricane during a seven day period.

Data Table

Day	Latitude	Longitude	Storm Classification
August 18	13° N	46° W	Tropical storm
August 20	19° N	59° W	Hurricane
August 22	25° N	66° W	Hurricane
August 24	25° N	78° W	Hurricane
August 26	28° N	90° W	Hurricane
August 27	32° N	91° W	Hurricane
August 28	34° N	86° W	Tropical storm

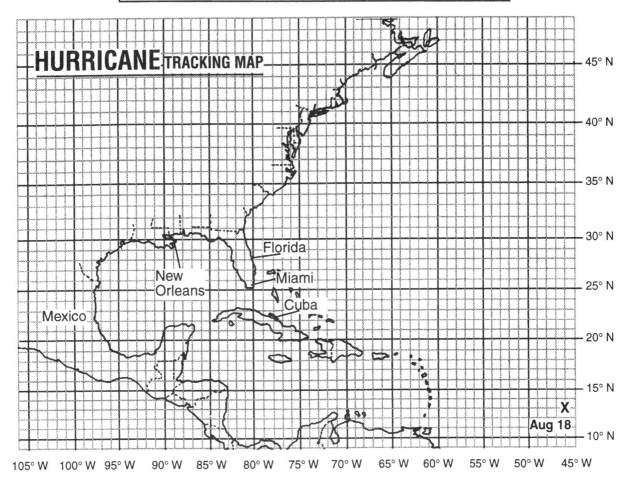

a. Plot the hurricane positions using the hurricane symbol: ❨

b. Connect the positions with a line. Use an arrow to show the direction of movement of the hurricane.

c. Name one specific land location that the hurricane affected.

location: _____ date: _____

d. Hurricanes form over warm, tropical oceans. The hurricane air mass would be classified as: (mP) (mT) (cT) (cP)

e. State TWO dangerous conditions that could cause damage as the hurricane strikes the shoreline.

(1) _____

(2) _____

f. State TWO ways that you can prepare for a hurricane emergency if a hurricane warning is announced in your area.

(1) _____

(2) _____

46. A student would like to conduct an experiment that proves that more evaporation occurs when it is hotter.

a. Write a question for which the student is finding the answer. _____

_____

b. Name the variable the student will change. _____

c. List TWO factors that should not change in the experiment.

(1) _____ (2) _____

d. Write the steps in a procedure that the student could perform.

_____

_____

_____

_____

47. A student wants to prepare for the winter season. There were many snow and ice storms last year and meteorologists forecast the same for this winter. List FOUR preparations that the student and his family can make now before the winter storms arrive.

(1) _____

(2) _____

(3) _____

(4) _____

48. The map below shows a weather system affecting a part of the United States.

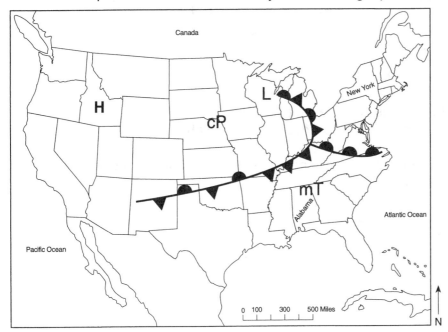

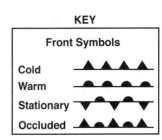

a. Lightly shade in the area where precipitation is most likely occurring at the present time.

b. Describe the weather conditions in Alabama. _____

_____

c. Write a weather forecast for New York which includes temperature, sky cover, and precipitation changes that may occur.

_____

d. Use a large double arrow (⟹) to show the direction in which the low pressure system will move.

e. Describe the present weather conditions at the **H**. Include temperature, sky cover, and precipitation.

_____

49. The graph shows the variations in Earth's monthly temperatures between January 1990 and January 1995.

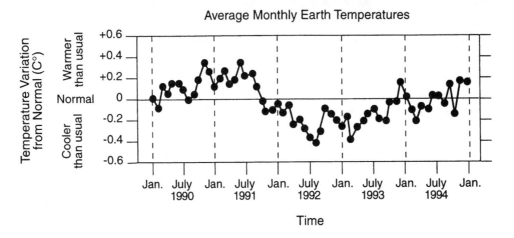

a. State the month and year of the lowest temperature. _____

b. The temperature in August 1990 can be best described as:
(normal)   (warmer than normal)   (cooler than normal).

c. In summer of 1991, Mt. Pinatubo, a volcano in the Pacific Ocean, exploded. State how the temperature was affected.

_____

_____

d. Explain the reason that this volcanic eruption affected the temperature in the way that it did.

_____

_____

50. The graphs below show the temperature changes that have occurred on Earth since 1860 and the changes in carbon dioxide that have occurred in the atmosphere during this same time.

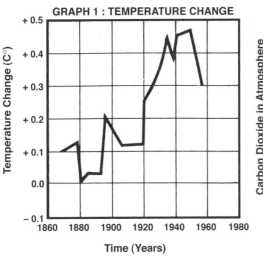

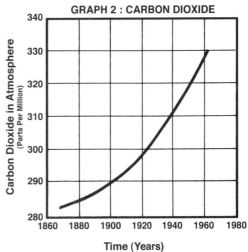

a. Based on the graphs, write one complete sentence that explains the relationship between temperature change and amount of carbon dioxide in the atmosphere.

_____

_____

b. Carbon dioxide is classified as a "greenhouse" gas. Explain what this means.

_____

_____

c. Name the human activity that probably caused the increase of carbon dioxide in the atmosphere.

_____

d. Propose one way we can help to decrease the amount of carbon dioxide in the atmosphere.

_____

_____

_____

NOTES

CHAPTER 10

GEOLOGY

The Lithosphere

The rock at Earth's surface forms a continuous shell around Earth called the **lithosphere**. Most of the lithosphere is covered by a thin layer of water called the **hydrosphere**. Oceans, lakes, streams, and fields of ice and snow make up the hydrosphere.

Rocks are made of minerals. There are a few common minerals that are found in most rocks. **Minerals** are identified by their physical and chemical properties. Physical properties include **streak**, the color of the powdered mineral, **hardness**, the resistance to being scratched, and **luster**, the reflection of light by the mineral. The reaction of a mineral to an acid is a chemical property that is often tested.

Rocks are classified according to how they formed. Most rocks show physical characteristics that give clues to their formation conditions. **Igneous rocks** form when hot, liquid rock material (magma or lava) cools and solidifies (hardens). This hot, liquid rock material is often found in regions of volcanic activity. If hot, liquid magma cools slowly below the surface, the igneous rock will have large mineral crystals. Igneous rocks that have small crystals formed when lava cooled and hardened rapidly on Earth's surface.

GRANITE
large mineral crystals

BASALT
small mineral crystals

FIGURE 1. IGNEOUS ROCKS

Sedimentary rock forms from sediment. Sediment can be rock fragments or pieces of organic matter such as seashells and plant leaves. These sediments over time will get buried, compressed and cemented together. Most sedimentary rock forms on Earth's surface or near water where sediment accumulates. As sediment accumulates many plants and animals are buried and become part of the rock. The remains of these organism may become **fossils** which are very common in sedimentary rock. Fossils are useful because they indicate past life forms, climates, and environments that once existed at the location.

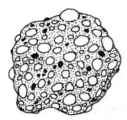

Conglomerate of rock fragments

Siltstone with fossils

FIGURE 2. SEDIMENTARY ROCKS

Metamorphic rock forms when pre-existing rock is exposed to intense heat and/or pressure. This usually occurs during mountain building or deep within Earth. Metamorphic rock may form when a small area of rock is in contact with hot magma.

GNEISS

FIGURE 3. METAMORPHIC ROCK

Changes in rocks are shown by the **rock cycle**. Each type of rock may be transformed or changed into another type of rock. For example, if a sedimentary rock melts and solidifies, it will change into an igneous rock.

FIGURE 4.
ROCK CYCLE

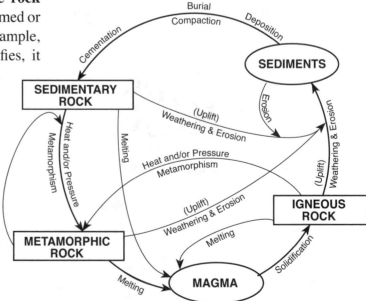

Review Questions

1. The layer of rock at Earth's surface is called the _____.

2. A large area of Earth's surface is covered with _____.

3. All rocks are made of solid compounds called _____.

4. A mineral can be identified by its _____ and chemical properties.

5. A mineral's _____ is the color of its powder.

6. Rocks are classified by their method of _____.

7. Place an "**X**" in the column for which the description is true.

	DESCRIPTION	Igneous	Sedimentary	Metamorphic
a.	Pebbles cemented together			
b.	Found in an area of volcanoes			
c.	Most common at surface near water areas			
d.	Contains fossils			
e.	Rock exposed to extreme pressure and heat			
f.	Layers of sand compacted together			
g.	Magma cooled and hardened			
h.	Made of minerals			

Weathering and Erosion

Many forces wear away Earth's surface and change its appearance. **Weathering** breaks rock into smaller pieces called **sediment**. **Soil** is made of weathered rock, organic matter, water, and air.

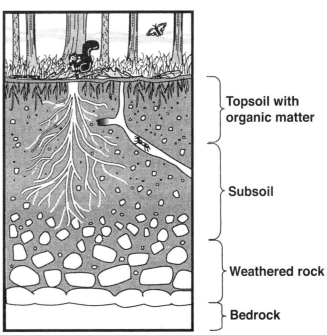

FIGURE 5.
SOIL PROFILE

Topsoil with organic matter

Subsoil

Weathered rock

Bedrock

Weathering occurs when rocks are exposed to atmospheric gases, water, and the weather. Weathering of bedrock is caused by the action of expanding ice, temperature changes, animal and plant activity, and the action of chemicals such as water or carbon dioxide. Weathering is most affected by climate. Air and water pollution have increased the rate of weathering in some locations.

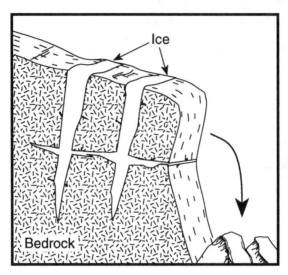

FIGURE 6. WEATHERING BY EXPANDING ICE

Erosion is the movement of sediment to a new location. The driving force behind erosion is gravity. Gravity can act directly or through agents of erosion such as moving water, wind, and glaciers. Gravity can act alone to move sediment downhill. Wind erosion occurs where soil is loose and unprotected. Wind erosion is common in dry climates and along beaches. **Glaciers** are masses of ice that move slowly downhill. As the mass of ice moves, the glacier pushes sediment ahead and carries sediment that is frozen in the ice.

AGENT	ACTION	EFFECTS ON SEDIMENTS	COMMON LOCATION
gravity	Pulls loose or wet materials down cliffs or steep slopes.	mixed sizes angular particles	hill slopes
moving water (streams, runoff, ocean currents)	Moves sediment, faster currents carry larger particles.	Particles are rounded, smoothed and sorted by size, density and shape.	worldwide the most common agent of erosion
wind	Moves loose, dry, fine sediment	Well sorted by size and density. Smallest particles can be carried long distances.	arid (dry) climates
glacier	Removes rock material off valley walls and floor. Drags sediment along bottom and in ice.	Rocks are scratched, flat sides produced. Mixed sizes, ranging from microscopic clay to boulders.	cold, humid climates

FIGURE 7. AGENTS OF EROSION

Moving water is the most common transporting agent of sediment on Earth. Rivers move sediment downstream toward the mouth of the river. At the shoreline, ocean currents and waves move sediment along the coast.

Deposition occurs when sediments are put down in place when the erosion agent stops or slows down. Erosion wears away Earth's surface and deposition builds it up.

Review Questions

8. Weathering breaks rocks into small pieces called _____.

9. Organic plant and animal matter are found in the _____.

10. The weathering of a rock by frost action is most common in _____ climates.

11. The force behind all transporting agents of erosion is _____.

12. Sediment is moved by _____ in a desert.

13. Most sediment on Earth's surface is moved by _____.

14. The _____ of sediment will build up the land.

Earth's Interior

The structure of Earth's interior is known by analyzing the behavior of earthquake waves as they travel through the inside of Earth. Earth is divided into four layers: crust, mantle, outer core, and inner core. Each layer has unique properties.

The **crust** is the thinnest, outermost layer, which completely surrounds Earth. It is the least dense layer. The crust is made of continental crust, which makes up landmasses, and ocean crust, which makes up the ocean floor.

The upper part of the **mantle** is a liquid-like plastic that the crust "floats" on. Beneath this the mantle is a stiff solid.

The **outer core** is above its melting point, therefore this layer is a liquid. Its composition is liquid iron. The **inner core** is very dense and very hot. It is solid iron and nickel. The elements that make up the core of the Earth are believed to be the same as those that are found in some meteorites.

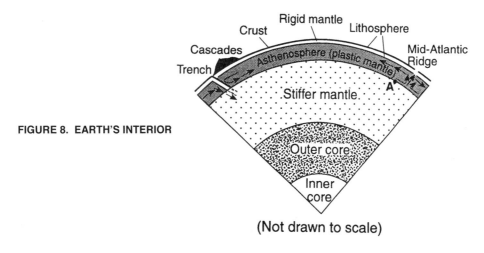

FIGURE 8. EARTH'S INTERIOR

(Not drawn to scale)

Review Questions

15. The structure of Earth's interior was discovered by studying _____ waves.

16. Earth's interior is divided into _____ layers.

17. The composition of Earth's core is inferred to be the same as _____.

18. The diagram shows the four layers of Earth's interior. Select the letter described.

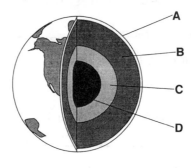

(Not drawn to scale)

a. Solid iron and nickel. _____

b. The ocean floor. _____

c. Crust floats on its "plastic" section. _____

d. Largest section of the interior. _____

e. Liquid iron layer. _____

f. The outer core. _____

g. The mantle. _____

Crustal Movements

There are many evidences that prove Earth's lithosphere has moved in the past. Displaced rock layers provide evidence for crustal movements. For example, marine fossil shells have been found high in the mountains, suggesting that this land was once below sea level and later uplifted. Some rock layers are observed to be **folded** (bent), tilted, or **faulted** (cracked).

**FIGURE 9.
CRUSTAL MOVEMENTS**

Normal, undisturbed Layers

Folded Layers

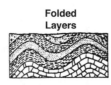

Tilted Layers

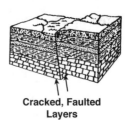

Cracked, Faulted Layers

Major crustal movements have affected large portions of Earth's lithosphere. The **Theory of Continental Drift** states that the present positions of the continents are different from those of the past. The continents were and still are moving. Evidence that the continents were once together is that the continents fit together like pieces of a jig-saw puzzle and there are similar fossils among different continents. Today, the continents have different plants and animals.

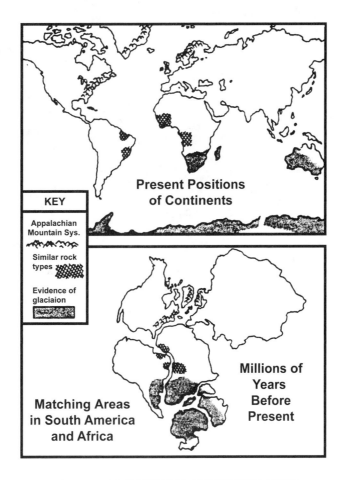

FIGURE 10. EVIDENCE FOR CONTINENTAL DRIFT

The ***Theory of Plate Tectonics*** explains that Earth's lithosphere is divided into a series of plates that "float" on the partially melted section of the upper mantle. The plates are constantly in motion due to **convection currents** in the mantle. Convection currents are caused by density differences. The flow of these convection currents move Earth's crust. Plate tectonics provides the mechanism that moves the continents.

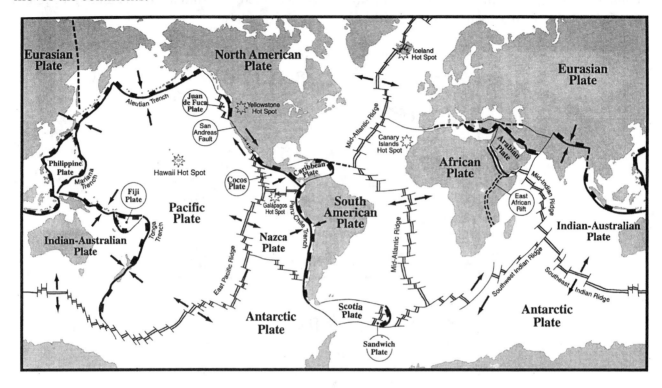

FIGURE 11. LITHOSPHERE PLATES

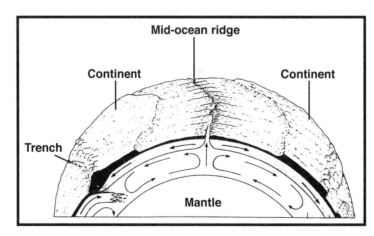

FIGURE 12. MANTLE CONVECTION CURRENTS

Crustal plates may collide or subduct and form mountains, slide past each other in fault zones, or move away from each other forming new ocean basins. The edges of plates are geologically active zones of crustal movement where earthquakes, volcanoes, and new mountains occur.

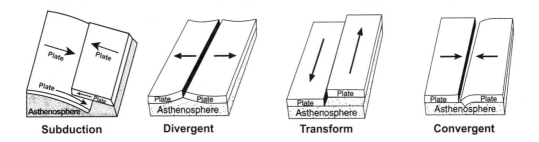

FIGURE 13. INTERACTIONS BETWEEN CRUSTAL PLATES

Review Questions

19. Folded, faulted, and tilted rock layers suggest that Earth's crust _____.

20. Evidence that the continents were once together is that their outlines appear to _____ together.

21. Another evidence that the continents were once together is that they have many of the same _____.

22. The *Theory of Plate Tectonics* describes Earth's lithosphere as being divided into separate sections called _____.

23. When two plates collide a _____ may form.

24. Volcanoes and earthquakes are common along the _____ of plates.

Earthquakes and Volcanoes

Volcanoes form in weak spots in the crust where molten material or magma comes to the surface. Lava that flows out of the volcano will harden and form new land. Ash, dust, rocks, water vapor, carbon dioxide, and other gases are thrown out of volcanoes.

Volcanoes are very hazardous. Lava will flow, setting fires and burying everything in its path. Ash can cover entire towns. Volcanoes can cause landslides and mudslides. Clouds of ash may be blown into the upper atmosphere and remain there for years. This can block sunlight and cause a colder climate.

Earthquakes are a natural shaking of Earth's crust. They can be caused by volcanic eruptions, the movement of rock along a fault, or plate movement. Earthquakes can cause damage to rock structures and buildings. Landslides may occur in areas where there are hills or loose soil.

Geologists have located the sites of volcanoes and earthquakes. They have observed that there is a pattern to where these occur. Most volcanoes and earthquakes occur at the edges of actively moving crustal plates. The most active sites border the Pacific Ocean, commonly known as the "Ring of Fire." Volcanoes and earthquakes are also common from the Mediterranean Sea to India and along the mid-Atlantic ridge.

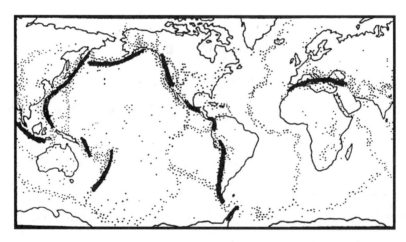

FIGURE 14.
THE DOTTED REGIONS ARE THE MAJOR EARTHQUAKE ZONES, THE SOLID LINES ARE THE MAJOR VOLCANIC BELTS

Review Questions

25. Volcanoes form in weak spots in the _____.

26. _____ can flow out of volcanoes and set fires.

27. The natural shaking of Earth's crust is an _____.

28. Volcanoes and earthquakes are common along the _____ of crustal plates.

29. The "Ring of Fire" refers to crustal activity along the edge of the _____ Ocean.

Topographic Maps

Topography refers to the shape of the land. Topography is caused by the actions of weathering, erosion, and deposition of sediment. Topography is also affected by crustal movements, earthquakes, and volcanoes.

The shape of the land is shown on **topographic maps**. Contour lines connect points of the same elevation on the map. Closely spaced lines on the map indicate a steep slope. Widely spaced contour lines indicate a gentle slope. Circular contour lines show a hill or mountain. Hachure marks show places of depression where the elevation goes down. Contour lines show the direction of stream flow because they make a "V" shape that points upstream.

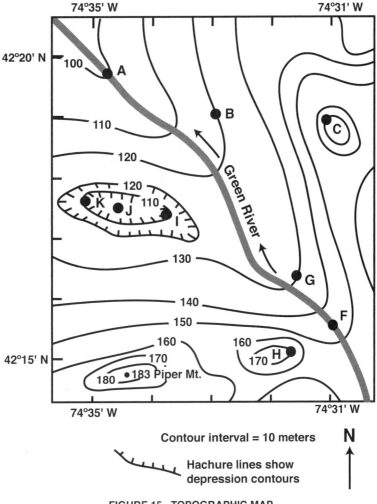

FIGURE 15. TOPOGRAPHIC MAP

Topographic maps show natural and man-made features of the land. The maps are color coded to show common features. For example, water areas are blue and forested areas are green. Symbols on the topographic map include benchmarks. A benchmark is a position where the exact elevation has been measured.

Review Questions

30. The shape of the land is shown on _____ maps.

31. Points of equal elevation are connected by _____ lines on a topographic map.

32. Closely spaced contour lines illustrate a _____ slope.

33. A benchmark indicates the exact _____ of a location.

34. Use the contour map below to answer questions a – e.

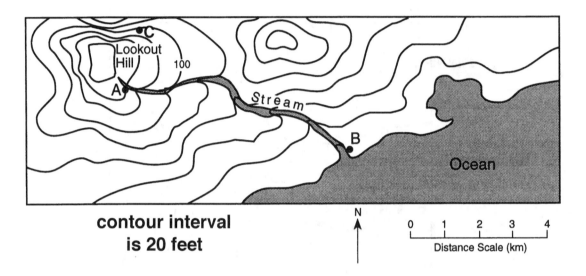

contour interval is 20 feet

a. Elevation at point **A** is _____ feet.

b. Approximate elevation of point **B** is _____ feet.

c. Steep slopes are nearest point _____.

d. The stream flows in a _____ direction.

e. The distance from **A** to **B** is _____ km.

continental drift

_____

convection current

_____

crust

_____

deposition

_____

earthquake

_____

erosion

_____

fault

_____

fold

_____

fossil

_____

glacier

_____

hardness

_____

hydrosphere

_____

igneous rock

_____

inner core

_____

lithosphere

_____

luster

_____

mantle

_____

metamorphic rock

_____

mineral

_____

organic matter

_____

outer core

_____

rock

_____

rock cycle

_____

sediment

_____

sedimentary rock

_____

soil

_____

streak

_____

Theory of Plate Tectonics

_____

topographic map

_____

volcano

_____

weathering

_____

1. The layer of rock and sediment on Earth's surface is the

   (1) atmosphere   (2) troposphere   (3) hydrosphere   (4) lithosphere

2. The hydrosphere is mostly

   (1) solid rock   (2) liquid rock   (3) liquid water   (4) gaseous water

3. Innermost layer of Earth is the

   (1) inner core   (2) outer core   (3) mantle   (4) crust

4. All rocks contain

   (1) fossils   (2) sand particles   (3) minerals   (4) air pockets

5. Rocks and minerals can be identified by their

   (1) color   (3) minerals

   (2) physical features   (4) mass

   Base your answers to **questions 6-7** on the diagrams below which illustrate three physical tests used to identify minerals.

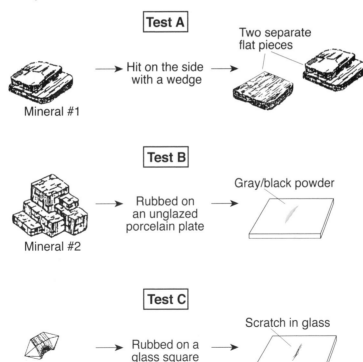

6. Which diagram illustrates the streak test?

   (1) Test A   (2) Test B   (3) Test C

7. Which diagram illustrates the hardness test?

   (1) Test A   (2) Test B   (3) Test C

Base your answers to **questions 8-12** on the diagram of the Rock Cycle below.

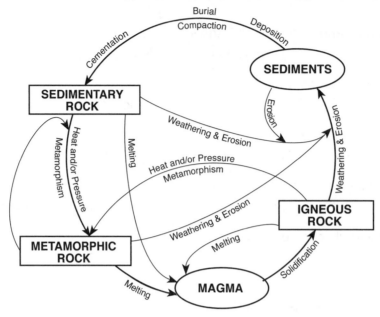

8. Igneous rocks form by the
    (1) cementing together of loose rock particles
    (2) cooling and hardening of liquid rock material
    (3) intense heat and pressure on rocks
    (4) compaction of sediment

9. Rocks that contain sand particles and fossils are classified as
    (1) igneous   (2) metamorphic   (3) sedimentary

10. Metamorphic rock can form from
    (1) magma and lava
    (2) deposited clay and sand particles
    (3) any type of rock
    (4) igneous rocks only

11. The diagram shows the formation of a sedimentary rock.
    Which two processes formed the rock?

    (1) heat and pressure
    (2) folding and faulting
    (3) compaction and cementation
    (4) melting and hardening

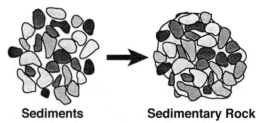

Sediments   Sedimentary Rock

12. Which processes change sedimentary rock into metamorphic rock?

    (1) erosion and deposition   (3) heat and pressure

    (2) melting and solidification   (4) evaporation and condensation

Base your answers to **questions 13-14** on the following diagram. This diagram is a geologic cross section of sedimentary rock layers **A**, **B**, **C**, and **D** which have not been overturned. Layer **E** is an igneous intrusion.

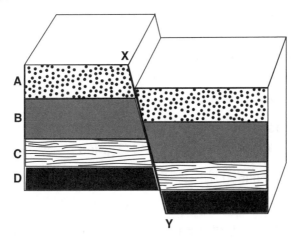

13. The oldest rock layer is:

    (1) A   (2) B   (3) C   (4) D

14. The rock feature from **X** to **Y** is a

    (1) fault   (2) fold   (3) ridge   (4) trench

15. The chart below classifies sediment according to size. A student measures a sediment to be 0.4 cm in diameter. This sediment would be classified as a

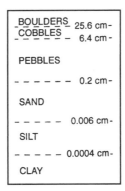

    (1) boulder   (2) cobble   (3) pebble   (4) sand

16. Which two processes cause the formation of soil ?
    (1) weathering of rock and decay of organic matter
    (2) weathering and faulting
    (3) decay of plant matter and condensation
    (4) evaporation and condensation

17. Which is an example of physical weathering?
    (1) cracking of a rock by freezing water
    (2) movement of sediment down a hill
    (3) reaction of limestone with acid rainwater
    (4) formation of a sandbar at the mouth of a river

18. The main force that causes movement of loose rock material over Earth's surface is
    (1) gravity   (2) glaciers   (3) wind   (4) ocean currents

19. Most erosion on Earth is caused by:
    (1) wind   (2) moving water   (3) glaciers   (4) ground water

20. The process that breaks solid bedrock into smaller pieces is known as
    (1) physical weathering   (3) erosion
    (2) chemical weathering   (4) deposition

21. The movement of loose sediment and rock material is known as
    (1) physical weathering   (3) erosion
    (2) chemical weathering   (4) deposition

Base your answer to **questions 22-23** on the following diagram which shows a stream entering the calm waters of a large lake.

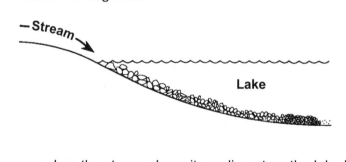

22. Which process occurs when the stream drops its sediment on the lake bottom?
    (1) physical weathering   (3) erosion
    (2) chemical weathering   (4) deposition

23. According to the diagram which size sediment is dropped first by the stream when it slows down?
    (1) very large   (2) large   (3) small   (4) very small

24. The diagram shows what happens to rock carried by a stream as time passes.

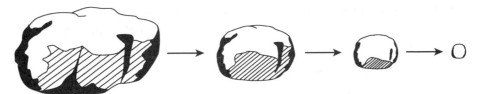

Which process of change is represented by the diagram?

(1) deposition

(3) condensation

(2) metamorphism

(4) weathering

25. Refer to the cartoon below.

The cartoon character on the right realizes that the sand castle will eventually be

(1) folded

(3) eroded

(2) metamorphosed

(4) deposited

26. The collision between two crustal plates can cause the formation of

(1) an ocean basin

(3) a mountain range

(2) a valley

(4) an island

27. Fossils of organisms that lived in shallow oceans have been found high up in mountains. This is evidence of

(1) erosion

(3) weathering

(2) crustal movement

(4) volcanic eruption

28. The diagram shows land features that have been displaced by

(1) faulting

(2) folding

(3) landslides

(4) deposition

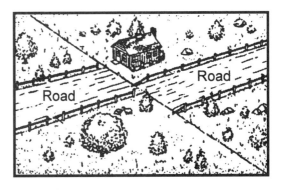

Base your answers to **questions 29-31** on the diagram below.

The diagram shows how scientists think some of the continents were connected in the past.

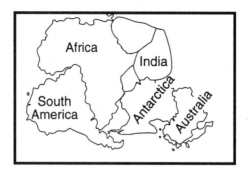

29. What evidence suggests that the continents were once joined?
    (1) shapes of the continents appear to fit together
    (2) same fossils of plants and animals are found on all these continents
    (3) same rock structures exist where continents would have been joined
    (4) all of these facts are evidence of contintental joining

30. For the past 250 million years, Africa and South America have
    (1) rotated around each other
    (2) moved further apart
    (3) moved closer together

31. The *Theory of Plate Tectonics* suggests that the continents move because of
    (1) Earth's orbiting of the Sun
    (2) Earth's rotation
    (3) the convection of heat energy in Earth
    (4) the Moon's gravitational pull on Earth

32. Which set of geologic events are found in the same geographic zones?
    (1) mountain building, earthquakes, volcanoes
    (2) mountain building, fossil formation, volcanoes
    (3) volcanoes, earthquakes, deposition of sediment
    (4) earthquakes, hurricanes, fossil formation

33. Which position is closest to a major earthquake and volcano zone?

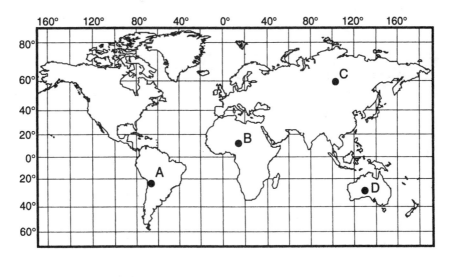

(1) A   (2) B   (3) C   (4) D

34. The diagrams show cross sections of exposed bedrock layers. Which cross section shows the *least* evidence of crustal movement?

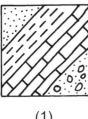

(1)   (2)   (3)   (4)

35. A student plotted the locations of a major earthquakes for the past twenty years. This map shows that most earthquakes occur

(1) near large rivers   (3) at the edges of crustal plates

(2) in the tropics   (4) in the inner core

Base your answers to **questions 36-40** on the map below:

Use the contour map of an island below . Points **A** through **G** are locations on the island. Elevations are in meters.

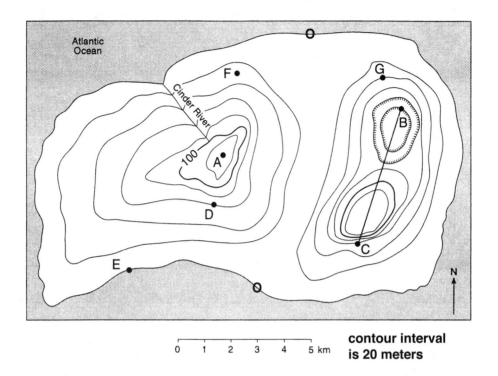

contour interval is 20 meters

36. Which point is nearest the steepest slopes?

    (1) F   (2) B   (3) C   (4) D

37. In which direction does Cinder River flow?

    (1) southeast   (2) southwest   (3) northeast   (4) northwest

38. What is the approximate elevation of point **F**?

    (1) 15 meters   (2) 20 meters   (3) 25 meters   (4) 30 meters

39. At location **B** the elevation is

    (1) decreasing   (2) increasing   (3) staying the same

40. If you were to walk from point **F** to **A**, the elevation would

    (1) decrease   (2) increase   (3) stay the same

41. The map below has isolines that connect points of equal earthquake intensity. Letters **A** through **H** are locations near the earthquake epicenter. The *Modified Mercalli Scale* classifies the effects produced by an earthquake.

Isoseismal Map

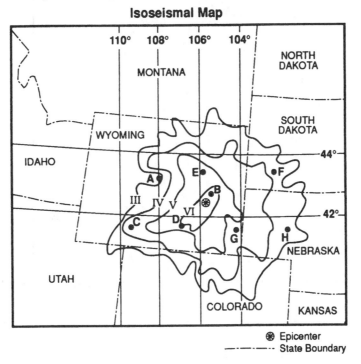

⊛ Epicenter
—·—·—·· State Boundary

Modified Mercalli Intensity Scale

INTENSITY LEVEL	EFFECT
I	Felt only by a few people
II	Felt indoors by a few people, especially on the upper floors of buildings
III	Vibration like that of a passing heavy truck; heavy objects swing
IV	Dishes, windows, and doors rattle
V	Dishes and windows may break; felt by nearly everyone
VI	Felt by all; heavy furniture may move

a. Write the letter that was closest to the epicenter of the earthquake. _____

b. State TWO lettered locations that felt the same effects from this earthquake.

_____ and _____

c. Write the letter of the location that would have felt a vibration similar to a large truck passing by. _____

d. Explain the most likely cause of an earthquake. _____

_____

e. State the approximate longitude for location **E.** _____

42. The diagram below represents the supercontinent *Pangaea* which began to break apart about 220 million years ago.

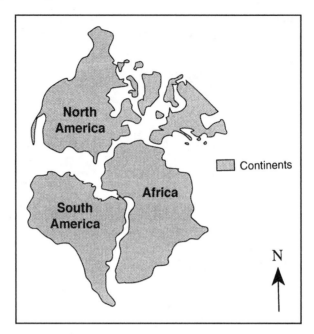

a. State TWO evidences that support the inference that *Pangaea* existed.

(1) _____

(2) _____

43. The diagram below represents the cross section of a mountain.

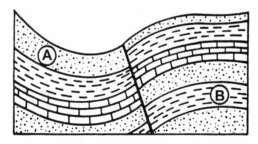

Name the TWO crustal movements shown in the diagram.

(1) _____ (2) _____

44. The data table below shows the percent use of salt in the USA.

SALT USE	PERCENT	HOW SALT IS USED
Water softening	9	Sodium ions in salt replace the calcium ions in water
Highways	69	Salt keeps roads clear of ice in winter
Agriculture	6	Salt is given to cattle and chickens to balance their diet
Foods	5	Humans use salt in their diet
Industry	11	Many industries, such as papermaking, use salt

a. Complete the pie graph to show the percent of each salt use. **Label** each section.

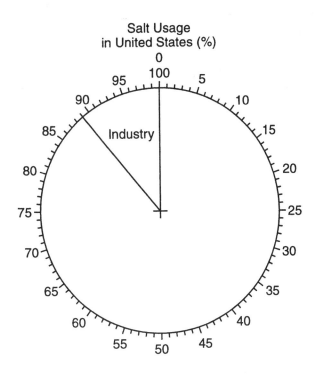

Salt Usage
in United States (%)

b. Based on the data table, explain the most common use of salt.

_____

_____

_____

c. How can the use of salt on highways threaten the environment?

_____

_____

45. The mineral sample shown is *Galena.* The chart lists the densities of several different minerals.

Mineral Sample Galena

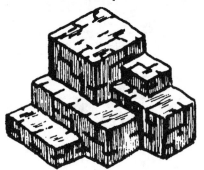

Mass = 210 grams

Mineral Density Table

Mineral	Density (g/cm³)	Mineral	Density (g/cm³)
Gypsum	2.3	Hornblende	3.2
Orthoclase	2.6	Chalcopyrite	4.2
Quartz	2.7	Pyrite	5.0
Calcite	2.7	Magnetite	5.2
Dolomite	2.9	Galena	7.5
Fluorite	3.2	Copper	8.9

a. Calculate the volume of this sample below.

b. Explain how was the mass of 210 grams measured. _____

_____

c. Explain the technique that could be used to measure the volume of this sample.

_____

_____

_____

d. A different mineral has a mass of 40.0 grams and a volume of 8.0 mL.

This sample is most likely the mineral _____.

Show your work below and explain your choice! _____

_____

_____

46. The diagrams below are four rock samples sketched by a student.

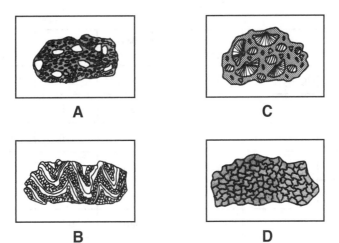

A

C

B

D

a. Select the rock sample that is most likely sedimentary. _____

b. Explain. _____

_____

47. The chart below lists the physical properties of nine minerals.

Mineral	Color	Luster	Streak	Hardness	Density (g/mL)	Chemical Composition
biotite mica	black	glassy	white	soft	2.8	$K(Mg,Fe)_3(AlSi_3O_{10})(OH_2)$
diamond	varies	glassy	colorless	hard	3.5	C
galena	gray	metallic	gray-black	soft	7.5	PbS
graphite	black	dull	black	soft	2.3	C
kaolinite	white	earthy	white	soft	2.6	$Al_4(Si_4O_{10})(OH)_8$
magnetite	black	metallic	black	hard	5.2	Fe_3O_4
olivine	green	glassy	white	hard	3.4	$(Fe,Mg)_2SiO_4$
pyrite	brass yellow	metallic	greenish-black	hard	5.0	FeS_2
quartz	varies	glassy	colorless	hard	2.7	SiO_2

Definitions

    Luster: the way a mineral's surface reflects light
    Streak: color of a powdered form of the mineral
    Hardness: resistance of a mineral to being scratched
             (soft — easily scratched; hard — not easily scratched)

Chemical Symbols

Al	— Aluminum	Pb	— Lead
C	— Carbon	Si	— Silicon
Fe	— Iron	K	— Potassium
H	— Hydrogen	S	— Sulfur
Mg	— Magnesium		
O	— Oxygen		

a. Name a mineral that has a green streak. _____

b. Name the mineral that contains iron, has a metallic luster, and has the same color and streak. _____

c. Name the TWO minerals with the same composition.

    (1) _____ (2) _____

d. Name a mineral that is a source of lead. _____

e. Kaolinite will weather very easily. Explain how the chart indicates this. _____

_____

48. Use the topographic map below.

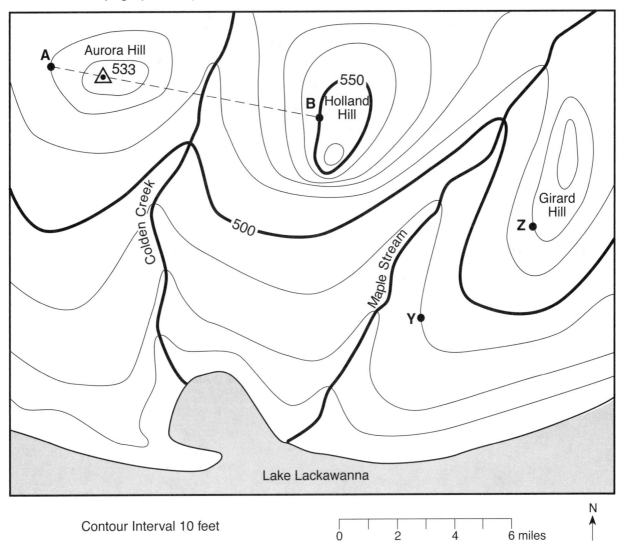

Contour Interval 10 feet

0   2   4   6 miles

N

a. Explain the meaning of the symbol ⚠ 533 on Aurora Hill. _____

_____

b. Measure the distance from A to B. _____ miles

c. Place an "**X**" on the map where the steepest slope is located.

d. Use an arrow (⟶) to show the direction in which Maple Stream flows.

e. The elevation of location **Z** is _____ feet.

f. Name the highest hill on this map. _____

49. The diagram shows the collision of an oceanic plate with a continental plate.

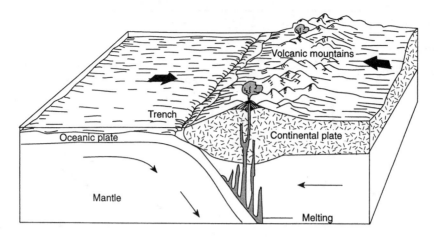

a. Compared to the oceanic crustal plate, the continental crustal plate is

(thinner) (thicker) (the same)

b. Other than volcanic activity, name another geologic event that is most likely to occur in

this area. _____

c. When the two plates come together, the oceanic plate goes under the continental plate because the oceanic plate is

(less dense) (more dense) (hotter) (lighter)

50. For each geologic event state ONE safety precaution that could be taken to prevent or reduce property damage or injury during a future event.

a. Volcanic eruption. _____

b. Earthquake. _____

c. Landslide. _____

d. River flood. _____

CHAPTER 11

ENERGY – FORCES – MOTION

> - **THE PHYSICAL SETTING: KEY IDEA 4**
>   *Energy exists in many forms, and when these forms change energy is conserved.*
> - **THE PHYSICAL SETTING: KEY IDEA 5**
>   *Energy and matter interact through forces that result in changes in motion.*

Forms of Energy

Energy is the ability to do work. Energy explains why an object is at rest or in motion. Energy is needed for matter to move.

Energy can be measured, but it is invisible. We can only observe the effects of energy. We see a tree swaying because of energy in the atmosphere, we cannot see the energy. There are many forms of energy.

FORM OF ENERGY	SOURCE	EXAMPLES
Mechanical	moving parts	muscles, machines, wind, rivers, waves
Chemical	molecules, compounds, elements	fossil fuels, food, batteries
Solar	energy from the Sun	heat, light, and ultraviolet radiation
Electrical	movement of electrons	lightning, electric current
Heat (thermal)	movement of the particles in a substance	heat lamp, fire, infrared radiation
Nuclear	atomic nuclei	uranium fuel
Geothermal	heat from inside Earth	hot springs, geysers
Sound	vibration of matter	thunder, piano, guitar
Light	waves of energy bundles called photons	Sun, light bulb

Review Questions

1. The major source of energy for Earth is the _____.

2. Oil and coal are forms of _____ energy.

3. The result of atoms splitting apart is _____ energy.

4. Energy from the inside of Earth is _____ energy.

5. The vibration of matter is _____ energy.

6. The movement of air molecules causes _____ **energy.**

7. The Sun gives off heat, light, and _____ radiation.

8. An infrared lamp gives off _____ energy.

Energy Transformations

Most activities in everyday life involve one form of energy being **transformed** (changed) into another. For example, the chemical energy in gasoline is transformed into mechanical energy in an automobile engine. When you exercise, you transform chemical energy from digested food to mechanical energy in your muscles. In chemical reactions, energy is transferred into or out of the chemical reaction. This may involve the transfer of light, electricity, or mechanical motion.

During energy transformations, heat is always produced. Some transformations produce a large amount of heat, others very little. When you walk, your feet produce heat as they rub against the ground. A lamp transforms electrical energy to light energy, but heat is also produced so the lamp gets hot. During energy transformations energy is not created or destroyed, it only changes form. This is the *Law of Conservation of Energy*.

Review Questions

9. Most activities involve one form of energy being _____ to another form.

10. When energy transformations occur _____ energy is always produced.

11. The *Law of Conservation of Energy* states that energy cannot be created or

_____.

12. Complete the chart for energy transformations that occur in different devices.

Device	Starting Energy	Changes to...
Battery	a.	Electrical energy
Clothes dryer	Electrical energy	b.
Car engine	Chemical energy	c.
Fireplace	d.	Heat Energy
Fan	Electrical energy	e.
Drum	f.	Sound energy

Kinetic and Potential Energy

All forms of energy exist as kinetic or potential energy. **Kinetic energy** is the energy of a moving object. A speeding car and a rolling ball both have kinetic energy. **Potential energy** is found in a resting object in the form of stored energy. A parked car has potential energy, a moving car has kinetic energy. A battery has potential chemical energy. A waterfall has kinetic mechanical energy.

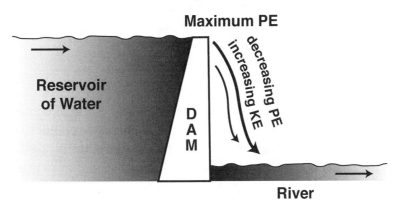

FIGURE 1. POWER DAM

The potential energy an object has is often a result of its position. The higher up an object is, the more potential energy it has. Water at the top of a power dam has potential energy equivalent to the height. When the water is allowed to fall through the dam the potential energy is converted to kinetic energy.

Review Questions

13. The wind has _____ mechanical energy.

14. A battery has _____ chemical energy.

15. At the top of a roller coaster, the car has the most _____ energy.

16. As a skier goes down a hill, potential energy will _____.

Forces

A **force** is a pull or a push that affects an object. A force can cause movement, stop movement, or change the speed and direction of movement. The amount of force applied is measured with a **spring scale**. The metric unit of force is the newton (N).

There are many types of forces. Electric force is caused by the electric attraction between positive and negative charges. This holds matter together and causes static cling on clothing.

Magnetism is the force of attraction of some materials to a magnet. A magnet attracts certain materials and either attracts or repels other magnets. A magnet has a north pole and a south pole. North poles repel each other and attract south poles. South poles repel each other and attract north poles. The attractive force of a magnet is greatest at its poles. Our Earth acts like a giant magnet, it has a north magnetic pole and a south magnetic pole.

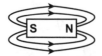

FIGURE 2. MAGNET

Electric currents and magnets can exert a force on each other. If a wire connected to a battery is wrapped around a nail, the nail will become a temporary magnet. The electric current has caused a magnetic field around the nail. This type of magnet is called an **electromagnet**. An electromagnet can be made stronger or weaker by changing the strength of the battery or the number of coils around the nail. It can also be turned off.

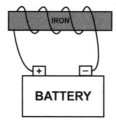

FIGURE 3. ELECTROMAGNET

Gravity is the attractive force between two objects. Gravitational force depends on how much mass the objects have and how far apart they are. The larger the mass, the greater the force. The closer the objects, the greater the gravitational pull. Gravity is one of the forces acting on orbiting objects such as satellites. Gravity also acts on projectiles, such as a thrown baseball. On Earth gravity is a force that acts on all objects at all times.

Friction occurs when two objects rub against each other. It produces heat energy. Friction is a force that opposes motion. It will cause a moving object to slow down.

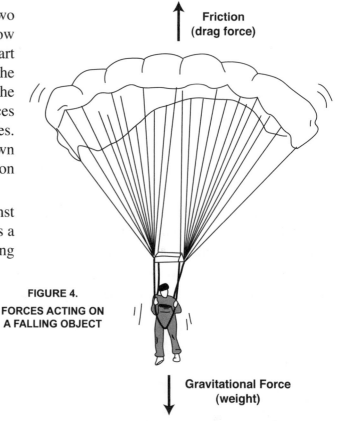

FIGURE 4.
FORCES ACTING ON
A FALLING OBJECT

Friction
(drag force)

Gravitational Force
(weight)

17. When you pull a wagon you are exerting a _____ on the wagon.

18. Positive and negative charges exert an _____ force on each other.

19. The North Pole and the South Pole of Earth have the strongest _____ force.

20. An electric wire wrapped around a nail can cause a _____ force.

21. Gravitational force is greatest when two objects are _____ to each other.

22. The gravitational force of a large planet is _____ than a smaller planet.

23. The force that will slow down motion is _____.

24. When two objects rub against each other _____ energy is produced.

Static Electricity

Electrical force is the attraction between two pieces of matter that are electrically charged. It is caused by positive and negative charges in matter. Matter is made of atoms. Protons are found in the nucleus of atoms. They have a positive charge. Neutrons are in the nucleus, and have no charge (neutral). Electrons orbit the nucleus, are free to move, and have a negative charge. It is the movement of these electrons which causes electrical force.

Static electricity is the presence of an electrical charge in matter. Static electricity does not flow through a wire, it is temporary.

Most matter is electrically neutral, the number of protons is equal to the number of electrons. Friction or rubbing can cause electrons to leave or enter matter, so a charge is built up. When matter loses electrons, it becomes positively charged. If matter gains electrons, it becomes negatively charged. For example, object A and object B are rubbed together. If A loses electrons to B, then A will become positive and B will become negative.

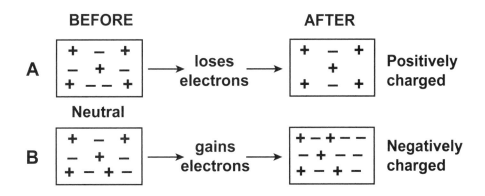

FIGURE 5. LOSS OR GAIN OF ELECTRONS

The *Law of Electric Charges* states that like charges repel each other, and unlike charges attract each other. If two objects both have a positive charge, they will **repel**, or move away from each other. Two negatively charged objects will also repel each other. If one is positively charged and the other is negatively charged, they will **attract** or move toward each other. An object which has no charge, will be attracted to both positively and negatively charged material.

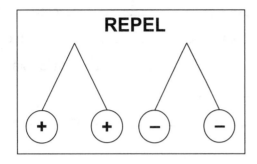

FIGURE 6. LIKE CHARGES REPEL

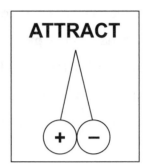

FIGURE 7. UNLIKE CHARGES ATTRACT

Electric discharge is the release of an electric charge that was built up in an object. This is why you get a shock after rubbing your feet on carpet. Lightning is a discharge of negative charges built up in clouds by the convection and friction between air molecules and raindrops.

Review Questions

25. The proton in an atom has a _____ charge.

26. When you brush your hair, the _____ of each atom will move out of your hair.

27. If an object gains electrons, it becomes _____ charged.

28. If an object loses electrons, it becomes _____ charged.

29. A positive charge and a negative charge will _____ each other.

30. Objects that have equal positive and negative charges are _____.

Electric Current

Electric current is the flow of electrons through a circuit. Electricity flows through conductors, such as a metal wire. Insulators stop the flow of electricity. The plastic coating on wires does not allow electricity to flow out of the wire.

Electric circuits provide a means of transferring electrical energy. The source of electricity could be a battery or an outlet. Wires carry the flow of electrons to the load, which uses the electricity. An appliance, a light, or a motor are examples of loads. There is usually a switch which controls the flow of electricity. The energy available to move electrons through a circuit is measured in volts by a **voltmeter.**

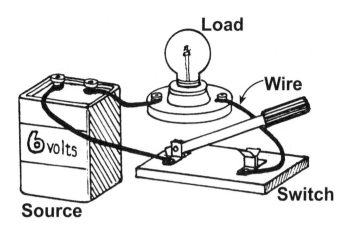

FIGURE 8. ELECTRIC CIRCUIT

There are two types of electrical circuits. A series circuit only has one path for electrons to flow through. The loads all share the circuit, so if one goes out, they all go out. Parallel circuits have many different paths for the electricity to follow. Each load has its own circuit, there is no sharing of electricity. If one appliance goes out, the others are not affected. Homes and schools are wired with parallel circuits.

Review Questions

31. Electric current is the flow of _____.

32. Electricity can not flow through an _____ such as a plastic.

33. On a circuit, a motor is classified as the _____.

34. A _____ circuit has only one path for electrons to follow.

35. A parallel circuit has _____ paths for electrons to follow.

36. Your home is wired in _____ circuits.

Motion

Motion is a change in position relative to a stationary reference point. When we are driving in a car, we know we are in motion because the scenery changes. The motion of an object can be described by its position, direction, and speed. **Speed** is the rate of motion. It is the distance traveled in a given time. For example, a car which traveled 100 miles in two hours had a speed of 50 miles an hour.

$$\text{Speed} = \frac{\text{distance}}{\text{time}}$$

FIGURE 9. SPEED EQUATION

ENERGY – FORCES – MOTION

An object's motion is the result of the combined effect of all forces acting upon the object. A moving object that is not affected by an unbalanced force will continue to move at a constant speed in a straight line. An object at rest will remain at rest unless an unbalanced force is applied to the object. An unbalanced force is needed to change motion. This can cause a change in speed or a change in direction called **acceleration**. For example, when lifting weights you must push up with a force greater than the downward force of gravity. Force is directly related to an object's mass and acceleration. Large masses need more force applied to change their position. The greater the unbalanced force, the greater the acceleration of the object and the greater the change in its motion.

Forces never exist alone, they always act in pairs. For every action there is an equal and opposite reaction. For example, when you kick a ball, the ball goes forward, and you move backward. A rocket's engine gases go backward, so the rocket goes forward.

Review Questions

37. A change in position is called _____.

38. Motion can be described by _____, direction, or speed of motion.

39. If no unbalanced force acts on a resting object, the object at rest will not _____.

40. The force needed to move an object is related to an object's _____ and acceleration.

41. For every action, there is an equal and _____ reaction.

Work, Power, and Machines

Work is done when a force makes the object move. Work changes the kinetic or potential energy of the object. For work to be done, a force must be applied and the object must move. When you push a cart, you are doing work. When you push on a wall, the wall does not move, so you are not doing work.

Power is the rate at which work is done. For example, you move a desk 10 meters in five seconds. The unit of power is the watt (W).

A **simple machine** is a device that helps us do work. It makes work easier to do because the machine increases our effort force. There are six types of simple machines: the inclined plane, wedge, pulley, wheel and axle, screw, and lever. A **complex machine**, like a bicycle, is a combination of interacting simple machines. Bicycles have a wheel and axel, screws, and levers.

FIGURE 10. SOME SIMPLE MACHINES

A RAMP IS AN INCLINED PLANE

**WITH THE HELP OF A LEVER
IT IS MUCH EASIER TO MOVE A BOLDER**

PULLEYS ARE OFTEN USED TO LIFT HEAVY OBJECTS

Machines transfer mechanical energy from one object to another. They can change the direction, distance, speed, or amount of force required to do work. For example, a pulley changes the direction of force and an inclined plane changes the distance of the force.

No machine is one hundred percent efficient. Some of a machine's energy is always lost as heat energy due to friction. By oiling, lubricating, or waxing a surface of a machine friction can be reduced making the machine more efficient.

Review Questions

42. A complex machine is a combination of many _____ machines.

43. Machines transfer _____ from one object to another.

44. Machines can change the direction or amount of _____ applied.

45. A machine produces heat energy due to _____.

46. Friction can be reduced by _____ a surface.

Energy Sources for Human Activities

Human activities such as transportation, manufacturing, construction, and farming require energy. This energy can come from renewable and non-renewable energy resources.

Non-renewable resources are fossil fuels such as coal, oil, and natural gas. These fuels were formed millions of years ago in the crust of Earth. They are the remains of ancient plants and animals. Once they are used up, there is no way to make a new supply of these fuels. Natural gas and oil are becoming more expensive as supplies are being used up.

Renewable resources are those which can be replaced in a relatively short period of time. Energy from the Sun is a renewable resource. Wind, the heat trapped inside of Earth (geothermal), and ocean tides are renewable energy sources. Many people do not use renewable energy sources. The technology for using these renewable resources is often expensive. However, as fossil fuels get more expensive and scarce, we will have to turn to renewable energy resources.

Conservation of energy will extend the supply of the resources which exist on Earth. Decreasing our use of fossil fuels will make them last longer. The burning of fossil fuels releases many air pollutants which are seriously affecting health, ecosystems, and climate. More efficient cars, better-insulated homes, and better design of devices that consume less fuel will save energy resources. The development of technology making better use of renewable sources of energy and finding other energy sources may be necessary in the near future.

Review Questions

47. Fossil fuels come from decayed _____ and _____ matter.

48. A _____ resource will be replaced by nature in our lifetime.

49. Conservation is to use _____ of the energy resources.

50. For each statement place an **"X"** in the correct column.

Description	Renewable	Non-renewable
Hot springs and geysers		
Can not be replaced in our lifetime		
Oil and gasoline		
Wood		
Solar energy		
A windmill		
Needs to be conserved		

acceleration

_____

attract

_____

balanced force

_____

complex machine

_____

conservation

_____

current electricity

_____

electric current

_____

electrically charged

_____

electromagnet

_____

energy

_____

force

_____

fossil fuel

_____

friction

_____

geothermal energy

_____

gravity

_____

kinetic energy

_____

magnetism

_____

mechanical energy

_____

motion

_____

non-renewable resource

_____

nuclear energy

_____

potential energy

_____

renewable resource

_____

repel

_____

simple machine

_____

speed

_____

spring scale

_____

static electricity

_____

transformed

_____

unbalanced force

_____

voltmeter

_____

work

_____

1. What type of energy does a moving river have?

   (1) chemical   (2) mechanical   (3) electrical   (4) thermal

2. Which type of energy is contained in a tank of gasoline?

   (1) chemical   (2) mechanical   (3) electrical   (4) thermal

3. Thermal pollution refers to the harmful addition of what type of energy to the water and air?

   (1) heat   (3) nuclear

   (2) ultraviolet radiation   (4) electrical

4. The heat energy in magma beneath Earth's surface is classified as:

   (1) nuclear   (2) solar   (3) mechanical   (4) geothermal

5. Which of the following is a force?

   (1) gravity   (2) temperature   (3) heat   (4) sound

6. What is the energy transformation that occurs in a ceiling fan?

   (1) electrical to chemical   (3) mechanical to electrical

   (2) electrical to mechanical   (4) mechanical to thermal

7. What energy transformation is occurring in a campfire?

   (1) chemical to thermal

   (2) chemical to mechanical and thermal

   (3) chemical to light and thermal

   (4) thermal to light

8. What energy transformation occurs in a green plant on a sunny day?

   (1) light energy to mechanical energy

   (2) light energy to chemical energy

   (3) chemical energy to light energy

   (4) chemical energy to mechanical energy

9. What energy transformation occurs when you rub your hands together?
   - (1) mechanical energy to heat energy
   - (2) mechanical energy to chemical energy
   - (3) chemical energy to heat energy
   - (4) heat energy to mechanical energy

10. Stored energy is
    - (1) friction
    - (2) potential energy
    - (3) kinetic energy
    - (4) gravitational energy

11. Which of the following groups all have kinetic energy?
    - (1) falling rock, rolling ball, burning log
    - (2) piece of coal, falling rock, rolling ball
    - (3) piece of coal, parked car, battery
    - (4) battery, falling rock, rolling ball

12. On a windy day a spinning windmill has
    - (1) potential mechanical energy
    - (2) kinetic mechanical energy
    - (3) kinetic thermal energy
    - (4) potential thermal energy

13. The diagram below shows the side view of a stream moving down a hill. At which position will the water in the stream have the most potential energy?

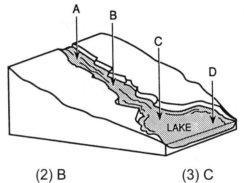

(1) A   (2) B   (3) C   (4) D

14. The diagram shows a swinging pendulum. At which point does the pendulum have the most kinetic energy?

   - (1) A
   - (2) B
   - (3) C
   - (4) D

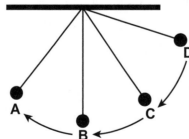

15. The diagram shows a kitten jumping from the top of the refrigerator to the kitchen counter.

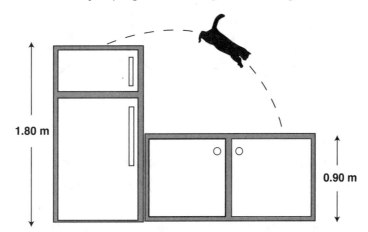

Compared to the kitten's potential energy at the top of the refrigerator, its potential energy on the counter is:

(1) less   (2) more   (3) the same

16. Which energy transformation occurs as a rock rolls down a mountain?

(1) The rock's potential and kinetic energy decreases
(2) The rock's potential energy decreases and kinetic energy increases
(3) The rock's potential energy increases and kinetic energy decreases
(4) The rock's potential and kinetic energy increases

17. Which force causes avalanches and landslides?

(1) gravity   (2) magnetic   (3) electrical   (4) friction

18. Which force causes a ball rolling down the street to slow down?

(1) gravity   (2) magnetic   (3) electrical   (4) friction

19. Which diagram correctly shows the magnetic field around a bar magnet?

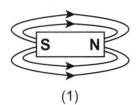 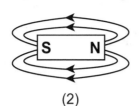 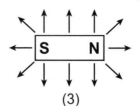 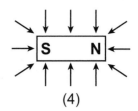

(1) (2) (3) (4)

20. The magnetic field of a magnet:
(1) affects all objects near it
(2) is visible to the observer

(3) only affects magnetic materials
(4) has no effect on a directional compass

21. Two bar magnets of equal strength are positioned as shown. How will the two magnets react to each other?

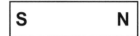   

(1) they will move toward each other
(2) they will move away from each other
(3) there will be no force of attraction between them

22. A wire is wound an iron bar as shown below. When the switch is closed the iron bar will

(1) begin to melt
(2) start to spin
(3) become magnetized
(4) glow

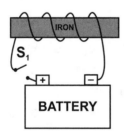

23. The diagram shows the relative sizes of four planets. Which has the greatest gravitational force?

 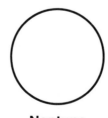

Mercury   **Venus**   **Neptune**   **Pluto**

(1) Mercury   (2) Venus   (3) Neptune   (4) Pluto

24. The diagram shows a space craft returning to Earth for landing. At which position is the gravitational attraction between the spacecraft and Earth the least?

(1) A
(2) B
(3) C
(4) D

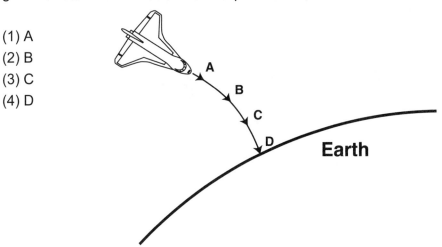

25. An inflated balloon that has been rubbed against a person's hair is touched to a neutral wall and is attracted to it. Which diagram correctly shows the charge distribution in the balloon and the wall?

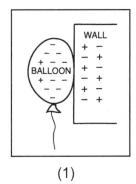 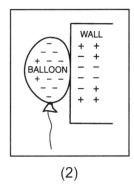 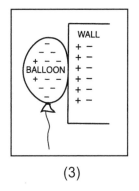 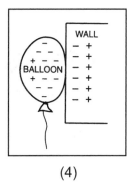

(1) (2) (3) (4)

26. Which of the following is a good insulator for electric wires?

(1) copper (2) aluminum (3) silver (4) rubber

27. Which atomic particle has a negative charge?

(1) proton (2) neutron (3) electron

28. When a glass rod is rubbed with a silk cloth it loses electrons. The glass rod will become

(1) negatively charged (2) positively charged (3) neutral

29. A neutral object will have

(1) equal amounts of positive and negative charges
(2) unequal amounts of positive and negative charges
(3) large amounts of negative charges
(4) large amounts of positive charges

30. Two plastic spheres are held near each other. If sphere A is positive and sphere B is negative, then they will

(1) move toward each other
(2) move away from each other
(3) not move at all

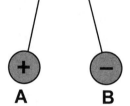

A   B

31. The best conductors of electricity include:

(1) copper, aluminum, plastic
(2) rubber, plastic, glass
(3) aluminum, plastic, rubber
(4) aluminum, copper, gold

32. Which of the measuring devices shown below are most likely to be used to determine the speed of a ball rolling down a ramp?

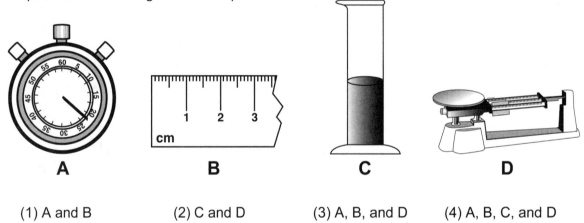

A   B   C   D

(1) A and B   (2) C and D   (3) A, B, and D   (4) A, B, C, and D

33. The diagram below shows the forces acting on an object. Which describes the motion of the object?

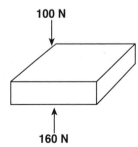

(1) the object will not move   (3) the object will move down
(2) the object will move up

34. Which action requires no work to be done on an object?

(1) lifting the object from the floor to the ceiling

(2) pushing the object along a floor

(3) decreasing the speed of a moving object

(4) holding an object stationary above the ground

35. The diagram shows a student moving a cabinet up a ramp. What two simple machines are being used?

(1) inclined plane and pulley

(2) wheel and axle and pulley

(3) wheel and axle and inclined plane

(4) inclined plane and wedge

36. Which of the following is a complex machine?

(1) doorstop   (2) knife   (3) shovel   (4) scooter

37. The amount of work done by a machine is never larger than the work put into a machine. Some of the input work is lost because of:

(1) gravity   (2) static electricity   (3) magnetism   (4) friction

38. Fossil fuels, such as oil and coal, formed over

(1) two years

(2) two hundred years

(3) two thousand years

(4) two hundred million years

39. Which of the following lists include renewable energy resources?

(1) coal, oil, natural gas

(2) coal, oil, solar

(3) solar, wind, running water

(4) solar, coal, running water

40. Which of the following actions helps to conserve our natural resources?

(1) placing cans and glass bottles in the garbage can

(2) driving down the street to visit a friend

(3) insulating the walls and ceilings in your home

(4) using the air conditioner every day in the summer

41. The eruption of Mt. St. Helens in 1980 resulted in the movement of volcanic ash across the northwestern United States. The movement of the ash is shown by the shaded path on the map. The times marked on the path indicate how long it took the ash to travel to each location from the volcano.

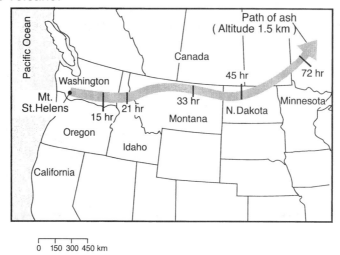

a. Calculate the speed that the ash cloud moved in the first 15 hours.

b. State the direction towards which the ash cloud moved. _____

c. Propose a reason that the ash cloud moved in this direction. _____

_____

d. Name the force that will eventually cause the volcanic ash to settle to ground.

_____

_____

e. Explain the effect that the settling ash had on the green plants that were covered by the ash.

_____

_____

f. Explain why a volcanic eruption is most likely to occur in the state of Washington.

_____

_____

42. A student is sledding down a long snowy hill. Students along the slope record the distance that the sled travels each minute.

Time (min)	Distance from start (m)
1.0 min	10.6 m
2.0 min	22.5 m
3.0 min	29.8 m
4.0 min	41.0 m
5.0 min	54.3 m
6.0 min	63.6 m
7.0 min	68.7 m

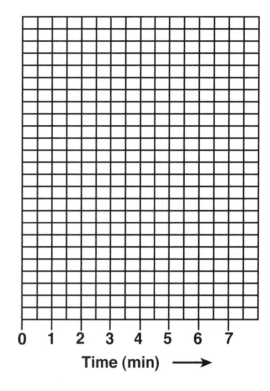

Distance (m)

Time (min)

a. Set up the vertical axis for distance.
b. Plot the data points with a dot " . " and connect with a line.
c. Label the line "sled with one person."
d. Draw a **dashed** line to show where the data would plot if the sled's metal runners were greased.

e. Write a title for this graph. _____

f. State the responding (dependent) variable. _____

g. Name one constant in this experiment. _____

h. If sand were placed on the hill, explain how the distance would be affected.

_____

i. Name the force that was acting on the sled to move it down the hill.

_____

j. The students took turns sledding down the hill. After ten runs the students noticed that the snow was melting where the sled rubbed against the slope. Explain the cause of this.

_____

_____

43. The diagram below shows three planets and their moons. The diagrams are drawn to scale.

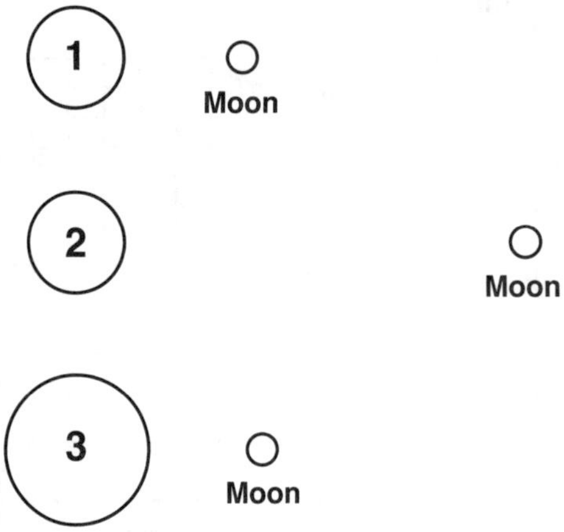

a. Write the number of the planet-moon system with the greatest gravitational force. _____

Explain._____

_____

b. Write the number of the planet-moon system that has the least gravitational attraction

between them. _____

Explain._____

_____

44. The diagram shows a green plant in the sunlight.

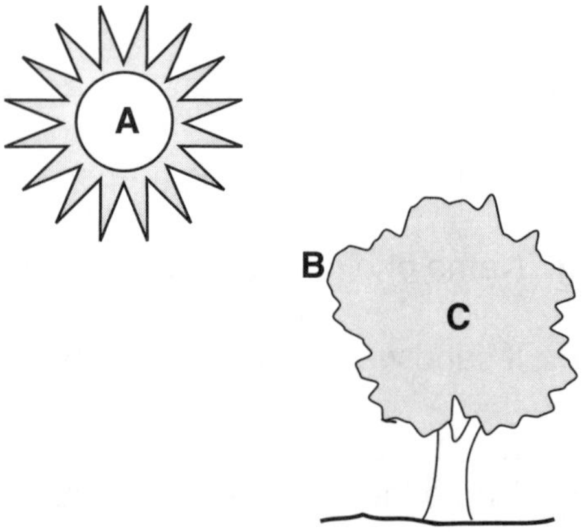

a. Name the source of energy for this system.

_____

b. Name the type of energy the plant is using at **B**.

_____

c. Name the type of energy that the plant produces at **C**. _____

d. Name the pigment that the plant needs to complete the energy transformation.

_____

e. Name the process that the green plant uses to transform this energy.

_____

45. Explain why it is better to use a renewable resource than a non-renewable resource.

_____

_____

46. The diagram shows a set-up of an electric circuit.

a. Describe what will happen to the light bulb when the iron sample is placed in the clips.

_____

b. Explain why this will happen.

_____

_____

c. Describe what would happen to the light bulb if a wooden stick was used instead of the iron.

_____

_____

d. Write the word that describes the role of the iron in this experiment.

_____

47. Name ONE method of producing electricity that uses a renewable resource.

_____

48. Explain TWO ways that your family can conserve electricity in your home.

(1) _____

(2) _____

49. A student's brother drives 75 miles each day to get to his full-time job.
Describe TWO ways that the student's brother could conserve on his gasoline usage each day.

(1) _____

(2) _____

50. A student is rolling a ball down a ramp to see how far it will travel in ten seconds. The student would like to change the experiment to get different results. List TWO variables that the student could change, and explain the effect it would have on the distance the ball travels.

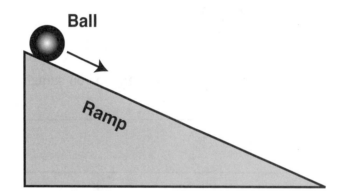

	Variable to change	Effect on distance the ball rolls
1		
2		

CHAPTER 12

SOUND AND ELECTROMAGNETIC ENERGY

> • **THE PHYSICAL SETTING: KEY IDEA 4**
> **Energy exists in many forms and when these forms change energy is conserved**

Waves

Waves are disturbances that transfer energy from place to place. If you throw a stone into a pond, circular waves move along the surface. When the stone hits the pond, it has kinetic energy. Some of the kinetic energy of the moving stone is transferred to the water, causing the water to move.

The substance through which some waves travel is a **medium**. This can be a solid, liquid, or gas. Air is usually the medium for sound waves. Light does not need a medium to travel through, it can travel through empty space (**vacuum**).

There are two types of waves. Transverse waves are waves in which the particles move up and down at right angles to the direction of the wave motion. Compressional waves are waves in which the particles move back and forth, in the direction of wave motion.

Wave A - Compressional

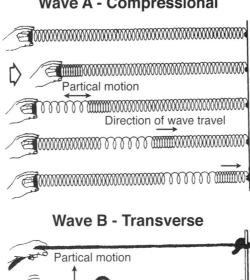

Wave B - Transverse

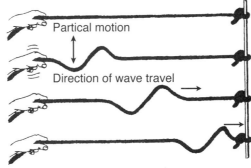

FIGURE 1. TRANSVERSE & COMPRESSIONAL WAVES

Transverse waves have a number of features. These include the crest, trough, and wavelength. The crest is the top of the wave. The trough is the bottom of the wave. The distance between two adjacent crests or troughs is known as the **wavelength**. The number of waves that pass a specific location in one second is the frequency.

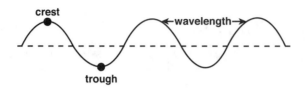

FIGURE 2. PARTS OF A TRANSVERSE WAVE

Waves can be reflected, refracted, or diffracted. **Reflection** is the bouncing back of a wave after striking a barrier or surface. Light waves are reflected off a mirror, so we see our image. An echo is reflected sound waves.

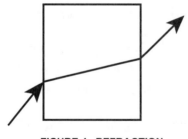

FIGURE 3. REFLECTION

Refraction is the bending of waves as they move from one medium to another. Light is refracted when it goes through a prism. When light moves from the air to the glass , the light wave will bend.

FIGURE 4. REFRACTION

Diffraction is the bending of waves around a barrier. This is why you can hear noise from around a corner.

FIGURE 5. DIFFRACTION

Review Questions

1. Waves are disturbances that transfer _____.

2. The material that a wave travels through is called a _____.

3. Light can travel through a _____.

4. The distance from a crest to the next crest is the _____.

5. Select the diagram that illustrates:

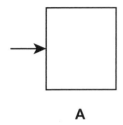  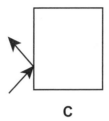 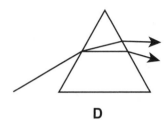

| A | B | C | D |

   a. reflection _____   **b.** refraction _____   **c.** diffraction _____

6. In the diagram below, the wavelength is between letters _____ and _____.

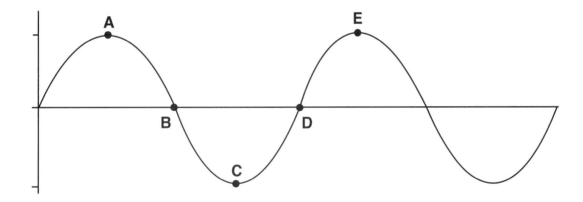

Sound

Sound is a form of energy that travels as a compressional wave. Sound cannot travel through a vacuum, it needs a medium (substance) to travel through. **Sound** travels through the medium by vibrating the particles of that substance. When sound travels through air it vibrates the air molecules. As sound travels into your ear, it vibrates the bones and tissues of your inner ear.

Sound travels much slower than light. This is why you see lightning before you hear thunder. Sound travels at different speeds through different mediums. It travels slowest through gases and fastest through solids. The speed of sound also depends on the temperature. As temperature increases, molecules move faster and there are more collisions, so sound travels faster. On a cold winter day sound will travel slower.

The intensity of sound is the amount of energy it has. Sound is measured in decibels (dB). A whisper is 10 dB but a jet plane is 170 dB. Continuous exposure to loud sounds can cause health problems such as increase in blood pressure and a loss of hearing.

Review Questions

7. Sound cannot travel though a _____.

8. Sound is caused by the _____ of particles.

9   The speed of light is _____ than the speed of sound.

10. Sound travels fastest through _____ materials.

11. Sound travels faster when the temperature is _____.

12. Constant exposure to sounds of more than 90 dB can cause _____ loss.

Electromagnetic Energy

Electromagnetic energies can travel through a medium (material) or through a vacuum (empty space). All electromagnetic energies travel at the speed of light which is more than a million times faster than sound. Electromagnetic energy includes microwave, infrared (heat), visible light, ultraviolet, x-rays, and gamma rays. These energies travel as transverse waves. Each type has a different wavelength. The shorter the wavelength, the more dangerous the electromagnetic energy.

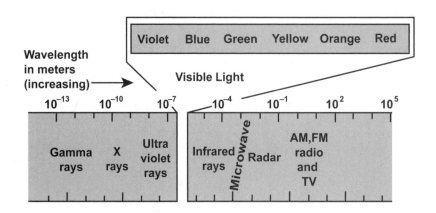

FIGURE 6. ELECTROMAGNETIC SPECTRUM

Gamma rays have the shortest wavelength. They are very dangerous and are used to destroy cancer cells. They are given off by radioactive elements and nuclear explosions. X-rays have great penetrating power and are used to examine bones, teeth, and luggage.

Ultraviolet radiation (UV) is found in light from the Sun. It causes sunburn and skin cancers. Ultraviolet radiation can damage the immune system, cause damage and cataracts in the eye, and stunt plant growth. Ozone in the stratosphere blocks out most of the UV radiation from the Sun.

Visible light is the only electromagnetic energy we can see. Each color we see has a different wavelength. Red is the longest, and blue the shortest wavelength.

Infrared radiation produces heat energy. Earth receives infrared radiation from the Sun. All objects give off heat or infrared radiation. Earth radiates heat to space, our bodies radiate heat to a room.

Microwave radiation is used in communications, cell phones, satellites, and in cooking. It is absorbed by food, which causes the food to heat up.

Radio waves have the longest wavelength. They are used to transmit radio and TV signals. Reflected radio waves can give us ground images in the dark or through clouds.

Review Questions

13. Electromagnetic waves can travel through a medium or through a _____.

14. Each type of electromagnetic energy has a different _____.

15. Cancer cells are destroyed by _____.

16. The only electromagnetic energy that we can see is _____.

17. Ozone blocks out _____ rays.

18. Heat is _____ radiation.

19. Name the type of energy used or given off.

   a. a warm kitten _____   d. a television antenna _____

   b. image of a broken arm _____   e. cooks food quickly _____

   c. sunburn _____   f. the colors we see _____

Light Energy

Light waves travel as transverse waves. Light does not need a medium or a material to travel through, it can travel through a vacuum. The speed of light is 300,000 km/sec.

Light is the only energy we can see. Some objects are luminous and give off light such as the Sun or a lamp. Other objects reflect light. We see the Moon and each other because of reflected light.

Light can be reflected, or bounced back unchanged. Reflection is best off a smooth, light-colored surface. Light can be absorbed, or taken into an object and then changed to heat energy. Dark, rough objects absorb light energy the best and therefore become warm very quickly.

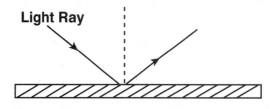

FIGURE 7. REFLECTION OF LIGHT

Refraction occurs when light enters a new medium causing its speed and direction to change. Refraction results in the bending of light rays. We see rainbows because of the refraction of sunlight as it passes through ice crystals and water droplets in the atmosphere. Objects appear bent when they are viewed in water. A pencil in a cup will appear to bend at the point that the water and air meet.

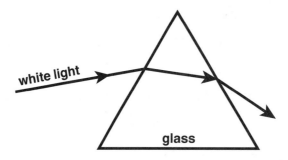

FIGURE 8. REFRACTION OF LIGHT

Light can be transmitted or passed through a material. Window glass allows light to be transmitted.

Review Questions

20. Light can travel through a medium like glass or through a _____.

21. We see objects because the objects _____ light.

22. The bending of light is _____.

23. A light colored, smooth surface will _____ light more than a dark, rough surface.

24. A black shirt will tend to _____ light energy.

25. Clear glass will _____ light.

Heat Energy

Another form of electromagnetic energy is infrared radiation, also known as **heat.** Matter is made up of tiny particles. These particles are always in motion. Heat or thermal energy makes the particles of matter move faster. The particles move faster and further apart as heat is added. Most substances **expand** when heated. When heat energy is removed from a material, the particles will move slower and closer together. Most materials will **contract** when cooled. Water is the exception, it expands as it cools and changes to ice.

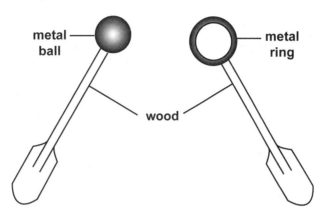

FIGURE 9. WHEN THE BALL IS COOL IT WILL PASS THROUGH THE RING. WHEN THE BALL IS HEATED, IT EXPANDS, AND WILL NOT FIT THROUGH THE RING.

Heat is a form of kinetic energy. Heat and temperature are not the same. **Temperature** indicates that heat energy is present. Heat affects the temperature of a substance. When heat is added, the temperature usually increases. When heat is removed, the temperature usually decreases. Heat moves in a predictable way. It flows from warm objects to cooler ones, until both reach the same temperature.

The unit of heat is the calorie. It takes one calorie of heat to raise the temperature of one gram of water by 1 degree Celsius. You may be familiar with food Calories. Food Calories are equal to 1000 calories.

Substances will heat faster or slower, depending on their color, texture, and type of material. Dark colors absorb energy faster than light colors. Black asphalt will heat faster than sand. Rough textures will absorb faster than smooth surfaces which reflect energy. Soil will heat faster than water.

26. Heat is a form of electromagnetic energy known as _____ radiation.

27. Most substances will _____ when heated.

28. When a material is cooled, the substance will usually _____.

29. When heat is removed, the temperature _____.

30. For each statement select the process that is occurring.

	Description	Reflection	Absorption
a.	A shiny, smooth surface		
b.	We see the Moon at night		
c.	A dark shirt becomes very warm		
d.	We see our face in a mirror		

Changes in the Phases of Matter

Matter can change state or phase when heat is absorbed or released. This is a physical change, there is no chemical change in the substance. When heat is added, molecules gain energy from the environment. As heat is added to water, the molecules move faster and further apart. They finally move fast enough to escape from their container as vapor. Energy is absorbed when a solid changes to a liquid (melting), or when a liquid changes to a gas (**evaporation**). When heat is removed, the particles of matter lose energy. Heat is removed when gases change to a liquid (**condensation**), or a liquid changes to a solid (**freezing**).

A substance's **freezing point** is the temperature at which its liquid form changes to a solid. Liquid water changes to ice at 32°F or 0°C. Every liquid has its own freezing point. Alcohol freezes at –117°C, and ocean water at –1°C. The melting point is the same as the freezing point. Melting will occur when heat is added, freezing will occur when heat is removed.

A substance's **boiling point** is the temperature when it evaporates, or changes from a liquid to a gas. Alcohol boils at 78°C; water boils at 100°C. Water vapor will condense at 100°C when heat is removed.

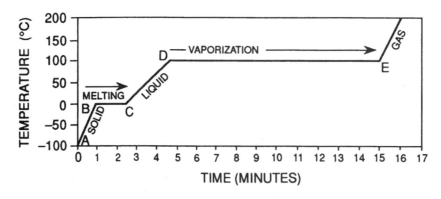

FIGURE 10. PHASE CHANGE

Review Questions

31. The phase change from solid to liquid is _____.

32. During melting, heat is _____.

33. Energy is _____ when a gas changes to a liquid.

34. Energy is released when a liquid changes to a _____.

35. Molecules of a _____ have the most heat energy.

36. The graph shows the heating of a solid material until it becomes a gas.

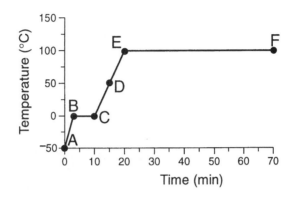

   a. Temperature when the solid melts is _____

   b. Letter at which all the material is a liquid _____

   c. Letter where the material has the least energy _____

   d. Letter where the material begins to boil _____

Methods of Energy Transfer

All types of energy can be transferred between locations, objects, or through matter in three ways: conduction, convection, and radiation. Energy is transferred through empty space by **radiation**. During radiation energy moves from one object to another without direct contact or matter in between. This is how electromagnetic radiation from the Sun reaches Earth.

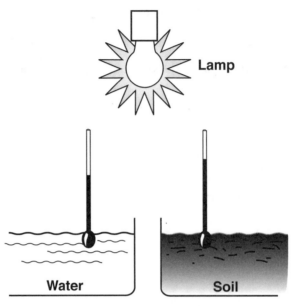

FIGURE 11. RADIATION

Conduction is the flow of energy through a solid by the collisions of its atoms or molecules. Energy is transferred by direct contact. The handle of a pot on the stove may get hot, even though the flame is not near it. Conductors are materials that allow energy to move through easily. This is why metal pots are used in cooking. Poor conductors are called insulators. They keep heat in and prevent heat from moving from place to place. This is why pot handles are often made of wood or plastic.

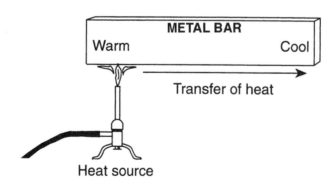

FIGURE 12. CONDUCTION

Convection is the flow of energy within a gas or a liquid. It is caused by density differences. Cold, dense air and water will sink causing the less dense, warm air or water to rise. This circulation of energy causes **convection currents**. This is why you are instructed to drop to the floor in a fire. The cooler air is at the bottom of the room.

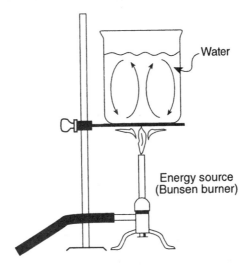

Water

Energy source
(Bunsen burner)

FIGURE 13. CONVECTION

Review Questions

37. Energy is transferred by direct contact during _____.

38. Hot air is _____ dense than cold air.

39. Heat circulates through the air in a classroom by _____.

40. Place an "**X**" in the column for the method of energy transfer described.

	Description	Radiation	Conduction	Convection
a.	Radio waves travel through space			
b.	Heat travels through a metal spoon			
c.	Electricity travels through an electric cord			
d.	Food is warmed in a microwave			
e.	Ocean water circulates by currents			
f.	Sunlight passes through a window			

absorb

_____

condensation

_____

conduction

_____

contract

_____

convection

_____

convection current

_____

diffraction

_____

electromagnetic energy

_____

evaporation

_____

expand

_____

freezing point

_____

heat

_____

infrared radiation

_____

light

_____

medium

_____

melting point

radiation

_____

reflection

_____

refraction

_____

sound

_____

temperature

_____

ultraviolet radiation

_____

vacuum

_____

visible light

_____

wave

_____

wavelength

_____

1. An echo is an example of
   (1) reflection   (2) refraction   (3) diffraction (4) absorption

2. When you sit in a room you can hear noises in the hallway because sound is
   (1) reflected   (2) refracted   (3) diffracted (4) absorbed

3. Sound is produced when particles of matter
   (1) vibrate   (2) change phase   (3) evaporate   (4) chemically react

4. Through which material will sound travel the fastest?
   (1) cold solid   (2) hot solid   (3) hot gas   (4) cold gas

5. Which of the following is true about sound?
   (1) Sound will travel slower in a vacuum.   (3) Sound will not travel through a vacuum.
   (2) Sound will travel faster in a vacuum.

   Base your answers to **questions 6-9** on the diagram below which shows the types of electromagnetic energies.

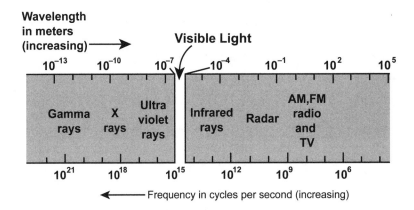

6. Based on the diagram which statement is true?
   (1) X-rays have a shorter wavelength than visible light.
   (2) Visible light has a shorter wavelength than gamma rays.
   (3) Infrared radiation has a shorter wavelength than gamma rays.
   (4) Radio waves have a shorter wavelength than infrared radiation.

7. What is the difference between ultraviolet, visible, and infrared radiation?
   (1) temperature   (2) wavelength   (3) speed of travel   (4) density

8. Which energy is not classified as electromagnetic?
   (1) radar   (2) sound   (3) television (4) heat

9. The electromagnetic energy that allows us to see objects is
   (1) gamma rays   (3) ultraviolet radiation
   (2) x-ray radiation   (4) visible light

10. A surface reflects 90 percent of the light that hits it. This surface is most likely:
    (1) dark colored and rough textured
    (2) dark colored and smooth textured
    (3) light colored and smooth textured
    (4) light colored and rough textured

11. Compared to a dull and rough surface, a shiny and smooth surface will most likely cause sunlight to be
    (1) reflected   (2) refracted   (3) scattered   (4) absorbed

12. Changing the color of the roof of a house from light to dark would probably increase the amount of solar energy that is
    (1) reflected   (2) created   (3) refracted   (4) absorbed

13. On a sunny day changing your shirt from a light color to a dark color would make you feel
    (1) cooler due to reflection
    (2) cooler due to absorption
    (3) warmer due to absorption
    (4) warmer due to reflection

14. The diagram below shows the path of visible light as it travels from air through water. The light did not travel in a straight line because of

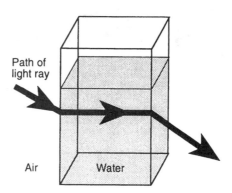

Path of light ray

Air   Water

    (1) reflection   (2) refraction   (3) diffraction   (4) convection

15. If you can not remove a metal cap from a glass jar, it might be helpful to place the cap under hot water. Which of the following supports this advice?
    (1) Heating causes metal to contract faster than glass.
    (2) Heating causes metal to expand faster than glass.
    (3) Heating does not cause metals or glass to change.

16. Complete the statement: Cooling is to contracting, as heating is to
    (1) vibrating   (2) expanding   (3) shortening   (4) boiling

17. Which diagram correctly shows the processes that change the states of matter?

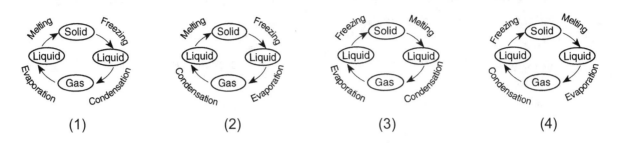

(1) (2) (3) (4)

18. The change in phase from gas to liquid is called

(1) evaporation (2) condensation (3) precipitation (4) transpiration

19. Water releases energy when it changes phase from

(1) liquid to solid (2) solid to liquid (3) liquid to gas (4) solid to gas

20. The diagram below shows the movement of crustal plates. The arrows in the mantle indicate the flow of heat energy by:

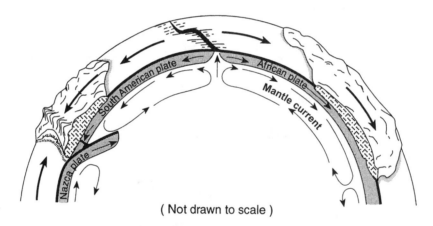

(Not drawn to scale)

(1) conduction (2) convection (3) radiation (4) refraction

21. On a clear summer night the ground cools off by

(1) conduction (2) convection (3) radiation (4) refraction

22. On Earth the movement of air by winds and currents is due to

(1) conduction (2) convection (3) radiation (4) refraction

23. Light from *Polaris*, the North Star, travels to Earth by

(1) conduction (2) convection (3) radiation (4) refraction

24. A piece of plant in a fish tank moved up and across the tank away from the water heater. When the plant reached the other side of the fish tank, it sank. What type of energy transfer does this movement show?

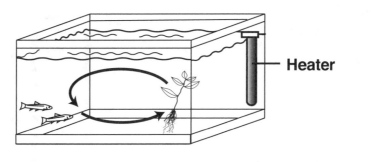

(1) convection   (2) conduction   (3) refraction   (4) radiation

25. The map shows four locations with the temperature of each given in Celsius. Heat will flow from:

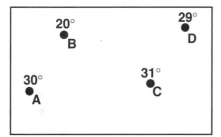

(1) A to B
(2) A to C
(3) B to D
(4) D to C

26. During a sunny afternoon it will become warmer because air molecules

(1) move faster   (2) move slower   (3) stop moving

27. Which action would help an air-conditioner use less energy on a hot, summer day?

(1) opening the curtains and blinds
(2) opening the windows
(3) turning on the lights and stove
(4) adding extra insulation in the walls and ceiling

Base your answers to **questions 28-29** on the diagram of temperature scales below.

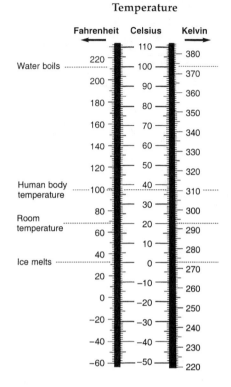

28. A temperature of 65°C
    is approximately equal to:
    (1) 17°F
    (2) 21°F
    (3) 145°F
    (4) 150°F

29. Average room temperature
    should be about:
    (1) 68°C
    (2) 68°F
    (3) 98°C
    (4) 270°K

30. The diagram below represents the four processes that can occur when water changes phase.
    Which letter represents condensation?

(1) A   (2) B   (3) C   (4) D

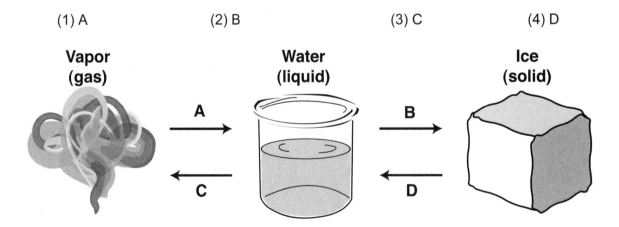

Base your answers to **questions 31-33 on** The graph below which shows the heating of a solid material for 200 minutes until it became a hot gas.

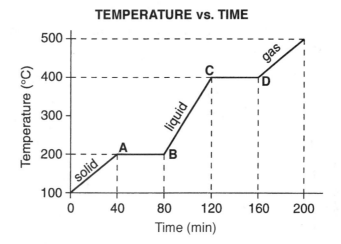

TEMPERATURE vs. TIME

31. The temperature at which the material began to melt was
    (1) 100°C   (2) 200°C   (3) 400°C   (4) 500°C

32. Why did the temperature remain at 200° C for 40 minutes?
    (1) no heat was being added during this time
    (2) the particles began to release heat energy
    (3) energy was used to change the particles' positions
    (4) energy was used to increase the kinetic energy

33. If heat energy was removed, then condensation would occur from letter
    (1) A to B   (2) C to B   (3) C to D   (4) D to C

34. The diagram below shows a cross section of a solar collecting system in the wall of a house in New York. The table gives the house temperatures during a spring day. No other heat source is available for the house.

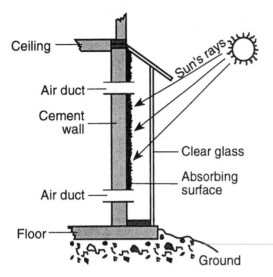

Time of Day	House Air Temperature (°C)
6 a.m.	12
8 a.m.	14
10 a.m.	16
noon	19
2 p.m.	22
4 p.m.	20

a. Describe the color and texture that the wall must be for maximum absorption of the

   sunlight. _____

b. State the time of day when the Sun is highest in the sky. _____

c. According to the data table, state the time when the house was the hottest.

   _____

d. The homeowners are heating the home by using an energy resource which is (renewable) (non-renewable).

e. In New York this solar collecting wall should face the _____

35. On a trip to Florida, a student notices that most of the houses and buildings are painted very light colors. Explain a possible reason for this.

   _____

   _____

36. One summer night a student is awakened by a storm. While the student sits in a dark room he observes the lightning flashes before he hears the thunder. State the science concept that this observation proves.

   _____

37. A hot cup of water and a cold cup of water are connected by metal bar.

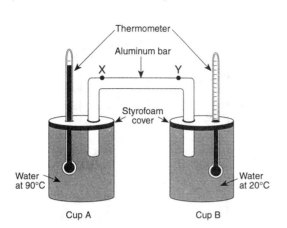

Minute	Temperature of Water (°C)	
	Cup A	Cup B
0	90	20
1	88	20
2	86	20
3	85	21
4	83	21
5	82	22
6	81	22
7	80	22
8	79	22
9	78	23
10	77	23
11	76	23
12	75	23
13	74	23
14	73	23

a. State the method of heat transfer. _____

b. Graph data for the hot cup using a solid line. Label the line *HOT CUP*.

c. Graph data for the cold cup using a dashed line. Label the line *COLD CUP*.

d. State the responding (dependent) variable _____

e. Name TWO constants during this experiment. (1) _____ (2) _____

f. Write a conclusion based on the data _____

_____

g. Compare the amount of degrees that **A** went down and **B** went up. _____

_____

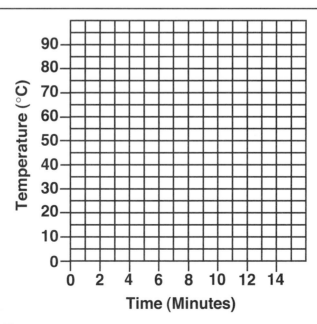

38. The diagram below shows the movement of water in a beaker which is being heated by a flame.

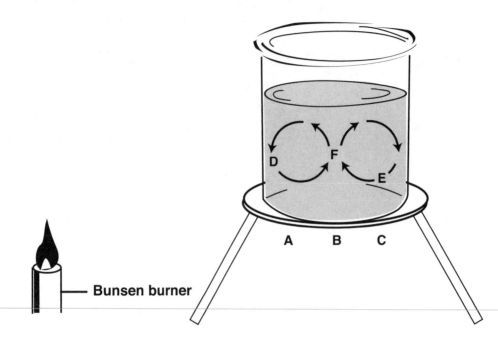

a. State the letter where the flame must be located. _____

b. State the letter where the water is the least dense. _____

c. Name the method of energy transfer occurring in the water. _____

39. The diagram below shows the percentage of sunlight reflected by different Earth surfaces when the Sun is overhead.

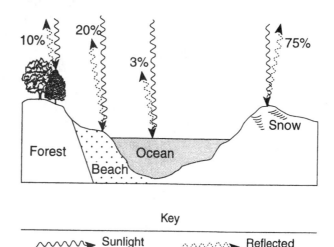

a. Name the surface that reflects the most light energy. _____

b. When light hits the surface of the ocean, very little of it is reflected. Explain why.

_____

_____

_____

c. Based on this data, explain why it is colder over a glacier than over the frozen tundra soil.

_____

_____

_____

d. A forest reflects 10% of the sunlight and absorbs 90% of the sunlight. Explain what a forest does with the absorbed light energy.

_____

_____

_____

40. The diagram below shows three different materials representing the three states of matter.

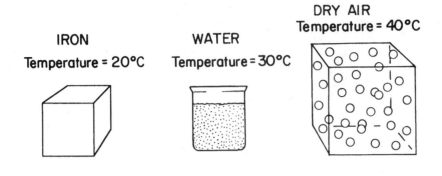

IRON
Temperature = 20°C

WATER
Temperature = 30°C

DRY AIR
Temperature = 40°C

    a. Name the substance that has a definite shape and volume _____

    b. Name the substance in which the particles have the most kinetic energy.

    _____

    c. Name the substance that can be produced by melting. _____

    d. Name the substance that will have the same volume as the container it is in.

    _____

    e. Name the substance through which heat will travel by conduction. _____

41. A student wants to find out which brand of light bulbs lasts the longest. She designs a scientific experiment.

    a. State the problem. _____

    _____

    b. State the manipulated (independent) variable. _____

    c. State TWO factors that should remain *constant* during the experiment.

        (1) _____ (2) _____

    d. Describe the expected outcome. _____

    _____

    _____

42. Read the following passage:

To Tan or Not To Tan

Around 1870, scientists discovered that sunlight could kill bacteria. In 1903, Niels Finsen won the Nobel prize for the use of sunlight therapy to treat infectious diseases. Sunbathing came into wide use as a treatment for tuberculosis, Hodgkin's disease, and skin wounds. The discovery of vitamin D, the "sunshine vitamin", reinforced the healthful image of the Sun. At the time, the link between skin cancer and exposure to the Sun was not known.

In the early 1900s people believed that a deep tan was a sign of good health. However, in the 1940s, the rate of skin cancer began to increase and reached large proportions in the 1970s. Scientists began to realize how damaging the Sun could be.

Since then knowledge connecting the Sun to skin cancer has greatly increased. Many deaths due to this type of cancer can be prevented. The cure rate for skin cancer is almost 100% when treated early.

---

a. State ONE known benefit of daily exposure to the Sun. _____

_____

b. Explain ONE precaution that you can take to decrease your risk of skin cancer.

_____

c. In the first paragraph, the term "*infectious*" refers to diseases that are _____

_____

43. Refer to the phase change diagram of a solid material that is heated from **A** to **E**.

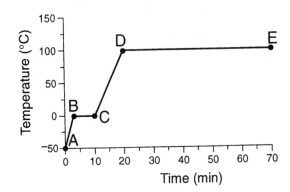

a. Explain what is happening to the substance between letters **B** and **C**.

_____

_____

b. State the phase(s) present between **C** and **D**. _____

c. At letter **A** the material has the least kinetic energy. Explain why. _____

_____

d. The starting temperature was _____

e. This substance is water. Explain how you know that this statement is true. _____

_____

_____

44. Diagram shows the heating of two containers which have equal amounts of soil and water.

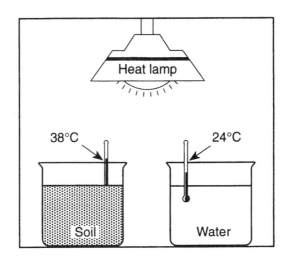

a. Explain the characteristic that causes the soil to become hotter than the water.

_____

_____

b. Name the method of energy transfer that occurs between the lamp and the containers.

_____

_____

_____

NOTES

CHAPTER 13

GENERAL SCIENCE SKILLS

- *THE PHYSICAL SETTING SKILLS based on Standard 4 : 10,11*
- *THE LIVING ENVIRONMENT SKILLS based on Standard 4: 1,2,5,6*
- *THE GENERAL SKILLS based on Standard 4: 1,2,3,4,5,6,8*

Mathematical Skills

Science often involves the collection of numerical data and the interpretation of that data. Numbers in science are sometimes expressed to the nearest tenth. For example, a length measurement may be written as l45.7 m.

To round a number to the tenth place, you need to look at the number in the hundredth place. If that number is 5 or above, round up. If that number is 4 or less, leave it alone. For example in the number 36.82, since the number in the hundredth place, "2," is less than five, then the number is expressed as 36.8.

Review Questions

1. Round the following numbers to the nearest tenth:

   a. 6.54 = _____   f. 232.55 = _____

   b. 12.37 = _____   g. 10.23 = _____

   c. 1.89 = _____   h. 9.52 = _____

   d. 3.61 = _____   i. 8.66 = _____

   e. 5.98 = _____   j. 29.47 = _____

2. Use a calculator to solve the following problems. Round all answers to the tenth.

   k. 6.3 x 0.9 = _____   q. 4.5 ÷ 1.1 = _____

   l. 1.2 x 7.9 = _____   r. 9.5 ÷ 23.7 = _____

   m. 3.8 x 32.7 = _____   s. 3.7 ÷ 7.9 = _____

   n. 23.3 x 48.9 = _____   t. 5.6 ÷ 2.5 = _____

   o. 8.5 x 3.4 x 1.2 = _____   u. 43.8 ÷ 8.4 = _____

   p. 4.3 x 3.8 x 2.6 = _____   v. 4.6 x 4.6 x 4.6 = _____

3. Use a calculator to express the following fractions as decimal. Round to the tenth.

   a. $\dfrac{8}{6}$ = _____   c. $\dfrac{10.8}{14.3}$ = _____

   b. $\dfrac{5}{7}$ = _____   d. $\dfrac{29.6}{13.2}$ = _____

Measuring with a Metric Ruler

The metric system is based on the number ten. This makes it easy to read the scale of a metric instrument. Measurements in science are usually written to the nearest tenth and must include a unit of measurement. For example, the length of a pencil could be measured as 12.6 cm. The unit of measurement is centimeter (cm). Another metric measurement, mass, would be written as 45.3 g. The unit of measurement is gram (g).

Review Questions

4. The diagram below shows a metric ruler. For each lettered position along the ruler, write the measurement to the nearest tenth of a centimeter; include the unit of measurement.

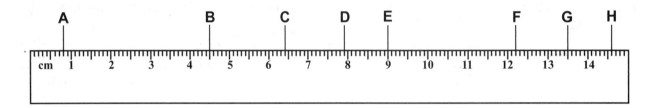

a. A = ___0.8___

b. B = _____

c. C = _____

d. D = _____

e. E = _____

f. F = _____

g. G = _____

h. H = _____

5. Use a metric ruler to measure the length of each line to the nearest tenth of a centimeter. *Write your answer on the line.*

a. _____

b. _____

c. _____

d. _____

e. __

f. _____

Determining Volume

Volume is the amount of space that an object occupies. Volumes of irregular shaped objects and liquids are measured by using a graduated cylinder. The volume of a regular-shaped object is calculated by using the equation:

Volume = Length x Width x Height

If the length, width, and height are measured in centimeters, the unit of volume is a centimeter cubed (cm^3).

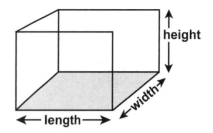

Review Questions

6. Calculate the volume of each of the regular-shaped objects pictured below to the nearest tenth of a centimeter cubed (cm^3). In each problem, show your work using the format provided in **6a**.

---

a. Volume = length × width × height

Volume = _____ × _____ × _____

Volume = _____

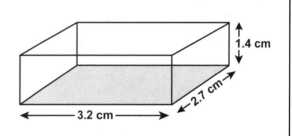

---

b. Volume = length × width × height

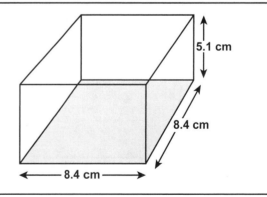

---

c.

Volume =

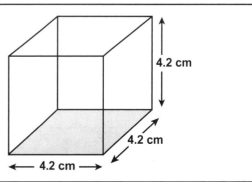

Measuring with a Triple Beam Balance

Mass is the amount of matter in an object. A triple beam balance is used to measure the mass of an object in grams (g). The riders on each beam must be set at zero before you begin to use the balance. Starting with the largest rider move the riders until the beam balances to zero. You read the mass by adding together the numbers from each beam.

Review Questions

7. The diagrams below represent the beams of three different balances. Record the mass to the nearest tenth (0.1) of a gram.

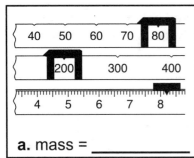

a. mass = _____

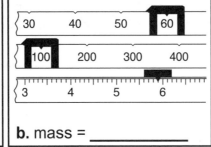

b. mass = _____

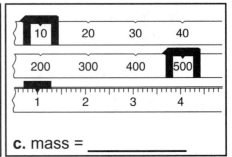

c. mass = _____

8. Measure the mass of four objects provided by your teacher to the nearest tenth.

Object's name	Mass (g)

Determining Density

Density is the concentration of mass in an object. Density is calculated by dividing the mass of an object by its volume. Mass is measured in grams using a triple beam balance. Volume is measured in cubic centimeters or millimeters (1 cm³ = 1 mL). The unit for density is g/cm³. The equation for density is:

$$D = \frac{M}{V}$$

Buoyancy is the tendency of an object to float or sink because of its density relative to the liquid it is in. In this diagram object **X** floats because it is less dense than the liquid it is placed in. Object **Y** sinks because it is more dense than the liquid.

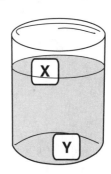

Review Questions

9. Calculate the density for four solid objects A to D. Express answers to the nearest tenth.

Object	Mass (g)	Volume (cm³)	Density (g/cm³)
A	46.2 g	36.5 cm³	1.3
B	3.2 g	5.7 cm³	
C	5.8 g	13.7 cm³	
D	129.6 g	128.7 cm³	

10. Below is a diagram of a container of water. Water has a density of 1.0 g/cm³. Based on the densities you calculated for objects A to D, place the letters A, B, C, and D where these objects would be if placed in the water.

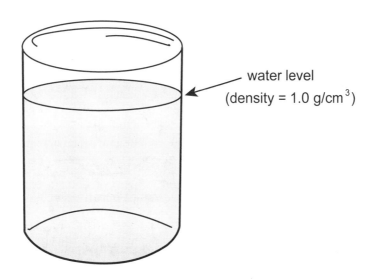

water level
(density = 1.0 g/cm³)

Measuring with a Microscope

A microscope is an instrument that magnifies small organisms and cells for detailed study. The circular area that you see when you look through the microscope is the *field of view*.

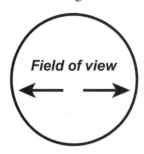

The diameter of the field of view is measured in millimeters (mm) by placing a metric ruler or grid under the microscope. If you know the field of view you can estimate the size of a specimen viewed under the microscope.

Review Questions

11. The diagrams show the field of view for different microscopes. A metric grid has been placed in the field of view. Each of the grid lines represent a millimeter (mm). Estimate the field of view to the nearest 0.5 mm for each diagram.

a. _____ mm   b. _____ mm   c. _____ mm   d. _____ mm

12. The diagrams show cells and micro-organisms viewed under a microscope. The field of view is given. Estimate the length of ONE cell or organism to the nearest 0.1 mm.

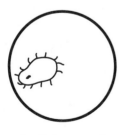 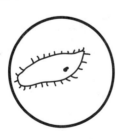  

←2.0 mm→   ←2.0 mm→   ←2.5 mm→   ←1.5 mm→

a. _____ mm   b. _____ mm   c. _____ mm   d. _____ mm

Measuring and Graphing Motion

When an object moves it changes its position in a period of time. A car moving down a highway will change its distance in a given amount of time. An object's motion is the result of the combined effects of all forces acting upon the object, such as gravity and friction.

Review Questions

13. The diagram shows a car that has moved down a ramp. The car was started from different points on the ramp. The diagram shows you how far the car moves from each starting point.

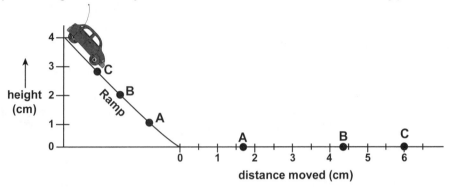

14. a. Complete the data chart with the missing information and answer the questions.

Release point	Starting Height (cm)	Distance moved along table (cm)
A		
B		
C		

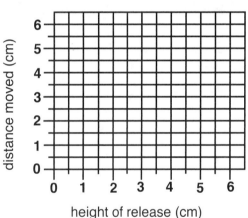

b. Construct a line graph of this data.

c. The manipulated (independent) variable was the _____

d. What force caused the car to move down the ramp? _____

e. What force caused the car to stop or slow down? _____

f. Based on your graph, if the height of the release point was 2.5 cm, the distance moved would have been _____ cm.

g. As height increased, the distance moved *(decreased), (increased), (remained the same)*.

h. If the mass of the car increased, the distance moved would *(decrease), (increase), (not change)*.

i. If the height of the ramp were less, the distance moved would *(decrease), (increase), (not change)*.

j. If the ramp surface were rougher, the distance moved would have *(decreased), (increased)*.

k. Draw a **dashed line** on the graph to show the movement of the car if the slope of the ramp had been steeper. **Label** this line "*steeper slope*."

Classification of Organisms

Living organisms are organized into categories for easier study. They are separated into groups based on **observable** physical characteristics.

Review Questions

15. Circle the terms that would be used to describe the <u>physical</u> characteristics of a **rabbit.**

big	hops	has fur	has four legs
two ears	bites	tail	eats carrots
smells	brown	soft	hibernates

16. Organisms are separated into groups based on physical features. To do this you must begin by asking a question that can be answered as **YES** or **NO**. Do this for the animals pictured below. Place the names of the animals in the correct box.

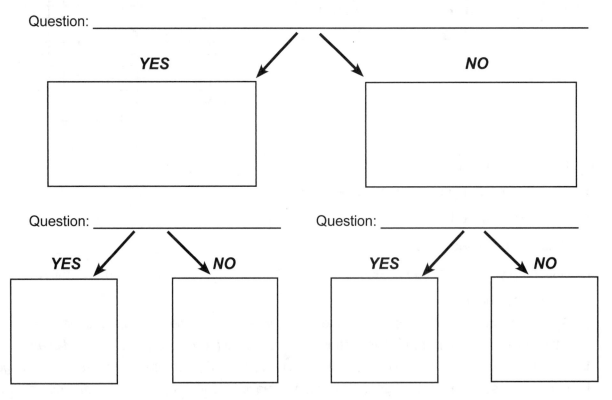

17. Place the word "**DOG**" in the boxes where it would be placed.

18. Place the word "**LIZARD**" in the boxes where it would be placed.

1. Which represents a number expressed to the tenth place?

   (1) 34.56   (2) 5.789   (3) 56   (4) 17.4

2. The number 654.763 correctly rounded to the tenth would be:

   (1) 654.0   (2) 654.7   (3) 654.8   (4) 654.76

3. What is the length of the garden snail from A to B?

   (1) 2.6 cm

   (2) 3.6 cm

   (3) 26.0 cm

   (4) 260.0 cm

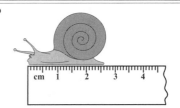

4. A paramecium is observed with a microscope. Its approximate length is:

   (1) 0.2 mm

   (2) 0.5 mm

   (3) 1.0 mm

   (4) 1.6 mm

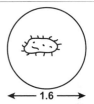

5. The volume of the solid cube shown is:

   (1) 1.2 cm^3

   (2) 1.7 cm^3

   (3) 2.4 cm^3

   (4) 3.6 cm^3

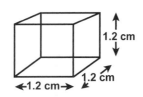

6. The mass of the object placed on the triple beam balance is?

   (1) 1.0 g

   (2) 11.0 g

   (3) 501.0 g

   (4) 511.0 g

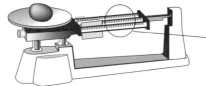

7. A solid object has a mass of 34.6 g and a volume of 40.0 cm^3. Its density is:

   (1) 0.9 g/cm^3 (2) 1.2 g/cm^3 (3) 5.4 g/cm^3 (4) 74.6 g/cm^3

8. The diagram shows three solid objects in a beaker of water.
   Which statement is true about the densities of the objects?

   (1) they are all less dense than the water

   (2) they are all denser than the water

   (3) **A** and **B** are denser than the water

   (4) only **C** is denser than the water

9. A ball is rolling down the street. What force will stop the ball?

   (1) gravity   (2) magnetism   (3) electrical   (4) friction

10. Organisms are placed into categories based on:

    (1) color   (2) shape   (3) habitat   (4) physical features

11. Solve the problem below: _____
(round to tenth)

$$8.65 \times 3.4$$

12. Express the fraction below as a decimal to the nearest tenth: _____

$$\frac{7}{9}$$

13. What is the correct length of the line below: _____

————————————————

14. What is the reading of point **A** on this metric ruler? _____

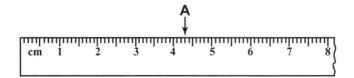

15. Calculate the volume of the box. _____
(round to nearest tenth)

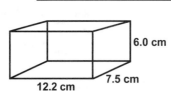

6.0 cm

12.2 cm   7.5 cm

16. What is the reading for this triple beam balance? _____

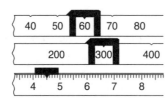

17. An object has a mass of 65.6 grams and a volume of 23.5 cm³.

    a. Calculate its density _____

    b. This object will *(float)* *(sink)* in water because _____

_____

18. A grid is viewed through a microscope as shown.

    a. The field of view is _____

    b. The organism below is viewed through this same microscope. Its approximate

       length is _____ .

19. Separate the animals below into two groups based on an observable physical characteristic.

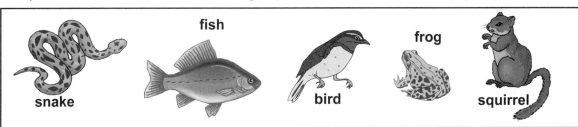

    a. **Question:** _____

             YES ↙   *NO* ↓

    b. Place this animal into one of the two groups above. Explain your reason.

                                                                   grasshopper

_____

20. A student collected data for three solid objects as shown below.

	Volume	Mass	Density
A	3.0 g	6.0 g	0.5 g/cm³
B	15.0 cm³	5.0 g	3.0 g/cm³
C	2.0 cm	8	4.0 g/cm³

    a. Correct all the mistakes in the chart.

    b. Which object(s) will float in water? _____ Why? _____

_____

NOTES

GLOSSARY

A

absorb – to take in

acceleration – a change in the speed or direction of moving object

adapt – adjust to a new environment

agent of erosion – any natural force which carries and moves sediment

air mass – large body of air with the same temperature and moisture throughout

air pressure – the force or weight of air pushing down on Earth's surface

altitude – height above sea level

anemometer – instrument that measures wind speed

asexual reproduction – type of reproduction where there is only one parent

asteroid – rock which orbits the Sun

atmosphere – thin layer of gases surrounding Earth

atom – smallest part of an element

attract – to draw to oneself

axis of rotation – imaginary line through an object that it spins on

B

bacteria – one-celled organism without an organized nucleus

balanced force – equal in value

barometer – instrument that measures air pressure

boiling point – temperature at which a substance changes from a liquid to a gas

buoyancy – the ability or tendency to float

C

Calorie – 1000 calories, used to measure heat energy in food

cancer – non-infectious disease which is the result of abnormal cell division

carbohydrate – sugar or starch, supplies energy to the body

carnivore – animal that only eats meat

celestial – of the sky

cell – smallest part of a living organism

cell division – when a parent cell splits into two new cells

cell membrane – outer covering of a cell which controls the movement of materials into and out of the cell

cell wall – rigid outer covering of a plant cell

chemical change – occurs when one type of matter is changed to a different type of matter

chemical property – describes how a material reacts with other substances

chemical reaction – process in which a chemical change takes place

chlorofluorocarbons (CFC'S) – man-made compounds that break down ozone in the atmosphere

chlorophyll – green chemical in the leaves of plants which absorbs light for photosynthesis

chloroplast – organelle in plant cells that contains chlorophyll, site of photosynthesis

chromosome – structure in the nucleus on which genes are located

circulation – movement of material within a cell or between parts of an organism

circulatory system – the system of organs which transports materials throughout the body

classification – to separate into groups based on similar characteristics

climate – the average weather of a region over a long period of time

clone – offspring that is identical to parent, result of asexual reproduction

comet – mass of ice and rock which orbits the Sun

community – all the different populations in a region

competition – the struggle among organisms for food, water, and space

complex machine – made of more than one type of simple machine

compound – substance that forms when two or more elements chemically combine

conclusion – outcome, result

condensation – the change in phase from gas to liquid

conduction –transfer of energy through a solid by the collisions of molecules

conservation – to use less of a natural resource

constant – remaining the same

consumer – organism which eats other organisms

continental drift – the idea that the continents move and change their positions

contract – to decrease in size, to compress

control – a set-up in the experiment in which no factor is changed

controlled experiment – experiment that tests only one factor

convection – flow of energy through a liquid or gas by currents

convection current – circular flow of energy caused by uneven heating and density differences

coordination – the even regulation of body systems as they work together

correlation – to match rock layers of the same age

crust – thin, outermost layer of Earth

current electricity – flow of electrons through a wire

cyclical change – any change that repeats in a predictable pattern

cytoplasm – watery substance that fills the cell

D

data – facts, observations that conclusions are based on

decomposer – organism that breaks down the wastes and dead remains of plants and animals

density – quantity that compares the mass of an object to its volume

dependent variable – the condition that changes or responds in an experiment, responding variable

deposition – the release of sediment when the transporting agent slows down or stops

development – a series of changes that occur after fertilization and gives rise to an adult organism

diet – what an organism usually eats

diffraction – when light and sound bend around a barrier

digestive system – series of organs that breakdown food into simpler forms so it can be absorbed into the body

disease – illness

DNA – molecule that carries genetic information

Dominant gene – trait that usually appears in an offspring

duplicated – copied

dynamic – related to energy and motion

dynamic equilibrium – a balance in energy, forces, or the environment

E

earthquake – shaking of the Earth's crust

eclipse – a temporary darkening of the Sun or the Moon

ecological succession – orderly process by which one biotic community is replaced with another

ecology – the study of the relationships between living organisms and their environment

ecosystem – the organisms in a community and the physical features of their environment

egg cell – the female reproductive cell

electric current – flow of electrons through a wire

electrically charged – matter with a positive or negative charge caused by the removal or addition of electrons

electromagnetic energy – energy that travels as waves at the speed of light, can travel through a vacuum

element – simplest form of matter, made of one type of atom

endocrine system – the glands which secrete hormones that regulate body functions

energy – the ability to do work

energy pyramid – shows the amount of energy available in the food chain as energy flows from one organism to another

environment – the surroundings in which an organism lives, includes living and non-living factors

equator – zero degree line of latitude, divides Earth into Northern and Southern Hemispheres

equinox – when the noon Sun is directly over the Equator, 12 hours day/night occurs worldwide, March 21 and September 21

erosion – to transport or move weathered rock and sediment

evaporation – change in phase from liquid to gas

evolution – changes in species over time

excretion – removal of gas and liquid wastes from an organism

expand – increase in size or volume

external fertilization – process in which eggs are fertilized outside the body of the female

extinction – when a species no longer exists

F

fat – source of stored energy for an organism

fault – crack in Earth's crust along which rock layers can shift

fertilization – the merging of an egg cell and a sperm cell

field of view – the diameter of the area you see under a microscope, measured in millimeters

flower – contains the reproductive organs of a plant

fold – the bending of rock layers

food chain – a series of organisms through which food energy is passed in an ecosystem

food web – interconnected food chains in an ecosystem

force – any push or pull that causes an object to move

fossil – evidence of an organism that lived in the past

fossil fuel – energy resource formed from the remains of dead plants and animals, includes coal,oil,natural gas

freeze – change in phase from liquid to solid

freezing point – temperature at which a liquid changes to a solid

friction – force that opposes and slows down motion

front – boundary between two air masses, results in a change of weather

fungi – group of non-green, plant- like organisms with simple structures and no chloroplasts

G

gas exchange – the replacement of carbon dioxide for oxygen

gene – a piece of hereditary information on a chromosome

genetic engineering – the process of altering DNA for heredity

genetic material – the hereditary information in the nucleus which is passed from generation to generation

genetic trait – characteristic of an organism controlled by genes

geothermal energy – heat from Earth's interior, can be used as a renewable energy resource

glacier – large mass of ice which moves due to gravity

graduated cylinder – instrument which measures liquid volume

gravity – force of attraction between two objects that have mass

greenhouse gas – carbon dioxide, methane, and water vapor which absorb and hold heat in the atmosphere

H

habitat – the part of the environment in which an organism lives

hardness – the resistance of a mineral to being scratched

hazardous weather – severe storms which are dangerous to humans and their properties

heat – energy caused by the motion of particles of matter, related to temperature

herbivore – animal that eats only plants

heredity – the passing of characteristics from parent to offspring by genes on the chromosomes

high pressure system – cool, dry with clear weather

homeostasis – the maintainance of a stable internal environment

hormone – chemical secreted by an endocrine gland that causes a specific effect

humidity – amount of water vapor in the air

hydrosphere – the water on Earth's surface

hypothesis – a proposed explanation to a question

I

igneous rock – rock formed by the cooling and hardening of lava or magma

independent variable – the condition in an experiment changed by the investigator, manipulated variable

infectious disease – disease caused by a microorganism that can be passed on to another organism

inference – conclusion made from known facts

infrared radiation – electromagnetic wave in the form of heat

inherited – characteristic passed on by heredity

inner core – innermost solid layer of Earth

insoluble – not able to dissolve in a given solvent

internal fertilization – process in which eggs are fertilized inside the body of the female

irregular shape – not straight or even sided

K

kinetic energy – energy of motion

kingdom – the largest group in the classification of living organisms

L

latitude – angular distance north or south of the Equator

law of conservation of energy – energy is not be created or destroyed, it can be changed from one form to another

leaf – flat, thin organ growing out of a plant stem, the location of photosynthesis

length – distance between two points

life cycle – the changes that an organism goes through during its lifetime

life processes – basic activities that all living organisms perform

light – massless bundles of particles that move as waves

lithosphere – the outermost solid rock layer of Earth

locomotion – movement from one place to another

longitude – angular distance east or west of the Prime Meridian

low pressure system – warm, moist with stormy weather

lubricate – to make slippery and reduce friction

luster – ability of a mineral to reflect light, shiny or dull

M

machine – device that transfers mechanical energy from one object to another

magnetism – the ability to attract iron or steel

manipulated variable – the condition in an experiment changed by the investigator, the independent variable

mantle – solid layer of Earth below the crust

mass – amount of matter in an object

matter – anything which has mass and volume

measurement – quantity or size as determined by an instrument

mechanical energy – energy of moving parts

medium – the substance a wave of energy travels through, can be solid, liquid, or gas

melting point – temperature at which a substance changes from a solid to a liquid

metabolism – all the chemical reactions of life processes in an organism

metal – shiny solid which is a conductor

metalloid – element which has properties of a metal and a non-metal

metamorphic rock – rock formed from intense heat and pressure on a pre-existing rock

metamorphosis – series of changes that some organisms undergo as they develop from egg to adult

meteor – streak of light observed when a meteoroid passes through the atmosphere

meteoroid – rock fragment in space

microbe – organism which can only be seen with a microscope

microorganism – organism that is too small to be seen with the unaided eye, a microbe

mineral – naturally occurring, inorganic compound found in rock

mixture – matter which contains more than one kind of substance, can be separated by physical means

molecule – smallest part of a compound

molten – melted

moon – an object which revolves around a planet

moon phase – the changes in the shape of the Moon as seen from Earth

motion – a change in position

multicellular – made of more than one cell

mutation – a change in a gene, can result in a changed trait

N

natural resource – available minerals, water, soil, and air used by organisms

natural selection – the idea that organisms with favorable traits are better able to survive and reproduce

nervous system – system which carries impulses throughout an organism, regulates and controls body functions

noble (inert) gas – a gaseous element that does not react with other elements

non-infectious disease – not transmitted or caused by a microorganism

non-metal – brittle, dull solid or a gas which is a poor conductor

non-renewable resource – resource that is not replaced by nature within the time span of human history

nuclear energy – energy produced by fission or fusion of atomic nuclei

nucleus – structure in a cell which controls cell activity and contains genetic material; center of an atom

nutrient – part of food that can be used by an organism

nutrition – process by which an organism takes in food and changes it to a usable form

O

observation – to use the senses or instruments to gather information

ocean basin – floor of the ocean

offspring – descendant of a parent

omnivores – animal that eats both plants and animals

orbit – the path of a planet around the Sun or a satellite around a planet

organ – group of tissues which work together to perform a specific function

organ system – group of organs which work together to perform a specific function

organic matter – material from a plant or animal

organism – a living thing

outer core – liquid layer in Earth between the mantle and inner core

ozone – compound of oxygen in the upper atmosphere which absorbs ultraviolet radiation

P

pedigree chart – model showing the traits of ancestors and descendants

phase (state) of matter – three forms of matter: solid, liquid, and gas

photosynthesis – the process by which plants absorbs sunlight to make food and oxygen from CO_2 and water

physical change – a change in matter that affects its physical appearance but not its chemical composition

physical environment – the non-living parts of the area an organism lives in

physical property – describes the appearance of matter such as color, phase, shape

plate tectonics – theory that Earth's lithosphere is broken into separate pieces that shift and move

pollen – produced in the flower, contains the sperm cell

pollination – transfer of pollen to the ovary of the flower so that eggs are fertilized

pollutant – harmful substance which contaminates the environment

population – group of organisms of the same species living together in a location

position – the place where an object is

potential energy – energy stored in an object as a result of its position

precipitation – the falling of liquid or solid water from clouds

predator – carnivore that attacks, kills, and feeds on its prey

pressure – the force on an object

prevailing winds – the general wind pattern in a specific latitude zone

primary consumer – animal that feeds on plants, a herbivore

producer – organism which makes its own food by photosynthesis, usually a green plant

property – characteristic of matter or an organism

protein – nitrogen compound needed for repair and growth of body tissues

Punnett square – diagram used to predict the probability of offspring inheriting a given trait

R

radiation – to give off or send out energy

recessive gene – gene whose trait is not shown if it is paired with a dominant gene

recycle – to reuse a material

reflection – when energy strikes a surface and is returned unchanged

refraction – the bending of a wave as it moves into a new medium

regeneration – to regrow a missing body part

regulation – to maintain a stable internal environment

renewable resource – a resource that is replaced by nature within the time span of human history

repel – to force away

reproduction – the process by which living things produce new organisms of their own kind

reproductive system – organs that produce egg and sperm cells

respiration – life process by which energy is released from food and used by the cell

respiratory system – organs which exchange gases between the organism and the environment

responding variable – the condition that changes or responds in an experiment, dependent variable

revolve – the movement of one object around another

rock – naturally formed solid made of minerals

rock cycle – model that describes how one rock type can be changed into another rock type

root – part of the plant which takes in water and nutrients from the soil

rotate – the turning of an object on its axis

S

scientific method – series of steps used to investigate and answer questions

scientific notation – a way to represent very large or small numbers using powers of ten

secondary consumer – animal that feeds on other animals

sediment – weathered rock particles

sedimentary rock – rock formed from the compaction and cementation of sediment or organic matter

seed – contains the immature embryo plant and nutrients

selective breeding – to choose the organisms with desired traits which will reproduce

sex cell – egg or sperm cell

sexual reproduction – type of reproduction in which there are two parents

simple machine – device which changes the direction or size of a force

skeletal system – bones and cartilage that support and protect the body of an organism

soil – loose sediment and organic matter on the surface of Earth that supports plant life

solar system – group of solid objects that orbit the Sun

solubility – amount of solute that can dissolve in a solvent

solute – part of a solution that is dissolved

solution – mixture in which the parts are evenly distributed throughout

solvent – part of a solution that dissolves a substance

sound – form of energy that vibrates the particles of a substance it moves through

species – all the organisms of one kind that can produce offspring

speed – the distance an object moves in a given time

sperm cell – the male reproductive cell

spherical – having a shape like a ball

spring scale – instrument used to measure force

star – gaseous body in space that produces energy by fusion of hydrogen

static electricity – temporary build up of electric charge in an object

stem – the supporting structure of plants through which materials are transported

stimulus – change in environment detected and reacted to by an organism

stratified – layered

stratosphere – atmospheric layer above the troposhere which contains ozone

streak – color of the powdered mineral

sublimation – the change in phase from gas to solid, or solid to gas

summer solstice – the noon Sun is overhead at the Tropic of Cancer (23½° North) usually occurs on June 21

survival of the fittest – the idea that individuals that are better adapted to their environment will most likely survive

T

temperature – average kinetic energy of the particles in a substance

tides – the rising and falling of water levels along the ocean shoreline

tissue – group of cells which work together to perform a specific function

topographic map – map which shows natural and man-made features of the land

transform – to change

transmit – to send

transpiration – process by which plants release water vapor to the air

triple beam balance – instrument used to measure mass

troposphere – lower layer of the atmosphere closest to the surface where weather occurs

U

ultraviolet radiation – shortwave energy emitted by the Sun

unbalanced force – not equal in value

unstable air – air that easily moves by convection causing storms

urban – of a city or town

V

vacuum – empty space, no matter present

variable – any factor in an experiment which affects the results of the experiment

variation – a trait or characteristic that is somewhat different from another organism of the same kind

vibration – a repeating up-down or back-forth motion

virus – disease causing microbe, does not have a typical cell structure

visibility – the distance that a person can see

visible light – form of electromagnetic energy we can see

vitamin – compound which is essential for the proper growth and functioning of an organism

volcano – opening in Earth's crust through which magma erupts

voltmeter – instrument used to measure electrical pressure

volume – amount of space an object occupies

W

waste removal – to take away materials that an organism does not need

water cycle – model used to show the movement of water between the air, land, and surface water

water vapor – the gas phase of water

wave – periodic motion or disturbance

wavelength – distance from one point on a wave to the same point on the next wave

weather – condition of the atmosphere at a given time and place

weathering – physical and chemical breakdown of rock

wind – horizontal movement of air

winter solstice – the noon Sun is overhead at the Tropic of Capricorn (23½° South) usually occurs on December 21

work – to use a force to move on object

NOTES

PRACTICE EXAM
SECTION

New York State
Intermediate-Level Science Test Sampler
Part A: Sample Questions 1–17

Directions (1–17): Each question is followed by four choices. Decide which choice is the best answer. Mark your answer in the spaces provided on the separate answer sheet by writing the number of the answer you have chosen.

1   Which part of a cell allows nutrients and other materials to enter or leave the cell?

    1 cytoplasm
    2 nucleus
    3 chloroplast
    4 cell membrane

2   Which human body system controls production of the hormones that regulate body functions?

    1 digestive
    2 endocrine
    3 respiratory
    4 skeletal

3   Hereditary information is found in a cell's

    1 chloroplasts
    2 chromosomes
    3 cytoplasm
    4 membranes

4   What is a major cause of variation within a species?

    1 sexual reproduction
    2 asexual reproduction
    3 extinction
    4 photosynthesis

5   Which process is shown in the diagram below?

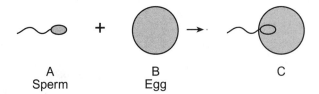

A
Sperm

B
Egg

C

    1 metamorphosis
    2 regulation
    3 fertilization
    4 respiration

6   A male chimpanzee has 48 chromosomes in each of his regular body cells. How many chromosomes would be found
     in each of his sperm cells?

     1 96
     2 48
     3 24
     4 12

7   The diagram below shows materials needed for survival being transported inside a plant.

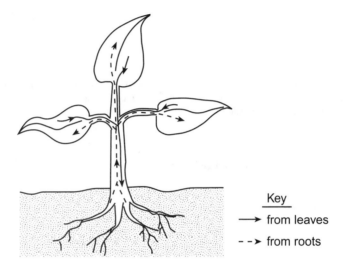

     Key
     → from leaves
     --→ from roots

     Which body system performs this function in humans?

     1 circulatory system
     2 digestive system
     3 excretory system
     4 respiratory system

8   The energy content of food is measured in

     1 ounces
     2 degrees
     3 grams
     4 Calories

9   The diagram below shows the Moon revolving around Earth as viewed from space.

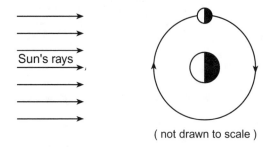

Sun's rays

(not drawn to scale)

What makes it possible to see the Moon from Earth?

1 The surface of the Moon emits its own light, which can be seen from Earth.
2 The Moon absorbs light during the day and emits the light at night.
3 Light emitted by Earth illuminates the Moon's surface, making it visible.
4 Light emitted by the Sun is reflected to Earth by the Moon's surface.

10   The solid part of Earth's surface is called the

1 hydrosphere
2 lithosphere
3 troposphere
4 atmosphere

11   A rock that contains fossil seashells was most likely formed as a result of

1 volcanic activity
2 sedimentation
3 heat and pressure
4 magma cooling

12   The diagram below shows the rock cycle.

Rock Cycle

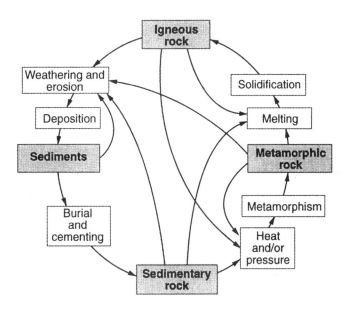

Which two processes result in the formation of igneous rocks?

1 melting and solidification
2 sedimentation and evaporation
3 crystallization and cementation
4 compression and precipitation

13   The cartoon below shows a humorous view of a scientific phenomenon.

What process is occurring that makes the child's breath become visible?

1 boiling
2 melting
3 condensation
4 evaporation

14   In which situation is a chemical reaction occurring?

    1 salt dissolves in water
    2 a nail rusts
    3 ice melts
    4 a glass breaks

15   As ice cream melts, its molecules

    1 absorb heat energy and move farther apart
    2 absorb heat energy and move closer together
    3 release heat energy and move farther apart
    4 release heat energy and move closer together

16   Which diagram best shows the property of refraction?

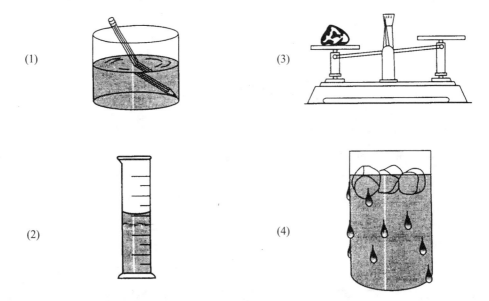

    (1)   (3)

    (2)   (4)

17   A student pushes against a wall with 20 N of force and the wall does not move. In this situation, the wall exerts

    1 0 N of force
    2 less than 20 N of force
    3 20 N of force
    4 more than 20 N of force

New York State
Intermediate-Level Science Test Sampler
Part B: Sample Questions 18–34

Directions (18–34): Each question is followed by four choices. Decide which choice is the best answer. Mark your answer in the spaces provided on the separate answer sheet by writing the number of the answer you have chosen.

18   The data table below shows the average distance of four planets from the Sun and the approximate time it takes those planets to orbit the Sun.

Planet	Average Distance from the Sun (millions of kilometers)	Approximate Time It Takes the Planet to Orbit the Sun (Earth days)
Mercury	57.9	88
Venus	108.2	225
Earth	149.6	365
Mars	227.9	687

Which statement is best supported by the data in the table?

1 Venus takes less time to orbit the Sun than Mercury does.
2 Mars takes less time to orbit the Sun than Earth does.
3 Mars takes more time to orbit the Sun than Earth does.
4 Venus takes more time to orbit the Sun than Mars does.

19   The data table below shows the masses and volumes of three objects (A, B, and C).

A	B	C
Mass = 4g	Mass = 6 g	Mass = 8 g
Volume = 2 cm^3	Volume = 6 cm^3	Volume = 4 cm^3

The formula for calculating an object's density is: Density $= \dfrac{\text{Mass}}{\text{Volume}}$.

Which statement about the densities of these three objects is correct?

1 B is more dense than A.
2 A is more dense than C.
3 B and C have equal densities.
4 A and C have equal densities.

20   The diagram below shows the frequency and wavelength of various types of electromagnetic energy.

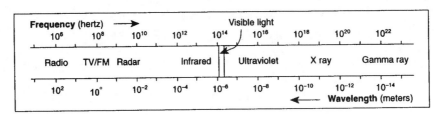

Which type of electromagnetic wave has a wavelength of approximately 10^{-10} meter and a frequency of 10^{18} hertz?

1 infrared
2 radio
3 X ray
4 radar

21   The graph below shows the distance and time traveled by four cars.

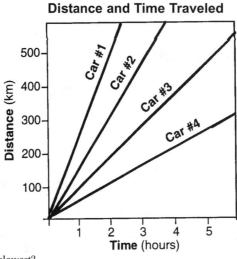

Which car traveled the slowest?

1 Car #1
2 Car #2
3 Car #3
4 Car #4

Directions (22–34): For each question, write your answer in the spaces provided on the separate answer sheet.

Base your answers to questions 22 through 24 on the diagrams and data table below.

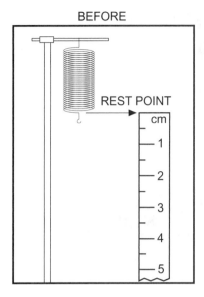

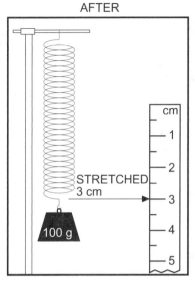

Attached mass (g)	Distance spring is stretched (cm)
100	3
200	6
300	9
400	12
500	15
1000	30

DATA TABLE

22   State the relationship between the mass attached to the end of the spring and the length the spring is stretched. [1]

23   Predict how many centimeters the spring will stretch if a total mass of 700 grams were attached. [1]

24   What mass would be needed to stretch the spring to a length of 60 cm? [1]

Base your answers to questions 25 through 27 on the Punnett square and information below.

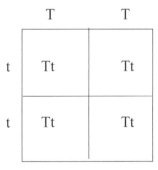

In a certain plant, the gene for tall height (T) is dominant over the gene for short height (t). The Punnett square shows the results of a cross between a pure tall plant and a pure short plant.

25   What percentage of the offspring would be tall plants? [1]

26   Use the Punnett square on your separate answer sheet to show the results of crossing two of the offspring shown in the Punnett square above. [2]

27   Which process is represented by the use of the Punnett square?

1   natural selection   3   pollination
2   sexual reproduction   4   mutation

Base your answers to questions 28 through 32 on the food web shown below.

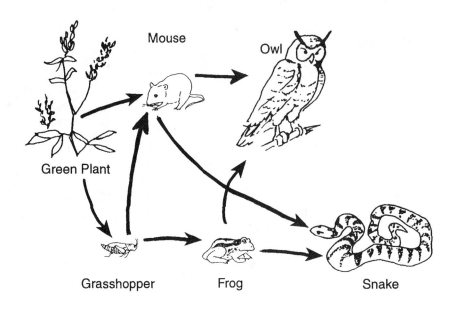

28   Identify a producer in this food web.   [1]

29   Identify an herbivore in this food web.   [1]

30   Identify a carnivore in this food web.   [1]

31   Identify an omnivore in this food web.   [1]

32   Explain why removing the snake from this food web might result in a decrease in the grasshopper population.   [1]

Base your answers to questions 33 and 34 on the diagram below, which shows a form of reproduction.

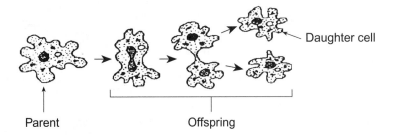

33   Which type of reproduction is shown in the diagram?   [1]

34   How does the genetic material of the daughter cell compare to the genetic material of the parent cell?   [1]

New York State
Intermediate-Level Science Test Sampler
Part C: Sample Questions 35–45

Directions (35–45): For each question, write your answer in the space provided on the separate answer sheet.

Base your answers to questions 35 and 36 on the charts below, which show two elements (iron and sulfur) and their properties. The arrows indicate that these elements may combine to form either a mixture of iron and sulfur or the compound iron sulfide.

ELEMENT	PROPERTIES
Iron	magnetic, black
Sulfur	nonmagnetic, yellow

physical change →

PROPERTIES OF IRON AND SULFUR MIXTURE
partially magnetic, black and yellow

chemical change →

PROPERTIES OF IRON SULFIDE COMPOUND
nonmagnetic, shiny, gray

35   How could a student use a magnet to indicate that combining iron and sulfur to produce the mixture of iron and sulfur is a physical change? [1]

36   What evidence indicates that a chemical change took place when the iron and sulfur combined to form iron sulfide? [1]

Base your answers to questions 37 and 38 on the diagrams below, which show two situations in which energy transformations are occurring.

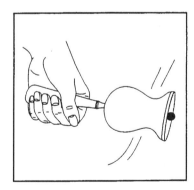

37   As the candle burns, which energy transformation occurs? [1]

38   As the bell rings, which energy transformation occurs? [1]

39   A student plays tennis several times a week. She notices that the tennis ball seems to bounce higher on some courts than on other courts. She wonders if this has something to do with the surface of the court. Design an experiment to see if her hypothesis is correct. Include these elements in your response:

- State the hypothesis. [1]
- Identify the factor to be varied. [1]
- Identify two factors that should be held constant. [2]
- Clearly describe the procedures. [1]

Base your answers to questions 40 through 42 on the graphs below, which show the laboratory growth of two microorganisms when provided with adequate food and grown in **separate test tubes**.

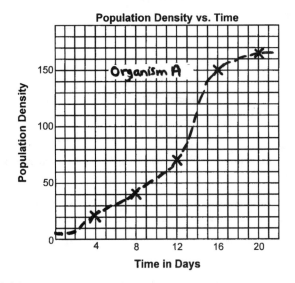

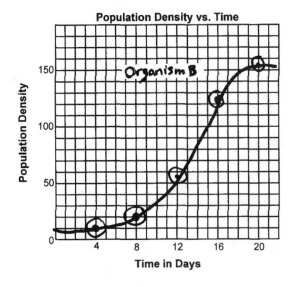

40   The data below were obtained when organism A and organism B were grown with adequate food in the **same test tube**.

Population density	Day					
	0	**4**	**8**	**12**	**16**	**20**
Organism A	5	50	100	75	25	10
Organism B	5	25	75	125	150	125

On the grid provided on your separate answer sheet, make a graph of the data from the table above according to the instructions below. [3]

a   Place an *X* to show the population of organism A for each interval in the 20-day period.

b   Connect the *X*'s with a *dashed* line. Make a key that indicates this line represents the data for organism A.

c   Place a dot in a circle to show the population of organism B for each interval in the 20-day period.

d   Connect circled dots with a *solid* line. Make a key that indicates this line represents the data for organism B.

41   State a relationship that may have produced the results shown when organism A and organism B were grown together. Explain your answer, using the graphed data. [2]

42   Based on your graph, predict the population density of organism A *or* organism B at day 21. Explain your prediction. [2]

Base your answers to questions 43 through 45 on the information below and on your knowledge of science. The page of notes shown below was made by a student doing a research project about hail.

Some Observations about Hail:

1   Hailstones are fairly round in shape.
2   When cut in half or held up to the light, layers can be seen in the hailstone.
3   Average diameter of hailstones found after last summer's storms:
        July 12 - 6 mm
        July 26 - 9 mm
        August 12 - 20 mm
        August 26 - 12 mm

Background Information Found in Science Book:

1   The precipitation dropped during a hailstorm is called hailstones.
2   Hail causes damage to crops, buildings, and vehicles.
3   Hailstones are usually more than 5 mm in diameter.
4   Thunderstorms form from tall clouds which have temperatures below 0°C in their upper regions.
        They have strong updrafts pushing the air toward the top.
5   The layers in a hailstone are caused by the path the hail takes as it falls.
6   A new layer forms each time the hailstone is pushed into the freezing zone.

43   On the diagram on your separate answer sheet, draw a path that would produce a hailstone that has three layers. You can practice on the drawing below. Be sure your path starts and finishes at the points shown. The dotted line separates the thunderstorm into Zone A, which is above 0°C, and Zone B, which is below 0°C. When you are satisfied with your path, copy it onto the diagram on your answer sheet. Your answer will be evaluated by how well the path you have drawn could produce a three-layer hailstone. [2]

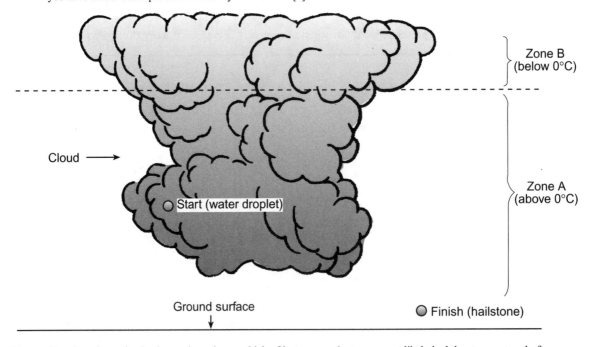

44   Based on the student's observations above, which of last summer's storms most likely had the strongest updrafts associated with it? Give two reasons to support your answer. [3]

45   Based on the background information in the student's notes above, identify one problem that can be caused by hailstorms. [1]

New York State
Intermediate-Level Science Test Sampler
Student Answer Sheet for Parts A, B, and C

Student Name _____

Directions (1–21): Each question is followed by four choices. Decide which choice is the correct answer. Mark your answer in the spaces below by writing the number of the answer you have chosen. (NOTE: A scannable answer sheet will be provided for the actual exam. This format is provided for the sampler only.)

1 _____	8 _____	15 _____
2 _____	9 _____	16 _____
3 _____	10 _____	17 _____
4 _____	11 _____	18 _____
5 _____	12 _____	19 _____
6 _____	13 _____	20 _____
7 _____	14 _____	21 _____

Directions (22–39): For each question, write your answer in the spaces below.

22 _____.

23 _____ cm

24 _____ grams

25 _____ %

26

27 _____

28 _____

29 _____

30 _____

31 _____

32 _____

_____

33 _____

34 _____

_____

35 _____

_____

36 _____

37 _____

38 _____

39 Hypothesis:_____

_____

Factor to be varied: _____

Two factors to be held constant:

     1 _____

     2 _____

Procedure: _____

_____

_____

_____

_____

_____

_____

40

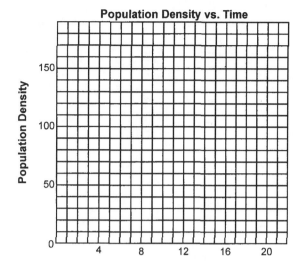

Population Density vs. Time

Population Density (y-axis): 0, 50, 100, 150

Time (x-axis): 4, 8, 12, 16, 20

41 _____

_____

42 _____

_____

43

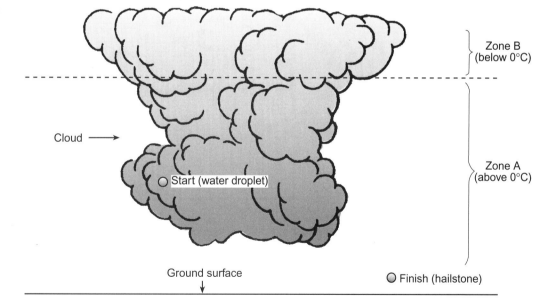

Zone B (below 0°C)

Zone A (above 0°C)

Cloud →

○ Start (water droplet)

Ground surface

◉ Finish (hailstone)

44 _____

_____

_____

45 _____

✂ CUT HERE

✂ CUT HERE

GRADE 8 - Intermediate-Level Practice Test #2

PART I

1. The diagram below represents a food chain.

   In the diagram, consumers are represented by the

   (1) sun and the corn plant
   (2) chicken and the boy
   (3) sun and the boy
   (4) corn plant and the chicken

2. All living things release energy from their food by a process called

   (1) respiration
   (2) photosynthesis
   (3) reproduction
   (4) irritability

3. Which of the following organisms can make their own food?

   (1) fungi
   (2) mushrooms
   (3) snakes
   (4) green plants

4. Adaptations enable an animal to

   (1) grow bigger
   (2) survive in its environment
   (3) absorb nutrients from the environment
   (4) make its own food

5. Which of the following organisms has had the most impact on the environment?

   (1) humans   (3) birds
   (2) earthworms   (4) green plants

6. Which human organ has a purpose similar to the function of the skin?

   (1) brain   (3) esophagus
   (2) kidney   (4) heart

7. Which of the following is in the correct order?

   (1) cells, organs, systems, tissues
   (2) cells, systems, organs, tissues
   (3) cells, tissues, organs, systems
   (4) cells, tissues, systems, organs

8. The body system responsible for the exchange of gases (oxygen and carbon dioxide) between the external environment and the body's cells is the

   (1) digestive system
   (2) respiratory system
   (3) circulatory system
   (4) excretory system

9. The graph below shows the levels of two hormones in the blood. Based on the data shown in the graph, which statement is true?

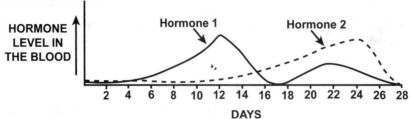

(1) Hormone 1 increases during the first 20 days.

(2) Hormone 2 remains the same throughout the 29 days.

(3) Hormone 1 decreases on the 20th day.

(4) Hormone 2 is highest on the 24th day.

10. Milk is heated and pasteurized in order to

(1) decrease the number of microorganisms

(2) decrease the amount of fat

(3) increase the vitamin content

(4) increase the number of calories

11. Which of the following statements is true?

(1) Sexual reproduction leads to the possibility of variation in the next generation.

(2) Asexual reproduction leads to the possibility of variation in the next generation.

(3) Sexual reproduction results in identical offspring.

(4) Sexual reproduction requires only one parent.

12. The crust of Earth is composed mainly of

(1) air   (2) shale   (3) rock   (4) water

13. Which of the following diagrams represents a fault?

A

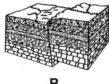

B

C

D

(1) A   (2) B   (3) C   (4) D

14. The table below shows how the hardness of four different minerals can be tested.

MINERALS	TEST FOR HARDNESS
Talc	Fingernail scratches it easily.
Gypsum	Fingernail scratches it.
Calcite	Copper penny scratches it.
Fluorite	Steel knife scratches it easily.

If a mineral can be scratched by a fingernail, the mineral can be

(1) talc, only

(2) calcite, only

(3) either talc or gypsum

(4) either gypsum or fluorite

15. Which processes form a metamorpic rock?

(1) cooling and solidification

(2) heat and pressure

(3) deposition and compression

(4) cementation and pressure

16. Which of the following is changed as air masses move across Earth's surface?

(1) daily weather

(2) seasons

(3) yearly climate

(4) amount of daylight

17. The boundary where two air masses meet is called a

(1) front

(2) low

(3) high

(4) weather system

18. Which of the following is *not* a hazardous weather condition?

(1) rain shower

(2) tornadoes

(3) hurricanes

(4) severe thunderstorms

19. Which of the following is *not* a weather condition?

(1) humidity

(2) temperature

(3) hours of daylight

(4) air pressure

20. In New York State, which side of a building gets the most direct sunlight at noon?

(1) north

(2) east

(3) south

(4) west

21. The following diagram represents Earth's movement around Sun.

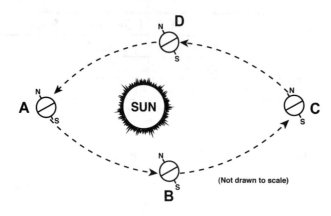

(Not drawn to scale)

When Earth is at Position C, the season in New York State is

(1) summer   (2) winter   (3) fall   (4) spring

22. Which of the following statements about planets is correct?

(1) Both Earth and Mars appear to support life.

(2) Earth is apparently the only planet that supports life.

(3) Jupiter has some evidence of life.

(4) Earth, Mars, and Jupiter appear to support life.

23. Which diagram best represents the shape of the most planets?

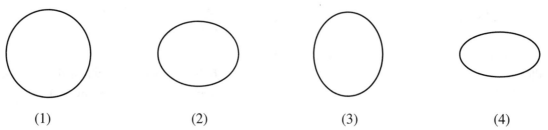

(1)   (2)   (3)   (4)

24. The diagrams below show boxes of the same mass being pulled up ramps. The ramps have the same lengths and heights. On which ramp would it be hardest to pull up the box?

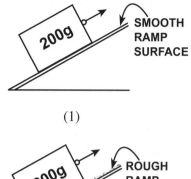

SMOOTH RAMP SURFACE

(1)

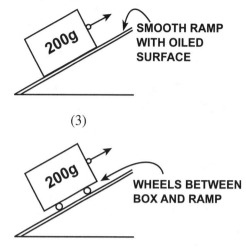

SMOOTH RAMP WITH OILED SURFACE

(3)

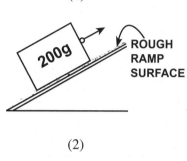

ROUGH RAMP SURFACE

(2)

WHEELS BETWEEN BOX AND RAMP

(4)

25. Which of the following is a result of two surfaces rubbing together?

(1) work
(2) friction
(3) chemical change
(4) physical change

26. The metal wires in an electrical circuit act as

(1) energy producers
(2) insulators
(3) transformers
(4) conductors

27. Which of the following statements about work is true?

(1) The amount of work done by a machine is always less than the amount of work put into the machine.
(2) The amount of work done by a machine is always greater than the amount of work put into the machine.
(3) The amount of work done by a machine is the same as the amount of work put into the machine.
(4) The amount of work done by a machine is not influenced by the amount of work put into the machine.

28. The following diagram represents

   (1) an inclined plane
   (2) a wedge
   (3) a lever
   (4) a wheel and axle

29. Which of the following is a good safety rule when using electricity?
   (1) Do not disconnect appliances before repairing them.
   (2) It is safe to turn on the radio while standing in water
   (3) Electrical appliances should be grounded.
   (4) Circuits should always be overloaded.

30. The force that keeps the solar system together is
   (1) electrical   (3) gravitational
   (2) magnetic   (4) nuclear

31. Condensation occurs when
   (1) a gas changes to a liquid
   (2) a liquid changes to a solid
   (3) a solid changes to a gas
   (4) a solid changes to a liquid

32. Which of the following would *not* be a safe laboratory procedure?
   (1) Place nose directly over container to smell it.
   (2) Always wear goggles when heating chemicals.
   (3) Never mix chemicals without your teacher's instructions.
   (4) Never taste chemicals in the laboratory.

33. Most of the energy used in the United States today is obtained from
   (1) nuclear fuels
   (2) fossils fuels
   (3) moving water
   (4) the wind

34. The data table below compares fuel sources which provided energy for the United States in 1982.

SOURCE	% ENERGY
Petroleum	39.3
Hydroelectric	5.7
Natural gas	26.3
Coal	23.8
Nuclear	4.9

   How much energy was from fossil fuels?
   (1) 90%   (3) 64%
   (2) 40%   (4) 24%

35. Base your answers to question 35 on the diagram below.

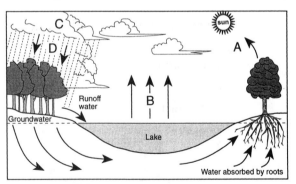

   Where is condensation occurring?
   (1) A   (3) C
   (2) B   (4) D

PART II

36. A food web is shown below.

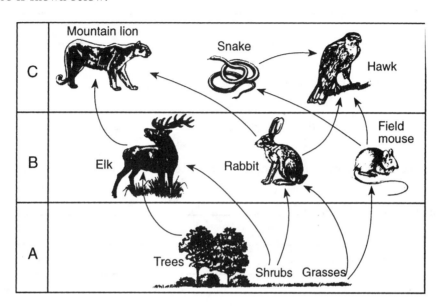

(a) Mountain lion is to carnivore, as elk is to ――――――――――― .

(b) The ecological term for trees, shrubs, and grasses is ――――――――――― .

(c) Name the organism missing from this food web. ――――――――――― .

(d) Complete the energy pyramid below:

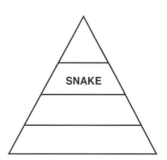

(e) Explain how the hawk's primary energy source is the Sun. ―――――――――――

――――――――――――――――――――――――――――――――――

――――――――――――――――――――――――――――――――――

37. A student wonders if the temperature on each shelf in the refrigerator is the same. The student thinks that the bottom shelf is colder.

(a) Write a hypothesis for an experiment the student could design to test this inquiry.

_____

_____

(b) State the manipulated (independent) variable _____

(c) State the responding (dependent) variable _____

(d) Name the scientific instrument the student could use to collect data. _____

(e) Write a procedure in a series of steps. _____

_____

_____

_____

38. Explain one change that occurs to the blood as it passes through the:

(a) kidneys _____

_____

(b) lungs _____

_____

c. small intestine _____

_____

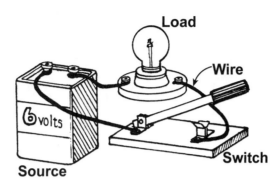

39. Describe an energy transformation that occurs in this circuit when the switch is down.

_____ energy is changed to _____.

40. Explain one method of producing electricity that uses a renewable resource.

_____

_____

_____

GRADE 8 - Intermediate-Level Practice Test #3

PART I

1. Which part of the diagram below represents a stimulus?

   LIGHT

   (1) soil   (3) light

   (2) leaves   (4) vase

2. Carbohydrates, fats and proteins are examples of

   (1) nutrients   (3) vitamins

   (2) minerals   (4) elements

3. Which of the following organisms are decomposers?

   (1) green plants   (3) fungi

   (2) producers   (4) fish

4. The following diagram represents a

   (1) succession   (3) reproduction

   (2) metamorphosis   (4) food chain

5. Which natural resource is nonrenewable?

   (1) plants   (3) minerals

   (2) soil   (4) water

Base your answers to questions 6 and 7 on the diagram below which represents reproduction.

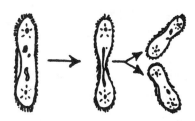

6. Compared to the size of the parent, the size of the offspring is

   (1) smaller   (3) the same

   (2) larger

7. The type of reproduction shown is

   (1) sexual

   (2) asexual

   (3) fertilization

   (4) metamorphosis

8. Which body system is represented by the diagram below?

   (1) digestive system

   (2) nervous system

   (3) endocrine system

   (4) circulatory system

9. Which of the following organs is not part of the circulatory system?

   (1) heart   (3) veins

   (2) blood   (4) trachea

10. Hormones are produced by the
    (1) nervous system
    (2) endocrine system
    (3) digestive system
    (4) respiratory system

11. Infectious diseases are caused by
    (1) deficiencies in the diet
    (2) allergies
    (3) microorganisms that can be transmitted from one organism to another
    (4) malfunctioning organs

12. The diagram below represents the formation of sperm cells in the human body.

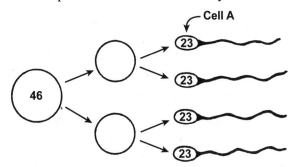

    The number 23 in cell A represents
    (1) genes   (3) chromosomes
    (2) nuclei   (4) chloroplasts

13. What is the length of the object represented in the diagram below?

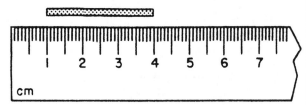

    (1) 1.0 cm   (3) 3.0 cm
    (2) 2.5 cm   (4) 4.0 cm

14. Traces of past life found in sedimentary rock are called
    (1) fossils   (3) sediments
    (2) minerals   (4) bedrocks

15. The diagram below represents a cross-section of soil. Which layer or layers formed because of weathering and the action of plants and animals?

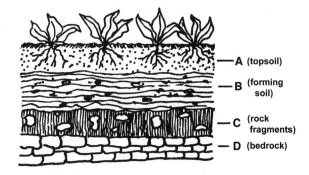

    (1) layer A
    (2) layer B
    (3) layer C
    (4) all three layers

16. The ocean floor is made up of
    (1) mountains only
    (2) valleys only
    (3) plateaus and plains only
    (4) mountains, valleys, plateaus, and plains

17. Which rock type forms when lava cools and hardens?
    (1) igneous
    (2) sedimentary
    (3) metamorphic

Base your answers to questions 18–20 on the map below of the United States which shows high pressure and low pressure areas.

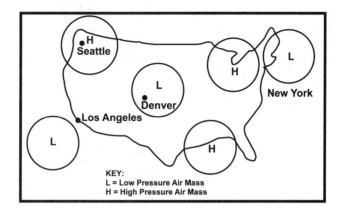

18. Which city is most likely to have clear and dry weather?
    (1) Denver   (2) Seattle   (3) Los Angeles   (4) New York

19. The low pressure system in Denver will move towards
    (1) Seattle   (2) Los Angeles   (3) New York

20. The low pressure southwest of Los Angeles is most likely
    (1) maritime tropical   (2) maritime polar   (3) continental polar   (4) continental tropical

21. Which of the following statements best describes weather changes?
    (1) Weather changes always occur suddenly.
    (2) Weather changes occur only in the morning.
    (3) Weather changes occur as new air masses move into a location.
    (4) Weather changes occur when the seasons change.

22. Water is returned to Earth's surface by
    (1) evaporation   (2) transpiration   (3) respiration   (4) precipitation

23. Which describes winter in New York?
    (1) high Sun, long daylight   (3) low Sun, short daylight
    (2) high Sun, short daylight   (4) low Sun, long daylight

24. Which of the following conditions causes the length of one day to be 24 hours?
    (1) Earth's rotation   (3) the Sun's rotation
    (2) Earth's revolution   (4) the Sun's revolution

25. At which position would a full Moon be visible to Earth?

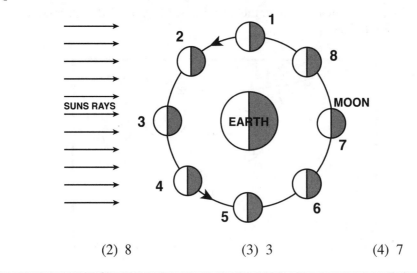

    (1) 1   (2) 8   (3) 3   (4) 7

26. The coils in an electric toaster change
    (1) electrical energy to light energy
    (2) heat energy to electrical energy
    (3) light energy to electrical energy
    (4) electrical energy to light energy and heat energy

Use the diagram below of a simple machine to answer question 27 and 28.

27. Which statement about simple machines best describes the diagram.
    (1) Simple machines need lubrication.
    (2) Simple machines can change the direction of a force.
    (3) Simple machines do not always make work easier.
    (4) Simple machines are not technological devices.

28. This simple machine is a(n)
    (1) pulley   (2) lever   (3) wedge   (4) inclined plane

29. Which of the following is *not* a result of matter vibrating?
    (1) light
    (3) music
    (2) noise
    (4) sound

30. What overall change takes place in an ice cube as it melts.
    (1) It loses energy and particles move closer together.
    (2) It loses energy and particles move further apart.
    (3) It gains energy and particles move further apart.
    (4) It gains energy and particles move closer together.

31. The melting of ice to water is an example of
    (1) evaporation
    (2) condensation
    (3) a physical change
    (4) a chemical change

32. A student could speed up a chemical reaction by
    (1) increasing the temperature.
    (2) decreasing the temperature.
    (3) increasing the size of the chemical particles.
    (4) removing one chemical.

33. Which term best completes the statement below?

    Graduated cylinder is to volume as balance is to

    (1) mass
    (3) force
    (2) temperature
    (4) length

34. Some people are against the building of nuclear power plants because they
    (1) use fossil fuels
    (2) produce hazardous wastes
    (3) have no safety systems
    (4) eliminate jobs

35. Which of the following is the primary source of energy for Earth?
    (1) the Moon
    (3) the planets
    (2) the Sun
    (4) green plants

PART II

36. Use the dichotomous key below:

MINERAL IDENTIFICATION KEY		
1	**a. Has a metallic luster**	**go to 2**
	b. Has a non-metallic luster	**go to 4**
2	**a. Has a red-brown streak**	**Hematite**
	b. Has a black streak	**go to 3**
3	**a. Attracted by a magnet**	**Magnetite**
	b. Does not attract a magnet	**Galena**
4	**a. Bubbles with acid**	**Calcite**
	b. Does not bubble with acid	**Quartz**

(a) Name *two* similarities between magnetite and galena

(1) _____ (2) _____

(b) Contrast hematite and magnetite

_____

(c) A student finds a metallic looking mineral that has a black streak and is not attracted to a magnet. This mineral is probably

_____

(d) Calcite will bubble when acid is placed on it.

This is a _____ property.

37. Adaptations are inherited traits. They improve the chances of a species surviving and reproducing. Adaptations also enable a species to survive environmental changes.

(a) Some green plants have a very thick waxy covering on their leaves. How does this help them survive if the climate becomes drier?

_____

_____

_____

(b) The colorful monarch butterfly is inedible to birds. The viceroy butterfly is edible but looks very similar to the monarch. Explain the viceroy's adaptation and how this helps them survive.

_____

_____

_____

(c) Wild mallard ducks are very common in ponds. The female is a dull brown but the male is very colorful with a green head, white neck ring and blue-purple outlined body feathers. Explain the reason for the difference.

_____

_____

_____

38. In guinea pigs, rough hair (R) is dominant over straight hair (r). A breeder of guinea pigs kept a pedigree chart for four generations of guinea pigs.

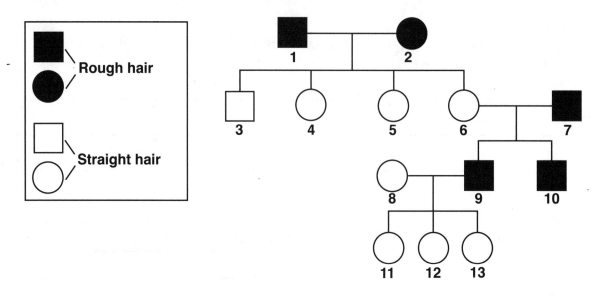

(a) Complete a Punnett square for the cross between #1 and #2 that would result in straight haired offspring.

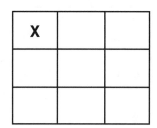

(b) Gene type for #9 is _____

39. The weather map below is for a low pressure system in Central United States.

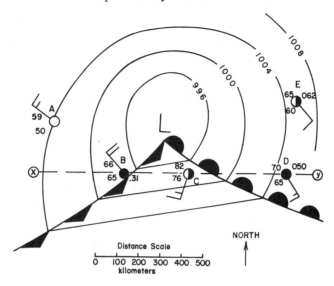

(a) Highest air pressure is at letter _____

(b) Strongest wind is at letter _____

(c) Distance in kilometers from A to B is _____ km.

(d) The cold front at B is moving in a _____ direction.

(e) The "L" indicates low _____.

40. The diagram below shows the position of Earth and the Sun's rays. On the diagram below, draw a small circle to represent the moon during a total lunar eclipse.

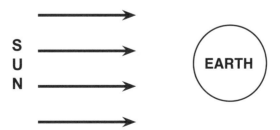

NOTES

NOTES

NOTES

NOTES

NOTES